PRAISE FOR UNSEEN WARFARE

Dr. Hakeem Collins allows us to understand the invisible world that is our real enemy. Better yet, his practical battleground prophetic teaching gift allows us to win every time!

SID ROTH

Host, *It's Supernatural!* Television Show

The Rules of Engagement are not the same for every battle. Nowadays, in modern warfare, drones are sent to spy out the land, next an actual air patrol followed by ground troops. Point is, there are specific battle plans you follow if you are going to succeed. As it is in the natural, so it is in the spiritual. We must first learn to *discern* the works of the enemy and not just aim at anything that moves. After properly discerning, you can shift into *disarming* the powers of darkness. But we must have a plan to maintain what we have attained and that brings us beyond disarming to *destroying* the works of the enemy. Jesus came to destroy the very works of the devil, not just displace them! Come on a journey with my friend Hakeem Collins and learn about this three-stage process and so much more in *Unseen Warfare*. Remember, we are called to enforce the victory of Calvary that Jesus Christ has already won!

DR. JAMES W. GOLL

Founder, God Encounters Ministries

GOLL Ideation LLC

Dr. Hakeem Collins, in his powerfully written book *Unseen Warfare: Rules of Engagement to Discern, Disarm, and Defeat the Work of the Enemy*, has done a masterful job explaining and revealing the unseen realm of the art of war that equips believers in invisible warfare. He tactfully provides spiritual strategies discovered in Scriptures that teach you the rules of engagement that afford perpetual victories and breakthroughs. Like the war pieces on a chess board, *Unseen Warfare* teaches the believer offensive and defensive approaches that anticipate the enemies' (devil's) moves before they happen. This book is timely and one of the most profoundly written about spiritual warfare on the market.

Unseen Warfare is a must-have for any Christian believer who desires to learn, understand, and engage fearlessly in supernatural warfare and how we can partner with unseen angelic forces in the same manner as Elijah the prophet prayed that the spiritual eyes of his servant be opened to see God's army in Second Kings 6:15-17. I highly endorse and recommend this literary work by Dr. Hakeem Collins as the battle and war plans for every believer to have in his or her spiritual arsenal for discerning, disarming, and defeating the works of the enemy.

Dr. Naim Collins
President, League of the Prophets
Author, *Realms of the Prophetic*

God desires for all of His children to live a free and victorious life positioned in the glory realm. In this book, Dr. Hakeem Collins shares supernatural strategies and navigational insights for living as an overcomer in *Unseen Warfare*. Through these teachings, Hakeem offers the reader basic training for rising up to prophetically discern, disarm, and defeat every assignment of the enemy. You will learn how to engage in true spiritual warfare that dispatches angelic armies, breaks soul-ties, and cancels every curse that has been spoken over your life. This is an important book for every believer who is serious about receiving their full inheritance that Christ paid for.

JOSHUA MILLS
Speaker and Bestselling Author, *Power
Portals* and *Seeing Angels*
International Glory Ministries
www.joshuamills.com

With *Unseen Warfare* happening around us daily, this book will give you wisdom from the Word of God, as well as supernatural strategies to defeat the warfare around you. The words written on the pages of this book are victory strategies that will cause you to go higher into all that God has for you. This is a "now" word to the Ecclesia— to take back cities, states, and nations for the glory of God. Every Christ follower should read this book and put into application what Dr. Hakeem Collins has masterfully put together. For every fivefold leader, this book will become a "go-to" resource for years to come.

PASTOR JOHN ORTIZ
Lead Pastor, The Gathering Place
www.tgp.church

I am both proud and excited to see men of God like Hakeem Collins continue the work of deliverance with *Unseen Warfare: Rules of Engagement to Discern, Disarm, and Defeat the Works of the Enemy*, spelled out so balanced and scriptural. This book exposes the "unseen war" with the enemy and gives readers powerful weapons to expose the enemy's cover and dismantle demonic operations with Kingdom authority! This is an excellent work, well-detailed and filled with tactical warfare methods. Well done, Prophet Hakeem Collins!

APOSTLE IVORY L. HOPKINS
The "General" of Deliverance
Overseer and founder of Pilgrims Ministry of Deliverance
Georgetown, Delaware

Dr. Collins has presented the Body of Christ with the needed tools to wage effective and potent warfare against the forces of darkness. *Unseen Warfare: Rules of Engagement to Discern, Disarm, and Defeat the Works of the Enemy* is as close to a combat textbook as you can get. It covers vital areas of victorious strategy from A to Z that when applied will show the manifested power of one of my favorite Psalms: *"Let* [watch] *God arise, and every* [satanic/demonic] *enemy be scattered"* (Psalm 68:1).

Bishop/Apostle J. Charles Carrington Jr.
Presiding Prelate: Full Gospel Christian Fellowship
Senior Pastor, Life Builders Church

Spiritual warfare is one of those topics that everyone experiences yet it is still one of the most overlooked topics taught in the Body of Christ. Dr. Hakeem has intricately and skillfully been able to take a rather complicated, scary topic and made it so practical. *Unseen Warfare* is a must-read. It is an answer key to some of the physical and spiritual challenges many are experiencing and is loaded with a lot of "aha" moments. This book is right on time and a major tool of empowerment to ensure we win in this season, and in the next.

Sharee Dorsett
Author, *Small But Mighty*
Associate Pastor, City of Love Church
Wilmington, Delaware

In his book *Unseen Warfare*, my friend Hakeem Collins releases revelation of the rules of engagement for displacing and destroying the works of the enemy. This book will give you wisdom and understanding of how to pray with discernment to outwit the enemy. You will learn how to pray and decree powerfully to release the truth of God's Word and Kingdom. Get ready, warrior, to have your skills sharpened and see the victory that is already yours.

STEVEN SPRINGER
International Speaker and Author
President and Cofounder, Global Presence Ministries
Apostolic Overseer, Global Presence Apostolic Network

Unseen Warfare is a must-have for every believer's spiritual arsenal, for on every page there is an explosive revelation. With astute precision, Dr. Hakeem Collins, a strong apostolic and prophetic voice to this generation, has laid out a guide map for you to follow, enabling you the ability to disarm the enemy and gain your victory. The insight given with each written line in this timely book will change your life. You will not be able to just simply read these words without experiencing the weighty power of them. Get ready to discern demonic attacks, plans, and schemes of the enemy and eradicate them!

ANDREW TOWE
Lead Pastor, Ramp Church Chattanooga
Author, *The Triple Threat Anointing*

We know from Scripture that we are in an invisible battle and that God has given us armor to wear and spiritual weapons to use. But do we understand the nature of this battle, how to use our weapons and how to walk in victory? Too many believers are ignorant of the enemy's devices and untrained in the art of spiritual warfare. Therefore, they remain susceptible to unnecessary harassment and hindrances from the kingdom of darkness. My friend Hakeem Collins has written a powerful manual on how to discern and defeat the works of the devil. *Unseen Warfare* equips you with biblical principles and practical tools to engage in the battle that rages around us daily. Being firmly rooted in Jesus' ultimate victory and your authority as a believer, you will learn how to use weapons of spiritual warfare to expose and dismantle the works of the enemy in your life.

JAKE KAIL
Lead Pastor, Threshold Church
Author, *Setting Captives Free*

We are living in unusual times and witnessing unprecedented events play out on the world stage. Clearly, there is a spiritual battle raging over the lives of people, regions, and nations. In *Unseen Warfare*, Dr. Hakeem Collins skillfully articulates the clash occurring behind the scenes, in the invisible realm. Furthermore, Dr. Collins provides powerful tools and strategies on how to outwit and overcome demonic forces and agendas operating in the world today. This is a book you need in your spiritual warfare prayer arsenal!

JOSHUA GILES
Pastor and Founder, Kingdom Embassy Worship Center
Founder, Joshua Giles Ministries
Author, *The Rise of the Micaiah Prophet*
www.JoshuaGiles.com

UNSEEN WARFARE

DESTINY IMAGE BOOKS BY HAKEEM COLLINS

101 Prophetic Ways God Speaks

Command Your Healing

Prophetic Breakthrough

Heaven Declares

UNSEEN WARFARE

RULES OF ENGAGEMENT TO DISCERN, DISARM, AND DEFEAT THE WORKS OF THE ENEMY

HAKEEM COLLINS

DESTINY IMAGE® PUBLISHERS, INC.

P.O. Box 310, Shippensburg, PA 17257-0310

"Promoting Inspired Lives."

This book and all other Destiny Image and Destiny Image Fiction books are available at Christian bookstores and distributors worldwide.

Cover design by Eileen Rockwell

Interior design by Terry Clifton

For more information on foreign distributors, call 717-532-3040.

Reach us on the Internet: www.destinyimage.com.

ISBN 13 TP: 978-0-7684-5258-7

ISBN 13 eBook: 978-0-7684-5556-4

ISBN 13 HC: 978-0-7684-5558-8

ISBN 13 LP: 978-0-7684-5557-1

For Worldwide Distribution, Printed in the U.S.A.

1 2 3 4 5 6 7 8 / 25 24 23 22 21

CONTENTS

FOREWORD

Early in my walk with God, I landed in a missions-oriented ministry that was partnering with churches and orphanages in Nicaragua. When I heard our leader planned to take a team to the Latin American nation in the summer, I was just hoping they'd let me go. I even did something I would never normally do: I asked.

The pastor said yes! Of course, I wasn't going to preach the Gospel in the stadium events, but rather to run the media operations since that was my predominant gifting at the time. My assignment was to create documentaries to show the donors the good work they were sowing into. I was so honored to serve God.

Being so young in the Lord at that time, I didn't know much about spiritual warfare. I had no earthly idea I would be met by fierce invisible enemies that I was ill-equipped to battle. (Somebody really should have warned me!) The devil wasted no time in saying hello. I remember being absolutely overwhelmed with witchcraft and a horde of other hellish opponents that I didn't discern—or at that time even knew existed.

That first trip to Nicaragua was beyond rough. Vain imaginations were ruling my mind. My body was under attack to the point that I could barely walk. I wasn't sleeping at night. The food made me sick to my stomach. Indeed, principalities, powers, rulers of the darkness, and spiritual wickedness in high places were having a field day with my ignorance. I just wanted to go home—but I was stuck.

After the first year and that first encounter with the spiritual onslaught, I didn't want to go back—ever. When the next summer came along, the pastor expected me to run the media in the 110-degree sun while battling unseen warfare. I had ideas of running somewhere else and had already made up my mind there was no way I would ever go back there—ever.

The Lord had different plans. As I was brushing my teeth, He said something to me that thrilled my heart: "I am going to send you to many nations…" I didn't know you could smile and brush your teeth at the same time, but I found a way. That smile, though, would soon evaporate when the Lord finished His sentence… "But I'm starting with Nicaragua."

My thoughts, "You've got to be kidding me!" Jesus triumphed over the principalities and powers in the earth, but during my first trip I felt like the principalities and powers triumphed over me. However, understanding the will of the Lord I went back to Nicaragua to film documentaries. Each year, I went back to that spiritual battleground called Nicaragua a little sharper and a little wiser until I was finally able to discern, disarm, and defeat the demon powers working to steal, kill, and destroy me—and help others defeat them, too. Before that assignment was up I was equipping leaders in prophetic ministry—and giving the devil a black eye.

During those eight years, I learned much of what Dr. Hakeem Collins teaches in this book. The unseen world is more real than what you can see, hear, or touch with your natural senses. Indeed, the enemy is roaming around like a roaring lion seeking someone to devour—but you can't always see him and you can't always hear him. You don't always know he's crouching at your door. The good news is, you can learn to discern the works of the enemy—and in *Unseen Warfare,* Hakeem equips you to become more aware of what you can't see with revelation and practical teaching. Read this book and you will come to understand just how armed and dangerous you really are. And that's where your victory begins.

Paul the apostle told us not to be ignorant of the devil's devices. This book rips the mask off your spiritual enemies and their devices at a macro level so that you can discern the ways of the enemy and stop demons dead in their tracks in your life. Once you understand the supernatural armor that has been allocated to you as a believer in Christ, you won't be afraid to run to the battle line. Once you catch the revelation of the weapons God has formed for your use, you will wield them with an assurance that your Goliath—or your Jezebel or Judas or whatever invisible enemy has set a snare for you—will fall on his face.

See, the devil sets you up to get you upset. But Jehovah Gibbor, our glorious warrior God, has set you up for success in every battle. He's given you His Son, His name, His blood, His weapons, His armor, His Word, the measure of faith, and His promise of victory. If you are not walking in consistent victory, it's an easy fix. Get better equipped so you can discern, disarm, and destroy the works, cycles, plans, and purposes of the enemy in your life. *Unseen Warfare* will help you see what you are up against so you can cut off the demonic swirl in the spirit realm before it ever manifests in the natural realm.

Hakeem's strategic warfare, prophetic prayer activations will give you a jump start when you are under attack. Read these out loud with fervor and authority and watch the devil flee. Then jump off from there to push back the darkness before it even forms. *Unseen Warfare* offers the inspiration, equipping, and revelation to form weapons that will prosper against the enemy before he can form weapons that try to prosper against you. Thanks, Hakeem, for adding this book to the library of great spiritual warfare classics.

JENNIFER LeCLAIRE
Senior Leader, Awakening House of Prayer
Bestselling Author, *Victory Decrees*

INTRODUCTION

Have you ever been somewhere and felt an eerie feeling, a presence that you couldn't quite identify? Or maybe you have been in the presence of someone and something they said or did set off "bells and whistles" in your spirit? Or have you personally, economically, or physically found yourself in a cycle of unexpected mishaps, misfortunes, or disappointments?

Perhaps, day after day you find yourself having to overcome insurmountable situations that were out of your control. Or maybe you are coping with unseen resistance, obstacles, persecutions, and unfortunate circumstances that have come to you unaware, unwarranted, and unwanted, leaving you feeling victimized, traumatized, and outright powerless and defeated. Are you tired of going through ongoing fights that you are unable to overcome? Do you feel that everything you do isn't good enough and that the enemy is playing mind games with you?

You don't have to succumb to the enemy's stick of dynamite attacks to bend your will to his. You can fight back by arming yourself with the armory of God to *discern, disarm, and defeat* the works of the adversary—the devil. If you are in the midst of any of these situations just mentioned, it may be a result of an unseen battle or invisible enemy working against you—and you don't even know it.

Never allow the enemy to pin you down in this wrestling match for your soul. You are victorious! And I will teach you in this book the strategies that I have learned through biblical sound teaching of the art of war and rules of engagement that will guarantee victory every time in the Holy Spirit against the devil. I don't want to bore you with naming every legion of demons or listing every Scripture to read on spiritual warfare. Rather, I want to specifically and strategically identify and expose the works of the devil and provide you the plan of action that works to defeat this nemesis of God and His people.

In this book, *Unseen Warfare*, we address and expose imminent unseen threats that are indirectly or directly diabolical that spiritually oppose God's people and oftentimes manifest in the natural to steal, kill, and destroy. Furthermore, when I think about warfare in itself, I am not limited in my understanding that there are just two types of war that goes on spiritually and naturally. We must know that there are various types of war or warfare that are occurring in and around us daily, knowingly or unknowingly.

You will also learn how to take your spiritual warfare tactics to the next level of potency. Not only will you identify the devil's strategies, you will know how to beat him at his own game. Like a chess match, you will be able to anticipate the next step of the enemy. No longer will you be manipulated, controlled, blindsided, bewitched, bewildered, confused, perplexed, fearful, doubtful, faithless, or become ensnared by the enemy's grip. No longer will you be outmatched and outwitted by the enemy—in this war you are guaranteed to win any and every time.

Every Christian believer must take full responsibility and equip themselves against the forces of darkness. Arming yourself with the proper spiritual artillery to ward off the enemy's attacks will save you time, money, headaches, and ultimately your life and the lives of those you love. Disarming yourself can become spiritually hazardous and pose a sudden threat to your spiritual longevity. In this current time and season, believers must be vigilant and alert as it pertains to any and all possible unseen and seen dangers and difficulties that may occur.

Before we get into topics pertaining to unseen spiritual or invisible warfare, we must first ask ourselves the following questions from a biblical and ancient standpoint:

- What does the Bible say about unseen warfare or spiritual warfare?
- How did the Lord Jesus Himself disarm and defeat the works of the enemy?
- What are the unseen adversaries and diabolical opposition we face daily?
- How do we as believers exercise our Kingdom authority and power by the Holy Spirit to disengage the enemy from a victorious place?
- What is the supernatural armor of God given to believers outlined in Scripture?
- What are offensive and defensive tactics believers can use to break irregular patterns, word curses, illicit, ungodly, illegal soul-ties, and unseen influences that hinder breakthrough, favor, and divine blessings?
- How can we break free from spiritual bondages and toxic relationships?
- How can we identify satan's bait and never fall for them?

- Why am I repeating bad habits and destructive life patterns and how can I overcome them?

- What are the strongholds of the enemy and how can I break free from them?

- How do I close doors that were open in the past and keep them closed?

- How can I break free from satanic strongholds, overcome personal sin, temptation, and safeguard myself and those I love?

- What spiritual significance and plan of action can I apply biblically to my life as I utilize each piece of the armor of God to disarm and defeat demonic activities posed against me?

- How do I resist the enemy and get an upper hand on the enemy of my mind, will, and emotions?

- How can I properly bind and loose and exercise my spiritual authority?

- What are satan's legal rights and how can I win spiritual war games?

- In what way can I break demonic mind control and overcome satan's insidious tactics?

- How do I identify demonic delays versus God delays and life pauses?

- Do I need to continue to forgive someone who continues to do me wrong?

- How can I be forgiven of my sin, however still experience the cause and effect?

The answer to these questions and more will be answered throughout this spiritual warfare manual. The Bible says that God does not want us to ignore enemy devices. There are no more excuses to why the enemy is holding back our destiny and creating demonic delays. I will go on to say that there are simple, potent, and proven biblical strategies to use if you are ready to engage spiritual warfare on the offense rather than defense.

There are three main principles and takeaways you will learn and gain after reading this spiritual warfare manual. You will learn how to:

1. **Discern** the works of the enemy.
2. **Disarm** the works of the enemy.
3. **Destroy** the works of the enemy.

As you keep these three principles in mind as you engage daily in some way or another in spiritual warfare with the unseen forces of hell, you will be well-equipped, empowered, and anointed by the Holy Spirit to win each battle. Discerning, disarming, and destroying the works of the devil are pivotal and vital to your spiritual well-being. You don't have to be on defense—you can be on the offense, beating the devil at his own game and wage warfare with boldness, confidence, wisdom, authority, and in the power of God. It is time to stand against the powers of satan with the power of God through the Holy Spirit.

Get ready to be supernaturally equipped to win the unseen battle against the devil with the spiritual rules of engagement through the Holy Spirit.

SECTION ONE

THE SPIRITUAL ART OF WAR

PART ONE

DISCERNING THE WORKS OF THE ENEMY

Chapter 1

BASIC TRAINING

For the moment all discipline seems painful rather than pleasant, but later it yields the peaceful fruit of righteousness to those who have been trained by it (Hebrews 12:11 ESV).

All Scripture is breathed out by God and profitable for teaching, for reproof, for correction, and for training in righteousness (2 Timothy 3:16 ESV).

When it comes to any field of occupation that we are involved in, training is necessary to complete the job responsibilities effectively and proficiently, especially when it comes to training in combat or war. All true believers are called into the armed services of God. In other words, every believer of God has a "call to arms" in His army! In the natural world, all armies have induction procedures, policies, and requirements. There are imperative requirements in order to join the armed forces.

We have a huge problem in today's society and churches because people would rather skip the training process. Therefore there are inexperienced, unequipped, and unprepared people in leadership roles and novices trying to lead. They engage in war without the proper warfare training and preparation. Readiness is key to success and allows an individual to gain all of the required essential training and education to avoid future errors, mistakes, and disasters.

PREPARATION IS ESSENTIAL

In addition, today's modern culture has turned some people into walking zombies; blindly pursuing immorality, worldly passions, political desire for power and financial status while totally checking out of the real world. People have become so blinded by their lust and greed for worldly and carnal possessions that they have become blind to the real unseen dangers and enemies that are out there lurking behind the scenes. There is a real battle and imminent threat going on, and God wants His people to be prepared for war and what lies ahead.

While modern society tends to believe that we are somehow more advanced than the previous generations, I believe we oftentimes lack the necessary knowledge and many skill sets that assisted past generations not only to survive, but to thrive in times of crisis. The fundamental principle of preparedness traces back to the beginning of time; its principles are found throughout the Word of God, with various passages of Scriptures that speak on preparedness, planning, and survival. Bible characters like Noah didn't wait for a flood to happen in his generation before he built a titanic-like ark for survival.

Moreover, the Lord doesn't want His people to fight a spiritual battle on the battlefield without proper training, readiness, preparation, and wisdom to discern, disarm, and destroy the works of the enemy. You don't get prepared while in the midst of a fight; we must prepare before a fight. Even though experience can teach us many things, we don't have to suffer the consequence of not having the necessary training, experience, and knowledge to counteract the enemy's attacks. However, experience with wisdom is key to personal survival and success before and after a war.

Discerning the Times and Seasons

Proverbs imply that knowledge without experience and wisdom is folly (see Proverbs 14:18; 16:22). In other words, the wise prepare, the fool goes blindly ahead to suffer the consequences. One of the things I have learned throughout many years as a believer and prophetic leader in the Body of Christ is that the only way you can truly become an effective, skillful, and a prepared warrior of God is that you must go through intense training and then be placed in the midst of combat.

People ask me why do I watch and read the latest news of current events. As a believer and prophetic voice, I must remain alert to what is going on in the world around me and what the enemy is up to. Believers must be prepared while discerning the current times. It's imperative to know your opposition, the enemy, to disarm his operations. What goes on in the natural realm parallels what's going on in the spiritual realm.

We must pay attention on what's going on in the world today as well as focus our prayer petitions, connecting to the pulse and heart of God to bring about real solutions and change. In other words, we must "pray attention" to what God desires to burden our heart with in prayer. Prayer changes everything! We must discern what is the will of God and the plan of the enemy and use the wisdom of God to outwit him. There is fake news being reported daily. However, whose report are we going to believe in times of crisis and uncertainty? (Read Numbers 13:30-33; Isaiah 53:1.)

Psalm 1:1-3 declares: *"Blessed is the one who does not walk in step with the wicked...but whose delight is in the law of the Lord...."* A lot of people may lend advice to things that are contrary to God's

Word but discernment is key to comprehending and recognizing it. Who are we going to believe—CNN, MSNBC, CBS, FOX, ABC News? Or the Good News of the Gospel?

Jesus says in Mark 1:15 (NKJV), *"The time is fulfilled, and the kingdom of God is at hand. Repent, and believe in the gospel."*

As Christian believers, if you want to discern the current times, I suggest like me you should relentlessly read, watch, or listen to the credible news, blogs, podcasts, books, social media news feeds, and reliable sources of information. Listening for information and believing in false reports are two different things. It's imperative to fact check sources for accuracy while also receiving prophetic intel and revelation from the Lord in regard to how to address issues in the secret place through fasting and prayer. The enemy has already devised a plan against God's people and humanity. It is vital to uncover the enemy's plan so you can take action to thwart it.

BOOT CAMP TRAINING

The Bible says in Amos 3:7 (ESV), *"For the Lord God does nothing without revealing his secret to his servants the prophets."* There are various biblical tactics and strategies that can be used in spiritual warfare; however the basic plan for Christian believers in basic training is discovered by observing how Jesus Himself dealt with the unseen adversary—the devil himself.

God reveals His plan to those who are His most trusted prophetic people and voices in every generation. The battle plan for basic training for all believers in spiritual warfare is based on six major points:

1. God's Word—the Bible—Scripture
2. God's delegated authority and power
3. Prayer

4. Fasting

5. Kingdom keys

6. The power in the name of Jesus

Moreover, to fully understand and embrace the necessity for basic training as it pertains to spiritual warfare is aligning ourselves with the plans and purposes of Jesus by accepting Him as our Lord and Savior, and also becoming a qualified trained soldier in His army that wars against satan and his demonic forces. Learning spiritual warfare tactics and strategy is to understand Jesus' original purpose, which becomes your purpose and sets you in a tactical position of direct opposition to the invisible enemy—the devil.

The war plans of the enemy are unmatched to the power and plans of God through His people. Keep in mind that Jesus already destroyed and exposed the works of the enemy, which caused Him to ensure rigor assaults throughout His earthly ministry and life. Satan's main objective and agenda against Jesus was to constantly attempt to destroy or prohibit Him from fulfilling the mission of the Father who had sent Him. When studying spiritual warfare, I have learned that God will avenge His people, and there is divine protection over you when you are in His care. The enemy cannot touch or harm those who are obedient children of God.

Deuteronomy 28:6-8 declares what God will do to our enemies: "*You will be blessed when you come in and blessed when you go out. The Lord will grant that the enemies who rise up against you will be defeated before you. They will come at you from one direction but flee from you in seven. The Lord will send a blessing on your barns and on everything you put your hand to. The Lord your God will bless you in the land he is giving you.*" Evil ones can try to come against you one way, but when God is finished with them they will be running away in seven different directions.

The enemy tried to trap Jesus, but it never worked. Every plot of the enemy against Jesus' life from the time He was born and throughout His public ministry failed and was aborted. This is the same plot against every born-again believer. Jesus was met with much resistance and opposition from religious leaders of His day, His followers, and satan and his demons.

Jesus is our war General and a great example of how to overcome the powers and wicked plans of the evil one. And the Lord has a counteractive plan against the enemy given to His prophets by divine revelation in and throughout His Word. The Lord will only respond after revealing His plan of action to His prophetic servants and believers.

I believe that this is one reason why God wants me to pay attention to what's going on in the natural realm as it pertains to current events, global crises, and economic uncertainty. You too should pay attention and keep up to date. Discerning the times and seasons is a skill that can be developed like any other.

Ecclesiastes 3:1 tells us, *"There is a time for everything, and a season for every activity under the heavens."*

DISCERNING WHAT GOD IS UP TO NEXT

The Holy Spirit will you lead into all truth as you understand the prophetic forecast of what God is doing. As soldiers in the army of the Lord, it's important to recognize "now seasons" to prepare for what's next. In other words, if it's winter we wouldn't wear summer apparel as we would need clothing to keep us warm. The Bible says that the sons of Issachar understood the chronological times, but they also understood spiritual and political time and seasons as well.

from Issachar, men who understood the times and knew what Israel should do—200 chiefs, with all their relatives under their command (1 Chronicles 12:32).

The sons of Issachar could discern what God was doing and when He was doing it. Just like in times of war, we must know what the enemy is doing and when he is doing it. Also, as believers we should discern when it's time to offensively or defensively fight or go to war and when it's time for peace, spiritually speaking.

Interestingly enough, this small tribe of Issachar knew when one move of God was starting and another one was ending. They could discern when a leader was falling and another leader was rising. They also possessed prophetic insight to share who the next leader should be. God gives us His heart toward a leader whom He has chosen.

The children of Issachar knew who to follow and when to follow the leader. Discerning the times and seasons in spiritual warfare engagement takes time and commitment in prayer in God's presence daily. I believe that understanding the unseen enemy requires discerning the demonic spiritual activity, patterns, and plots sent by the enemy.

GOD TRAINED ME PERSONALLY

How I was able to discern the times and what the enemy was up to after prayer was when God started training me in spiritual warfare at 20 years old when I attended Marshall University in Huntington, West Virginia, while there contending daily against witches that would perform astral projection. These witches would show up in my room while I was asleep to instill fear, intimidation, and doubt in the power of God and in the name of Jesus Christ.

I recall a time praying in my dorm room, going into my little closet full of clothes. I would pray for an hour at 3:00 a.m., being led by the Holy Spirit. I didn't understand why God would have me pray at that early hour when I had to be up at 8:00 for class and football practice. When I finished praying one time, I was extremely drained and sleepy so I went back to sleep. I was awakened by a dark spirit hovering over me. This evil spirit lurked in the darkness and was crouching on my chest. I couldn't breathe; it was choking me for some reason. While coming to myself and noticing this supernatural dark force on me, I clearly thought I was dreaming.

However, it was a real face-to-face encounter with a witch. As I tried to yell out the name of Jesus, the more this evil spirit muzzled my ability to say His name. I was afraid and didn't know what to do at that moment. The only thought that came to mind was the power in Jesus' name. The enemy also knows the power of His name. James 2:19 (GW) reveals, *"You believe that there is one God. That's fine! The demons also believe that, and they tremble with fear."*

Also, Matthew 8:29 says, *"What do you want with us, Son of God?" they shouted. "Have you come here to torture us before the appointed time?"* That is why the devil fears praying, fasting, and God-fearing men and women of God. The enemy wanted to instill fear and keep me from praying. Furthermore, as this evil spirit was choking me, I couldn't scream the name of Jesus in fear, nor could I speak the name of Jesus in faith in the power of God.

While being choked by this witch demon spirit, I heard the Spirit of God whisper to me saying "Hakeem, it's not in the volume of speaking My name, it's in the power of knowing what My name can do." During that moment of a spiritual warfare attack, I received a divine revelation. While being choked, I had a breakthrough revelation from the Lord through a whisper. I then whispered the name of Jesus and suddenly the witch left, and my room became bright like the sun—and I was able to breathe again.

I sat up on the edge of my bed thinking, *What just happened?* I looked in the mirror and there were many scratches on my neck and red hand marks. After that encounter I wanted to learn more about demons, witches, evil spirits, deliverance, spiritual warfare, and the kingdom of darkness. I wasn't afraid of the enemy after that near-death experience, but I was afraid that he cowardly caught me off guard while I was asleep.

Whatever illegal door I opened out of ignorance, I knew it was my job to close them and equip myself with the Word of God, Spirit-filled resources, books, and teachings on spiritual warfare. Since that day, I have never stopped driving out demons, healing the sick, prophesying, and equipping believers to arm themselves with the Holy Spirit and Word of God to discern, disarm, and destroy the works of the enemy. God wants you to be armed to disarm the enemy.

Be Sober-Minded

Keep in mind that in basic training in spiritual warfare you must equip yourself with knowledge through the Word of God to defeat the enemy at his plan. The enemy will play war games with those who are ignorant, vulnerable, and susceptible to the strategy and tactics of the devil. The enemy wanted me to walk in fear and anxiety after that attack in my dorm room. But I fought back with wisdom taken from God's Word. We are to be sober minded and stand alert in this hour. We are to stay focused and offensively be prepared daily. The Bible says in First Peter 5:7-9:

> *Cast all your anxiety on him because he cares for you. Be alert and of sober mind. Your enemy the devil prowls around like a roaring lion looking for someone to devour. Resist him, standing firm in the faith, because you know that the family*

of believers throughout the world is undergoing the same kind of sufferings.

We must keep our attention and hope in Jesus as we are sober-minded, and be on high alert of the enemy as well. First Peter 1:13 also says, *"Therefore, with minds that are alert and fully sober, set your hope on the grace to be brought to you when Jesus Christ is revealed at his coming"* (1 Peter 1:13).

The way the enemy can outwit a soldier of God or believer is to keep them unaware, unprepared, and uninformed of his schemes (2 Corinthians 2:11). The Lord was teaching me spiritual warfare and the severity of it while I was attending Marshall University. Training from the Lord Himself and through His Word can prevent unnecessary problems. The only weapon I had against the enemy when I was being choked alone in my dorm room was the power in the name of Jesus, which caused the demon spirits to flee.

Basically, I needed basic training in the knowledge of God's Word as it relates to spiritual warfare and the spiritual weapons allotted to me. However, discerning the times is also key to learning spiritual warfare. The Lord taught me how to look beneath issues of the day and understand the larger cultural moment.

DISCERNING THE SIGNS OF SPIRITUAL WARFARE

There is biblical precedent for the importance of discerning the times. Some of King David's men were trained and skilled in understanding the times *"to know what Israel ought to do"* (1 Chronicles 12:32). Mordecai correctly spoke these words to his cousin, Queen Esther, in her efforts to save the Jewish people, *"And who knows whether you have not come to the kingdom for such a time as this?"* (Esther 4:14 ESV).

Jesus consistently criticized the Pharisees and other religious leaders for failing to discern the times, and for not recognizing him as the Messiah: *"You know how to interpret the appearance of the sky, but you cannot interpret the signs of the times"* (Matthew 16:3 ESV).

Failing to discern the current times and seasons as it relates to spiritual warfare engagement can be disastrous. Yet accurately discerning the times can lead to freedom, influence, blessings, and redeemed time. Discerning the times is a skill developed like any other. Those who take advantage of developing it put themselves in the best position to make a significant contribution in the time in which the Father has appointed them to live (Acts 17:26).

The Bible is clear about the children of light pertaining to the time and seasons. Scripture declares in Ephesians 5:15-17: *"Be very careful, then, how you live—not as unwise but as wise, making the most of every opportunity, because the days are evil. Therefore do not be foolish, but understand what the Lord's will is."*

God desires us to pay attention and walk as those who are wise, redeeming the time. Knowing the will of the Lord is imperative as believers endure spiritual boot camp training. Like the sons of Issachar, I had to understand the times and the rules of engagement to spiritual warfare early in my Christian walk as a believer, which motivated me to have a newspaper in one hand and the Word of God—the Bible—in the other. This teaches me how to pray effective prayers that are targeted, not amiss. God loved the world so much that He gave us His only begotten Son to salvage what was lost.

Stay Awake to Stand Guard

We must pray that it is in the heart of the Father concerning our communities, cities, region, nation, and world. The enemy wants to gain and claim territories for himself to blind the minds of the people in them. We are at war and the Lord wants His people ready to defeat the works of the enemy here and now for His glory. We need to be awake and on guard to fight back against those who desire to destroy life and take us hostage as prisoners of war through demonic deception, strongholds, and bondage.

In God's family army, He protects those who are His. As you are preparing for spiritual warfare, you must know that the battle is not yours but the Lord's. We need to be prepared to protect our families and guide them through times of crises. We need to stand guard and remain on high alert! We can't blindly follow the zombies into the pits of hell; we must be alert, and ready for the real evils out there. The Bible declares in First Thessalonians 5:6 *"Therefore let us not sleep, as others do, but let us watch and be sober."*

Basic training in spiritual warfare engagement better prepares us, regardless of how long one has been saved. Moreover, there are believers today who say that we are not to get involved in spiritual warfare, but instead just trust and believe God and keep our gaze on Him. While the Lord should always be our primary focus, He has equipped each of us with the war tools to use that will bring victory in any area of challenge.

Likewise, when God has provided medical knowledge and training for us to use in the physical realm, we are to utilize these resources He has provided. I believe the Lord admonishes His people to be engaged in spiritual warfare (see 1 Timothy 6:12). We must understand that there is an invisible battle being waged in the spiritual realm. It's a daily battle between the flesh and the spirit.

War Alarm

God wants to equip His people in spiritual combat against the unseen warfare waged by evil supernatural powers. There are believers today who, when they gave their lives to Jesus as Savior, were surprised to know that they, too, had an invisible enemy—the devil. Perhaps they expected life to become instantly perfect after salvation and everything would be settled with no more issues or problems in life.

Salvation, though, doesn't end the battle. Truth be told, in many ways it is just the beginning of it. I recall when I gave my life to Jesus at a very young age and was excited about it until later my faith and salvation was tested daily. The enemy likes to catch new believers off guard while they are vulnerable after accepting Jesus as Savior over their lives. He entices them with worldly, fleshly, and carnal desires to draw them back into the old sin nature.

In the Old Testament era, a trumpet was blown to summon God's people to war. Today, there is a blowing of a trumpet in the spiritual realm sounding the alarm throughout the nations of the world. It is a summon to this unseen war between good and evil. Are you ready to respond to the Lord's summon, His call to arms? Are you ready to take your spiritual oath to serve your King and His Kingdom?

Furthermore, are you prepared to be used by the Lord in your generation to change the narrative of the enemy's plot and scheme against the church at large? Are you open to expose and eradicate demonic works? It's our spiritual duty to call for arms and go through spiritual boot camp.

> *Be on your guard; stand firm in the faith; be courageous; be strong* (1 Corinthians 16:13).

When unbelievers give their lives to the Lord and are born again by God's Spirit, they become believers in Christ—new creatures. However, they are not just believers, children of God, they are being prepared to become soldiers in the armed forces of the Kingdom. When they give their lives over to the rule of Christ and are grafted into God's Kingdom, they are given full rights, benefits, and privileges in the Kingdom of God, His Sovereign Government.

Furthermore, at the time of regeneration (being born again) believers are suddenly "drafted" into spiritual warfare service as soldiers-of-God-in-the-making on earth; later being equipped to fight against the kingdom of darkness. The Holy Spirit and learning the Word of God prepares believers for spiritual warfare. No one automatically becomes a great soldier in God's family army— they are trained to become one.

Kingdom Recruitment

Basic training is provided for an individual to understand the fundamentals of warfare, to become physically and mentally competent. An individual's overall fitness is imperative to endure strenuous times. Keep in mind that training alone is useless unless an army is mobilized. In other words, to "mobilize" means to "put in a state of readiness for active military service."

Likewise, it's imperative that no one skips spiritual boot camp in God's service. Over time with much experience gained in spiritual battles, soldiers typically receive advanced training in specific areas of combat and operations depending on their mission.

Spiritual basic training or spiritual boot camp is a phrase commonly and widely used rather than the term "recruit training." Through the Gospel of Jesus Christ being preached, recruits or unbelievers are welcomed into the Kingdom of God as believers of Christ. Understand that you were recruited by the Lord through the preaching and teaching of the Gospel to return to your rightful place as king-priests and children of God.

Because you were recruited by the message of the Kingdom of God, you are now being made into one of God's trusted warriors!

Spiritually speaking, every believer will go through spiritual boot camp, receiving initial instructions for new military personnel.

In the natural, basic training or boot camp is a physical and psychological intensive preparation process, which resocializes recruits for the rigorous demands of military service and special missions in warfare engagement. Boot camp could last for several weeks or months, and the common specifications and features in the training process include inspections, physical training, foot drills, weapons training, and a graduation parade. As believers we are being conditioned, prepared, and trained for spiritual warfare engagement.

In a natural army, "inspections" occur regularly to assess the soldier's preparation, readiness, and skill sets. In addition, there are tactical maneuvers in training when the soldiers apply what they have learned in actual combat conditions. Basic training also prepares a cadet for survival, war scenarios, exercises, and fitness readiness in regard to overall self-discipline, sacrifice, teamwork, and physical and mental acuteness.

LIFETIME OF SPIRITUAL WARFARE TRAINING

Basic training spiritually speaking continues throughout the life of believers. Ongoing, unseen battles require ongoing training and is provided by the Lord. In the natural, on-the-job training is common place. Employees receive continual training to stay relevant and up-to-date on system changes, etc.

Likewise, as a warrior of God in an invisible battle, regardless how long a person has been saved, basic training is required and a prerequisite for advanced training, just as it is for a job promotion. Spiritually speaking there is no difference in what type of basic training you received during your walk with Christ. All believers must be able to discern, disarm, and defeat the works of the enemy by the power of God through His Holy Spirit.

We have to know and learn the strategy of the unseen enemy—the devil. There's no purpose in understanding spiritual warfare if we don't know who we are fighting and why. God has a basic training manual outline in His Word—the Bible—the Scriptures. The early church in the 1st century viewed their spiritual encounters with unseen dark evil forces in terms of warfare.

As believers in the 21st century, we must get used to natural military terminology just as the early church throughout the New Testament understood it. Military armor serves as divine spiritual protection for God's people. The Word of God was compared to a sword. And fiery darts were considered weapons used by satan. Faith was the *"good fight"* and believers like you and I were encouraged to *"wage the good warfare"* (see 1 Timothy 6:12; 1:18 NKJV).

Today, there is no difference from the early believers who knew they were in one way or another engaged in intense spiritual conflict. The early church understood the weapons of their warfare were not carnal ones but mighty through the supernatural power of God.

However, using the weapons of God against demonic powers and strongholds require spiritual discipline and His wisdom.

LIFE OF WAR

I must say that a Christian life is a life of war. In other words, believers will encounter daily engagement whether they notice it in the natural or recognize it as spiritual warfare. As soon as believers come to grip and understand this, the better they can prepare for it and experience supernatural victories in Christ Jesus each and every day. Apostle Paul knew and warned the early church of perilous times to come (2 Timothy 3:1).

In other words, Paul knew that there would be terrible, tough times, hardship, difficult, and grievous moments that they would face in the 1st century. As believers and soldiers in God's army, we should keep at the forefront of our minds that at any time we can be open targets of the enemy. God doesn't want us to be fearful of the enemy but fearless—prepared to prevail over his evil works.

This concept and notion of the word "preparedness" is nothing new; in fact, long before the words "survivalist" and "prepper"— which are not synonymous terms—became part of the modern lexicon, the Word of God admonished wise people to study the dangers that lie ahead, and then take precautionary plans of action and necessary preventatives to protect themselves and their family from threats. A prepper is focused on stockpiling supplies to use when camping out, bugging in, or at a bugout location and have the skill set to use them.

However, more often than not, the quantity of supplies outweighs the quality of survival skills honed. On the other hand, a survivalist is more engaged and focused on the innate skills they possess to get them through a desperate situation or scenario with usually no more stockpiled preps that can be carried in a duffle bag, backpack, or rucksack on a person's back. This type of boot camp training is essential for the believer surviving and enduring spiritual warfare engagement by the enemy.

A prepper with essential survival skills at best can benefit from having the best of both worlds and will surely enhance one's chances of breathing longer during a catastrophic disaster. The term "prepper" was coined to describe individuals concerned with preparedness. I believe God wants us to be both, technically speaking. To prepare in times of crisis and to have the skill set to survive in strenuous and uncertain situations long term.

I am reminded of two Scripture passages: Philippians 4:6-7 (ESV) says, *"Do not be anxious about anything, but in everything by prayer and supplication with thanksgiving let your requests be made known to God. And the peace of God, which surpasses all understanding, will guard your hearts and your minds in Christ Jesus."* And in Psalm 46:1 (ESV) reveals, *"God is our refuge and strength, a very present help in trouble."* The Lord wants us to exercise and activate His wisdom through the Holy Spirit and prepare ourselves and take coverage. I love what the Bible says in Proverbs 27:12: *"The prudent see danger and take refuge, but the simple keep going and pay the penalty."*

Strategies and Safeguards for War

I believe that as we are in times of uncertainty it is imperative for today's believers to understand spiritual warfare now, rather than just in the early church era and history. God is giving us through His Holy Spirit and Word new strategies to discern, disarm, and destroy the works of the enemy. In military terms, the word "strategy" is the science of forming and carrying out a special military mission and operation. Proper training and using effective warfare tactics and strategies will assist you in war victories against our enemy, satan.

Military leaders do not engage in spiritual battles without a careful examination of their resources and development of combat strategies. One of the greatest weapons against believers is ignorance. The enemy wants God's people to be oblivious, unconcerned, unbothered, and ignorant of what is really going on in the spiritual world around them. The reality of the unseen realm and spiritual warfare becomes real when we consciously know that they exist.

We must stay awake, aware, and sensitive to these realities and prepare for them. In addition, the enemy wants God's people to be unprepared, unequipped, and perplexed about the war he is initiating, plotting, and launching against them. The enemy doesn't play by the rules. We must safeguard ourselves from the sudden or unpredicted attacks that come from the enemy at any time.

For example, a wise homeowner installs an alarm system to prevent burglars from breaking in. Having an alarm system could possibly prevent a family member from getting hurt or killed. Being prepared eliminates possible situations or scenarios. It is wise to envision harmful possibilities and plan ahead, including receiving proper training and arming yourself with a weapon to protect your loved ones, your home, property, and yourself.

We should never underestimate the enemy! God wants us to be prepared and sensitive to the Holy Spirit's checks and balances that go off within us to alarm us of any pending unseen dangers or possibilities. Better to be safe than sorry. We must hear the Holy Spirit's warning signs to better equip ourselves in a just-in-case situation so we can respond wisely, quickly, and effectively.

In spiritual basic training you will learn to identify and execute good judgment when put in an unexpected situation. Even in unexpected real-life circumstances and situations you will be ready when it happens.

Spiritual warfare training is imperative for every believer regardless how long they have been saved and served God. Warfare is unavoidable! Fortunately, you don't have to wrestle with day-to-day invisible conflicts and opposition alone. God will help you win the invisible battle on the invisible frontlines of the battlefield. The enemy wants to expose your weaknesses and leave you as open prey to unwarranted and unwanted attacks. He wants to keep you ignorantly vulnerable and defenseless to make you an open target for a barrage of fiery darts aimed your way. God will not allow that to happen when you focus on Him and His battle plan.

DELEGATED AUTHORITY AND POWER

The Lord wants to expose the enemy and his strategies, which is one of the greatest revelations of His Word. Furthermore, the greatest revelation is that every believer comes into the revelation that they have power over all the powers of the enemy. I want to encourage you as you continue to read the following chapters that will further equip you to become a supernatural warrior armed and dangerous against the forces of hell while you advance to a new level in spiritual warfare.

One major lesson I have gained in learning how to discern, disarm, and defeat the works of the devil raging in my life is that it is only when I find myself in the furnace of affliction and when all odds are stacked up against me and all hell is breaking loose around me, that I can truly appreciate the early training in the art of spiritual warfare and strategic prayers. God doesn't want us to get distracted and caught up in war games created by the enemy. This is the time to rise up as bold warriors of God—and like King David slay the giants in our lives.

Luke 10:19 (NKJV) says, *"Behold, I give you the authority to trample on serpents and scorpions, and over all the power of the enemy, and nothing shall by any means hurt you."*

Believers are given spiritual authority to engage in spiritual warfare. The Lord has given you authority to trample on serpents and scorpions, and over all the power of the enemy, nothing will harm you. We have been given: 1) authority and 2) power.

Knowing your authority in Christ makes the difference in how you effectively dismantle any and every demonic power working against you daily. The enemy only messes with those who don't know their authority and power in the Holy Spirit. Luke 10:19 clearly states that the Lord has given us authority to and authority over *all*, not some, of the power of the enemy.

The word "authority" is the Greek word *exousia* in (Strong's G1849). According to Vine's Expository Dictionary, "authority" means to "leave or permission," or liberty of doing as one pleases, it passed to that of "the ability or strength with which one is endued," then to that of the "power of authority," the right to exercise power, e.g., Matthew 9:6; 21:23; Second Chronicles 10:8; or "the power of rule or government," the power of one whose will and commands must be obeyed by others, e.g., Matthew 28:18; John 17:2; Jude 1:25; Revelation 12:10; 17:13.

The Lord has given you authority over all the power of the enemy. The word "power" in the Greek is the word *dynamis* (Strong's G1411) which means, according to Vine's Expository Dictionary, the "power, ability, physical or moral, as residing in a person or thing." We can see that the Father has granted us the delegated right to exercise power over all the ability and power that is released against us by the enemy.

The enemy possesses no authority. However, he has limited power. God is telling us that we have authority over all the power of the enemy. How wonderful is it to know that this unseen adversary doesn't have any authority and that you do—and your spiritual, delegated authority in Christ through the Holy Spirit trumps all the power of the enemy!

God's Word doesn't say some or a few powers (*dynamis*) of the enemy but *all*. It's the strategy of the enemy to keep you from knowing this truth, this principle. You must know what you possess and have been given to you by the Lord. In basic training spiritual warfare and through the Holy Spirit, God equips us with this understanding. I am reminded of a young good-looking shepherd boy whom God raised up as a man after His own heart—and whom the Lord later anointed as king over the nation of Israel.

Fearless Warriors

David was a skillful warrior and man of war. The Lord empowered him in the art and science of war as it relates to the rules of engagement in intense combat in his reign as king. His skill and expertise were acquired, given, and entrusted by the Lord, in His sovereignty, putting David in various battlefronts and combat zones throughout his development. He was able to ward off and defeat bears and lions and later decapitate Goliath who was considered a champion by the Philistines, but was an enemy of God and the children of Israel. David received boot camp training early as a shepherd boy to later become a victorious warrior king! He had a lion's heart and the Father's heart at the same time.

God is looking for fearless warriors who will be empowered by the Spirit of God to disengage the enemy. Are you ready to allow the Lord to teach you the warfare strategies and tactics that will yield flawless victories? David in Psalm 144:1-2 (NKJV) declares:

> *Blessed be the Lord my Rock, who trains my hands for war, and my fingers for battle—my lovingkindness and my fortress, my high tower and my deliverer, my shield and the One in whom I take refuge, who subdues my people under me.*

Clearly, this passage of Scripture from Psalm 144 reveals to us from King David himself stating that it was the Lord who taught his hands to war and fingers to fight. In other words, it was Jehovah-Gibbor, the mighty Man of War, who taught him the rules of engagement in spiritual warfare strategies and tactics. David goes on in adulation and honor of his Commander and Chief and war General the Lord Himself saying that the Lord is his:

- Rock
- Trainer
- Strength
- Steadfast Love
- Fortress
- High Tower
- Deliverer
- Shield
- Refuge
- Protector

Real kings recognize true kings. David gave honor to the One and only true King. David also faced many uncertain challenges and battles, including a personal warfare conflict with his own son Absalom, whose defiant insurrection almost cost and forfeited David's kingdom. In addition, personal imperfections and the fleshly war within himself included killing his lover's husband when he was supposed to be on the battlefield with his men.

THE WAR GAMES OF THE ENEMY

There is no perfect warrior or leader; however, the warfare intensifies with those who are called to leadership. That's why we need the wisdom of God and the Holy Spirit to address unresolved or unchecked areas of our hearts and souls. The enemy's war games are nothing to take lightly. This is a serious chess match between satan and those called to serve God in His Kingdom.

We must think like the enemy to defeat the enemy. In other words, believers must understand how the enemy thinks, anticipate his next move, and beat him at his own war games. This spiritual wrestling match is already a fixed fight. Jesus already defeated the works of the enemy on the cross at Calvary. In addition, Jesus also saw satan fall from heaven like lightning that predates the church, humanity, and earth. Jesus is undefeated in the ongoing war against the enemy. This spiritual battle and the main agenda are about who can control the world.

The devil wants to continue to control and influence the world system throughout every generation. He doesn't want to transfer or relinquish that power to the children of light, we believers. He wants to continue to pervert the kingdoms of men by trying to duplicate the Kingdom of God. In the world system, the devil wants to set up lawlessness, perversion, and chaos on the earth through false religion, society, governments, nations, and the seven mountain spheres or earthly domains. The Lord didn't give the world to man to rule, but the earth.

Sadly, the Bible is clear that satan is the god of this world, not the god of the earth, but the world that comes to blind the unbelievers. As children of God we are not the god of the earth, but we are to rule like God in the earth realm. To rule, govern, and execute like God on the earth. So that being said, we are to manage what goes on in the world system as well and execute God's justice.

We must understand that the Word of God goes on to say that satan is the prince and the power of the air (Ephesians 2:2-3 NKJV). What does that mean? The title translated in Greek implies a lesser ruler with an assigned authority in a lower realm. The phrase "god of this world "(or "god of this age") indicates that satan is the major influence on the ideals, opinions, goals, hopes, and views of the majority of people (2 Corinthians 4:3-4). His influence also encompasses the world's philosophies, education, and commerce. We will address this topic more in a later chapter.

INVISIBLE BREAKTHROUGHS

The enemy wants to control the air traffic in the spirit realm. Just like the tower at an airport that monitors the traffic of airplanes going in and out of territories, satan wants to control the world and the gates in certain regions and territories. That's why there is an unseen battle going on when a believer prays. We fight in an unseen battle when our prayers are ascending to the throne of God; satan tries to intercept our prayers by the principality and powers in the second heavens. These unseen demonic entities try to hinder your prayers from breaking through into God's throne-room. It doesn't matter how long, how much, and how powerful we can pray, there is an invisible war targeting every prayer petition and request being sent up. That's why we need breakthrough warfare-type prayers that bring results.

Daniel understood what was prohibiting his prayers from breaking through, but he met prayer resistance with even more prayer persistence to get his breakthrough. In other words, for you to counteract spiritual warfare through prayer, you pray through to break through. Don't succumb to the ongoing fight that occurs before, during, and after prayer. You can regain control spiritually speaking through the power of God when you receive commands from the watchtower in heaven to earth.

We are to regain control over the air traffic that the enemy (the power of the air) is trying to prevent prayers of God's will to be implemented on earth. The Lord needs you and me to partner with Him to police and enforce spiritual laws that govern how we advance the Kingdom and remove demonic interference, interruptions, and interceptions by the enemy.

The enemy wants to create air traffic jams and collisions so the saints' prayers are not answered. Prayer weapons in spiritual warfare are discussed more in an upcoming chapter. We are dealing with a real power that controls the air towers of this world, and he has to be removed so that the watchtowers of God will be established in full control.

Satan may be the prince of the power of the air, but he is not the king of the universe and creator of everything. The devil is real; and even though we don't see this unseen menace to the civilization and society, that doesn't mean his attacks are not real. These unseen weapons sent by the enemy have had destructive and deadly results.

FALLING LIKE LIGHTNING

We must know what we are up against and what are the preventative and safety precautions needed to safeguard and win against these unseen assaults, battles, and resistance tactics. I love what Luke chapter 10 says about the seventy-two disciples who were sent out by Jesus to cast out demons. When they returned, Jesus said that He saw satan fall like lightning from heaven. After that He goes on to tell them about the supernatural authority and powers given to them (Luke 10:17-20 ESV).

This passage of Scripture implies that when the disciples were sent by Jesus on their deliverance mission, rescuing people from demonic influence, at the same time, the power of the enemy was falling like lightning. Whenever the authority of God is executed and activated against satanic, demonic, or diabolical forces, the enemy loses its power fast, like lightning. The enemy's strongholds over regions, territories, and nations are dismantled and destroyed. We know that satan fell from his position in heaven when pride was found in his heart.

Later, however, satan, the god of this world, blinded the minds of those who don't believe. They are unable to see the glorious light of the Good News. They don't understand this message about the glory of Christ, who is the exact likeness of God. So that's why it is imperative to know the power and authority you possess in disarming the enemy and rising up in power. We will talk further about satan, demons, and his kingdom in a later chapter.

The authority and power of God that you possess strips off the enemy and his demonic forces from your life and those you love. The seventy-two disciples were given supernatural power to drive out the demon invasion and at the same time satan's strongholds in that area succumbed to the power of God. The following are several Scriptures to read and study in regard to satan:

> *The seventy-two returned with joy and said, "Lord, even the demons submit to us in your name!" He replied, "I saw Satan fall like lightning from heaven. I have given you authority to trample on snakes and scorpions and to overcome all the power of the enemy; nothing will harm you"* (Luke 10:17-19).
>
> *How you have fallen from heaven, you morning star, son of the dawn! How you have been cut down to the ground, you conqueror of nations!* (Isaiah 14:12 GW).
>
> *Jesus said to him, "Away from me, Satan! For it is written: 'Worship the Lord your God, and serve him only'"* (Matthew 4:10).
>
> *The great dragon was hurled down—that ancient serpent called the devil, or Satan, who leads the whole world astray. He was hurled to the earth, and his angels with him* (Revelation 12:9).

ADVANCE TRAINING

Satan is an ancient archenemy and will do anything he can to steal, kill, and destroy anything related to the Lord. You have to arm yourself with necessary combat training to be successful like King David in your generation. Basic training is key to the next level of training and in field operations.

In addition to any field of operation and work, everyone has to undergo some type of training, preparation, and educational placement assessment. Furthermore, in the armed forces recruits go through a physical and psychological evaluations and observation to determine if they are mentally and physically ready. Training and readiness are necessary and essential for the various and rigorous types of service operations into which a cadet will later be deployed. There are various levels of training required depending on assignment, role, and duties.

Christ Jesus was born and sent to the earth to destroy the works of satan. The main mission for every believer under the power of God is to have the same purpose with the help of the Holy Spirit. We cannot defeat the powers of darkness in our own strength or ability. It takes the spiritual weapons available to you to use to dismantle, disengage, and destroy the forces of hell by the supernatural power of God's Spirit through us. Christ Jesus finished His divine Kingdom mission at the cross—He disabled and destroyed sin itself that had rule over humanity.

SIDELINES TO FRONTLINES OF BATTLE

This is the time for every Spirit-filled believer to rise up and take their rightful position as God's Kingdom ambassadors and official representatives in the earth to activate and enforce God's delegated power and authority here and now! No longer will we stand on the sidelines watching the enemy steal, kill, and destroy what God has done for us.

God desires His people to come from the sidelines to the frontlines of this real battle raging all around us to win the war. The main objective of Christ was the exact antithesis of the enemy's. Jesus came so that we may have an abundantly full life. Contrarily, *"The thief does not come except to steal, and to kill, and to destroy. I [Jesus] have come that they may have life, and that they may have it more abundantly"* (John 10:10 NKJV).

The enemy is a thief whose plan is to make you a "casualty of war." Meaning that satan's plot against the children of God is to bring injury, mishap, failure, disaster, and death to those called to God. But—you will not become a prisoner of war or a casualty of war. God has anointed you with the Holy Spirit to overcome all the powers of the enemy. We must also keep in mind that the Bible declares, *"…The kingdoms of this world are become the kingdoms of our Lord and of His Christ, and He shall reign forever and ever!"* (Revelation 11:15 NKJV).

As we progress to the other chapters in this book, a foundational and fundamental principle must be established—the war is not yours but the Lord's. But the enemy is taking it out on you as God's children, so it is the time to fight the good fight of faith, which means we stand firmly anchored in the Word and in the power of God's Spirit, reckoning ourselves dead to our emotions, human reasoning, feelings, will, desires and not permitting sin to reign in our mortal bodies by being tempted and yielding to its lustful appetite. I am reminded of the Scripture in Matthew 16:23-25 that declares:

Jesus turned and said to Peter, "Get behind me, Satan! You are a stumbling block to me; you do not have in mind the concerns of God, but merely human concerns." Then Jesus said to his disciples, "Whoever wants to be my disciple must deny themselves and take up their cross and follow me. For whoever wants to save their life will lose it, but whoever loses their life for me will find it."

FAITH FIGHTERS!

Basically, to fight the good fight is to do what is right or the right thing and be a model to others to do the same. Someone who is fighting the good fight is working relentlessly daily to overcome and make life choices to bless, defend, and assist others. I must ask, how did the apostle Paul fight the good fight of faith? He stood firm in the faith, was alert in prayer and watchful and acted like a man of strength.

Paul the apostle, knew the reward of serving the Lord and thought of fighting the good fight as an honor. Therefore, Paul encouraged and admonished faithful believers of Christ to stay firm in the faith which we were called. As believers we should stand strong when trials, tribulations, and crisis come our way. Paul told Timothy, *"Timothy, my son, I am giving you this command in keeping with the prophecies once made about you, so that by recalling them you may fight the battle well"* (1 Timothy 1:18). I want you to look at this passage of Scripture in different Bible translations:

- 1 Timothy 1:18 King James Version, "This charge I commit unto thee, son Timothy, according to the prophecies which went before on thee, that thou by them mightest **war a good warfare.**"
- 1 Timothy 1:18 New American Standard Bible, "This command I entrust to you, Timothy, my son, in accordance with the prophecies previously made concerning you, that by them you **fight the good fight.**"
- 1 Timothy 1:18 New Living Translation, "Timothy, my son, here are my instructions for you, based on the prophetic words spoken about you earlier. May they help you fight well in the **Lord's battles.**"

There are different words and phrases pertaining to warfare:

- "fight the battle well"
- "war [wage] a good warfare"
- "fight the good fight"
- "fight well in the Lord's battles"

We can see the mind-set of Paul as he is encouraging his spiritual son in the faith that truth and the prophetic promises of God is what we use as weapons of warfare against falsehood, doctrinal error, heresy, and anything contrary to the Word and purposes of God. However, looking into this more closely we can see that the good fight or warfare is actually not our fight, per se, but it's the Lord's battles we are fighting. God is raising up what I call "faith fighters!" Are you a faith fighter who will trust the Lord in this spiritual battle?

If it's the Lord's battle, then the Lord has weapons we use to contend against evil. The enemy is after the prophetic purpose, destiny, and future of the church—and in the Lord's army we have a duty to uphold. Timothy was so often encouraged by the apostle Paul, his spiritual father on purpose by the Spirit of God.

Waging Prophetic Warfare

The early church understood what they were up against. Not just demons, supernatural evil powers and works, but also spirit of deception, error, apostasy, heresy, ageism, paganism, false doctrines of men and devils, charismatic witchcraft, the spirit of seduction, carnality, greed, perversion, division, and the spirit of the age.

There was so much the early church fathers and leadership had to fight against in the spiritual and natural. Apostle Paul stewarded his responsibility over Timothy as an apostolic voice to inform, impart, and inspire his spiritual son and resident apostle and overseer in this church. He charged him to wage a good war as he fulfills the call of God.

In light of all this, it is not surprising that Paul chose to close his introduction by emphasizing that the Christian life is a battle and encourages us to *wage the good warfare*. The word "good" means noble or excellent. In other words, Paul is saying that this is the most important war you can fight.

First Timothy 1:18-20 instills urgency to the mission Timothy was given in First Timothy 1:3, which is to guard against the false teachings Paul described. The key to this effort is maintaining the same faith that has been passed along. The apostle Paul encouraged his spiritual son to wage war with this prophetic word. We can use the prophetic Word of God in our lives to fight against the enemy. It is the prophecy that causes many people to go through some unseen affliction and conflicts. The enemy is threatened by those upon whom the Word of God is placed. Your prophetic word becomes a weapon of war against the enemy. Timothy was encouraged to use his prophecy in times of testing.

Timothy was instructed to use the prophetic charge spoken over him to persevere and aid him against false teachers, prophecies, etc. in the church. His prophecy was a weapon of truth to contend against falsehood. Never despise prophecy or God's prophetic word over your life. First Thessalonians 5:20 says, *"Do not treat prophecies with contempt."* In other words, don't kick it to the side or deem it worthless.

Timothy had to wield his prophecies against every lie that came from the enemy. The greater your prophecy, the greater the warfare that the enemy will send against you. How I use my prophecy as a weapon against the enemy is by obeying and fulfilling the Word of the Lord. I love the Amplified Version of First Timothy 1:18, *"This command I entrust to you, Timothy, my son, in accordance with the prophecies previously made concerning you, so that [inspired and aided] by them you may fight the good fight [in contending with false teachers]."*

We fight the good fight using the prophetic word of God and God's logos (written Word). That is why Jesus says in Matthew 4:4, *"It is written: 'Man shall not live on bread alone, but on every word that comes from the mouth of God.'"* We need both the spoken (prophetic and proceeding rhema word) and the written word (logos) of God to defeat the deceptive works of the devil. Take a look at what Romans 15:4 says, *"For everything that was written in the past was written to teach us, so that through the endurance taught in the Scriptures and the encouragement they provide we might have hope."*

As we move on to the next chapter, God wants us always to remember the He doesn't want you to be defeated by the enemy. Because He is for you, who can be against you? Being defeated is often a temporary condition; however, giving up is what makes it permanent. You are not defeated. Don't give up in the brunt of the battle—stand your ground and fight with the Holy Spirit's empowerment and authority.

You are a soldier anointed of the Holy Spirit to win every unseen battle of war! You are not alone! The God of war is with you to the end! When I am going through spiritual resistance from the enemy, I mediate on Psalm 68:1 (ESV) and declare: *"God shall arise, his enemies shall be scattered; and those who hate him shall flee before him!"*

Chapter 2

THE UNSEEN WAR

For we do not wrestle against flesh and blood, but against principalities, against powers, against the rulers of the darkness of this age, against spiritual hosts of wickedness in the heavenly places (Ephesians 6:12 NKJV).

When believers give their lives totally over to Christ's Kingdom, they automatically become direct enemies of the devil and his demons. You become an open target and are considered a traitor in the mind of the enemy. Also, you have committed treason against his demonic institution, kingdom, and rule when you transitioned from sinner to believer.

Colossians 1:12-14 (ESV) says, *"giving thanks to the Father, who has qualified you to share in the inheritance of the saints in light. He has delivered us from the domain of darkness and transferred us to the kingdom of his beloved Son, in whom we have redemption, the forgiveness of sins."* The Lord rescued you from the power of the darkness and brought you into the Kingdom of light of His beloved Son.

This is why satan knows that when you sin, he can go before the Lord to bring accusations against you to charge you of them so that you are penalized, judged, and sentenced for your war crimes before the courts of Heaven. Thank God for His Son—Jesus—who paid the price for the reparation of our sins and that we are blood-washed through the blood atonement. There is an unseen war going within and all around you.

One of the greatest decoy weapons against the Body of Christ is not the enemy we can see with the natural eyes but the ones we cannot see.

UNCOVER THE UNSEEN

Understand that the unseen enemies that go unnoticed and unchecked are the greatest threat to humanity, especially the Body of Christ of believers. To understand the unseen war, we must first understand the natural and spiritual realms. Beneath our tangible and natural landscape lurks an unseen spiritual realm where invisible battles rage. It's a dangerous sphere!

If you are truly prepared to remove the blinders and pierce into the invisible realm, God will begin to reveal to you and teach you through the truth in His Word about the archenemy and foe, satan, also known as lucifer, the serpent, son of the morning, and the great dragon.

The enemy's main purpose is to steal, kill, and destroy, and God uncovers in Ephesians chapter 6 satan's cunning and deceptive battle plan. We must understand first a biblical truth that the unseen or invisible world is just as real as the seen or visible world. This spiritual world is just as tangible as the natural one. There is a system, order, and protocol in this spiritual dimension. There are angelic beings and civilization beyond the natural one.

Humans exist between two worlds—the natural and the spiritual. The natural realm can be felt, heard, seen, tasted, and touched. There is a natural kingdom located in the natural world as well, residents who live in a natural kingdom. Whatever city, state, and nation you live in is considered part of the natural visible realm.

Daily you can see people and experience the natural elements, atmosphere, and environment all around you through sights, smells, and sounds. However, there is another world in which we also reside. This is the spiritual world we cannot see with our natural or physical eyes—yet it exists and is very much real. Apostle Paul reveals the natural and spiritual division.

First Corinthians 15:40 says there is a natural body and there is a spiritual body. If there is a natural body, then it will take a natural body to live in a natural world. However, humans are made up of three dimensions—they are spirit beings with an eternal soul and spirit. Humans are comprised of a body, soul, and spirit. Our spiritual being (soul and spirit) is composed of a spiritual realm, just as our natural bodies are composed of the natural world.

To understand the unseen war, we have to discern the invisible realm. We can see this in the Old Testament where the prophet Elisha was given prophetic intelligence from the Lord that frustrated a certain king's multiple plans against him in Second Kings chapter 6. The prophet was able to discern and see in the invisible realm a supernatural angelic army ready to go to war. Second Kings 6:8-18 (GW) says:

> *Whenever the king of Aram was fighting against Israel, he asked for advice from his officers about where they were to camp. So the man of God would send a message to the king of Israel, "Be careful not to go by that place. The Arameans are hiding there." Then the king of Israel would send someone to the place that the man of God told him about. Elisha warned them so that they would be on their guard. He did this repeatedly.*

The king of Aram was very angry about this. He called his officers and asked them, "Won't you tell me who among us is a spy for the king of Israel?" One of his officers answered, "No one, Your Majesty. Elisha, the prophet in Israel, tells the king of Israel everything you say—even what you say in your bedroom." The king said, "Find out where he is. Then I will send men to capture him." The king was told, "He is in Dothan." So the king sent horses and chariots and a large fighting unit there. They came at night and surrounded the city.

When the servant of the man of God got up in the morning and went outside, he saw troops, horses, and chariots surrounding the city. Elisha's servant asked, "Master, what should we do?" Elisha answered, "Don't be afraid. We have more forces on our side than they have on theirs." Then Elisha prayed, "Lord, please open his eyes so that he may see." **The Lord opened the servant's eyes and let him see.** *The mountain around Elisha was full of fiery horses and chariots. As the Arameans came down to get him, Elisha prayed to the Lord, "Please strike these people with blindness." The Lord struck them with blindness, as Elisha had asked.*

SEEING IN THE UNSEEN REALM

We can see specifically that the prophet prays for God to open the eyes of his servant that he may see. The prophet was really asking the Lord to open the spiritual eyesight of his servant so that he could see into the unseen realm. When God opened his eyes, he saw in a world beyond the natural that was in the spirit, but appearing natural. He saw in the spiritual realm the mountain full of horses and chariots of fire surrounding Elisha. There was more with them in the unseen realm than those who were coming against them in the natural realm. Many believers don't realize how powerful we are and what access we can tap into.

Interesting enough, when God opened the spiritual eyes of the young man, a supernatural exchange was happening as Elisha prayed to the Lord that his enemies would be blinded—and their natural eyes were suddenly blinded. The point is, there are two realities existing at the same time all around us. That is why it's important to discern spiritually so you can understand the resistance, mishaps, misfortunate, opposition, problems, and attacks that seem to come out of nowhere. You could be experiencing the result of something happening in the invisible sphere—spiritual warfare.

Spiritual warfare must be discerned and understood with a spiritual mind-set and with a biblical perspective. It will take a spiritual comprehension to understand not only spiritual warfare but spiritual things in general. A carnal mind doesn't comprehend spiritual things. In our natural, sinful state, there is no way we can discern spiritual things. First Corinthians 2:14 (ESV) says it like this: *"The natural person does not accept the things of the Spirit of God, for they are folly to him, and he is not able to understand them because they are spiritually discerned."*

DISCERNING SPIRITUALLY

Spiritual things must be spiritually discerned. The story of the prophet Elisha and his servant is a prime example of the spiritual discernment needed to better examine closely what was happening. There was a natural battle in which troops of the nation of Syria had surrounded the small town of Dothan, the residence of Elisha. When Elisha's servant, Gehazi, saw this great army host surrounding them, he became instantly fearful.

However, the prophet Elisha didn't flinch; rather, he prayed that God would open his servant's spiritual eyes. His servant needed to see what Elisha already knew existed in the spiritual world. God opened Gehazi's natural eyes and permitted him to see into the invisible world. He was able to visibly see for himself the superior host of angel armies of God aligned and armed for battle.

The unseen war is raging each and every day. You must ask the Lord to open your eyes to discern and to see into the spiritual world. God could open your natural eyes as He did with Gehazi. Or reveal it through a dream or vision or supernatural trance. Whatever method He sovereignly decides will show you there is a real world in the spirit.

I believe God wants to open the natural eyes of the Church at large to see into the world of the spirit. There is an army coming against the Body of Christ to cause fear to set in. But the Lord will raise up Elisha-type leaders who will equip us with the necessary war weaponry to discern and see the unseen war approaching. They will teach us how to see in the spirit and prepare for war as God will open the eyes of Gehazi-types of believers who will see that there is nothing to fear. There are more with you than against you.

Unfortunately, there are many individuals who, like those in the city of Dothan, are unprepared and spiritually asleep. They are unaware of the unseen threat they are facing and that the enemy has surrounded them and is positioned for an attack. We must always watch and pray.

However, there are those who will rise up in this hour and recognize by discerning that there is a spiritual conflict occurring, like Elisha who received prophetic intelligence of the king's warfare plots devised in his bedchambers. These Elisha-type leaders will identify and locate the enemy while recognizing the forces of God that will assure flawless victory.

Keep in mind that even though there is an unseen war happening each and every day around us in the spirit realm, the battle is not yours—it's the Lord's. Personally, I was encouraged when I read a simple but powerful passage of Scripture in Deuteronomy 20:4 (ESV) where it says, *"For the Lord your God is he who goes with you to fight for you against your enemies, to give you the victory."*

Clearly, God's Word says that He will go with you, to fight for you against your adversaries, to give you victory and to save you. There is nothing to fear when it comes to the spiritual world that you don't see. However, it's important not to be ignorant of what exists behind the unveiled spiritual realm.

That is why the enemy is fearful of a praying believer—because God will start to open your spiritual eyes or activate spiritual discernment into what the enemy is up to before the attack comes to you. Elisha knew what the king was up to before the enemy surrounded them. There is one Kingdom coming against another kingdom, and God's Kingdom always wins.

War in the Spirit, Not the Flesh

In Second Corinthians chapter 10, we see that even Paul writes a direct and assertive letter to the church at Corinth as it pertains to warfare going on there. He was basically saying that though we are carnal beings who walk in the flesh, we don't war after the flesh. He wrote:

> *For though we live in the world, we do not wage war as the world does. The weapons we fight with are not the weapons of the world. On the contrary, they have divine power to demolish strongholds. We demolish arguments and every*

pretension that sets itself up against the knowledge of God, and we take captive every thought to make it obedient to Christ. And we will be ready to punish every act of disobedience, once your obedience is complete (2 Corinthians 10:3-6).

Paul the apostle goes on to expressively compare the ministry of the Gospel to warfare, he uses a most apt similitude. The Christian life, it is true, is a perpetual war for whoever totally surrenders themselves to God's service. The call to arms will have no truce from satan at any time, he will constantly harass to no end.

Surrendered believers become ministers of the Word and leaders who are standard bearers on the frontlines of the battlefield, going ahead of others. Certainly there are none whom satan harasses more and are more severely assaulted, or that sustain in spiritual combat more numerous or more dreadful onsets. Seriously taking these things into account, the Gospel is like a fire that ignites satan's fury.

Apostle Paul faced this constant fury by the enemy while also defending his apostleship when speaking boldly to the church about what is happening to him in the flesh as well as being aware of the spiritual activities in the unseen realm. The unseen war is real for those called to minister the Word of the Lord. But! Paul says that we can use God's supernatural divine weapons that:

- Pull down and demolish strongholds
- Demolish arguments and false teachings
- Prepare us to use God's knowledge to defeat the enemy

We can see that these weapons have a divine purpose against demonic activity. The unseen spiritual war is a battle that involves all men and women, boys and girls as well. There is a daily invisible spiritual war going on around, a wrestling match between good and evil—there is also a war of wills between flesh and blood—each other. May we exhibit Jesus' love and compassion for one another (John 13:34-35).

Warfare Struggles

Ephesians 6:12 (GW) declares: *"This is not a wrestling match against a human opponent. We are wrestling with rulers, authorities, the powers who govern this world of darkness, and spiritual forces that control evil in the heavenly world."*

There is a constant struggle going on and the apostle Paul also emphasizes to this particular church that to wrestle with flesh and blood will not only be useless, but highly pernicious. One of the rules of engagement as it pertains to this situation is that we must be on the offense and attack the enemy first who wounds and tries to attack God's people from his concealment—who slays first and appears later. Paul goes on to highlight what those struggles are that we as believers will contend with:

1. Rulers
2. Authorities
3. Dark world powers
4. Spiritual forces of evil in heavenly places

It is the strategy of the enemy in this unseen war to invoke terror in the hearts of God's people. The apostle Paul describes our unseen enemy as formidable, not to overwhelm us with fear, doubt, and intimidation, but to quicken our ability in the Holy Spirit and confidence in God's power to be diligent and earnest; for there is a middle course to be observed. When the devil is unheeded, ignored, or neglected, he does his utmost to oppress us with sloth, and afterward disarms us by inflicting fear, terror, and anxiety hoping that his rules of engagement that he initiated will ultimately cause God's people to be left vanquished.

Paul relentlessly labors to keep the body of believers on high alert and informed of satan's unpredictable tactics. By speaking of the power of the enemy, Paul clearly employs readers to understand that this adversary is not to be ignored or even to be safely despised. Whether believers want to realize it or not, they are in the middle of a spiritual war. Only unbelievers are prisoners of war taken captive in bondage to evil and sin by the enemy forces. They are not just prisoners of war but victims of the war. However, every believer of Christ has been delivered, rescued, set free from the grips of the enemy through the sacrifice of Jesus Christ, and we are overcomers and victors!

THE ONGOING BATTLE

Even though believers are free from the enemy doesn't remove the fact that you are not entirely discharged from duty as a soldier in God's army. You are still engaged in the war raging against you even though you are set free by Jesus Christ. The wrestling match continues when you are a child of God (read Ephesians 6). When it comes to spiritual warfare as a believer when engaging the enemy, wrestling involves close contact. It's not social spiritual distancing! Rather, it's an ongoing warfare that no one is exempt from and cannot be watched from the sideline or in the bunker.

One of the obvious things the enemy attempts to do among Christian believers is to make us spiritual assailants against one another. He loves to see division, competition, jealousy, envy, unforgiveness, hate, pride, and so much more evil happen within the church community.

We must remember that our warfare is not against each other as believers—it's against the real enemy and instigator, the devil.

We must guard our hearts and watch and pray for each other. The enemy has the upper hand when he sees believers use their spiritual gifts against each other instead of using their gifts for the purpose God gave them to use sovereignly to edify each other.

We are at a disadvantage when we use the gifts of God to tear down each other or to control each other. Charismatic witchcraft and so much more is running rampant among different streams in the Body of Christ—and this should not be. I will talk about this more in a later chapter. The unseen war is presently active, and it will take spiritual discerning believers to carry out the duties of the King and His Kingdom.

Oftentimes when people think about spiritual warfare, they believe it to be some scary movie, like *The Exorcist* when I was growing up. But today there is so much darkness not only on the movie screen but also on television and on the Internet. Netflix has many series that glorify the demonic like Charmed, Merlin, The Witcher, The Order, The Magicians, Good Witch, Supernatural, Vampire Diaries that it seems everywhere you look there is something dark or works of evil.

But not all spiritual warfare is like that at all. The unseen warfare that is happening in and around us may at times be initiated by demonic spirits and those operating in witchcraft. Watching movies like these mentioned above as a believer can cause a Christian to be susceptible to the enemy's tactics and lies. We must guard our eyes and ear gates to these demonic frequencies and projections through certain television shows, networks, movies, paganistic holidays like Halloween and worldly activities that seems innocent but spiritually dangerous. God doesn't want us to be easily duped by methods of the enemy to lure us into sinful activities or open a door to demonic oppression and torments.

Two Spiritual Kingdoms

There is a natural kingdom where humans live. The Word of God speaks of these natural, visible kingdoms that have been for some time under the influence and power of the enemy—satan.

For example, satan tempted Jesus for forty days and forty nights while He was in the wilderness fasting and praying. Satan had a proposition for Jesus in Matthew 4:8-9: *"Again, the devil took him to a very high mountain and showed him all the kingdoms of the world and their splendor. 'All this I will give you,' he said, 'if you will bow down and worship me.'"* How was satan able to offer Jesus all the kingdoms of the world if he wasn't the god of this world.

> *Satan, who is the god of this world, has blinded the minds of those who don't believe. They are unable to see the glorious light of the Good News. They don't understand this message about the glory of Christ, who is the exact likeness of God* (2 Corinthians 4:4 NLT).

Satan has a spiritual kingdom. However, he has the ability and power to influence the natural kingdom of this world or age through humans. The world system has come under the rule of satan, the evil one. Other biblical writings explicitly teach that *"the whole world is under the control of the evil one"* (1 John 5:19), for satan is *"the god of the world"* (2 Corinthians 4:4 ESV) and the ruling *"prince of the power of the air"* (Ephesians 2:2 ESV).

Jesus addresses this evil "prince" as the leader of a relatively unified and pervasive army of spiritual powers and demons. You can see his rule infiltrating and influencing the seven spheres of society and culture. This is some very serious stuff to know—that the devil has a seat of power over the world system that has become his seat of rulership. We understand that he lost his position in Heaven and was later ejected and cast down to earth.

However, this banishment didn't happen in the first century, it predated the Garden of Eden and the unseen war started long ago before humans even existed. The Bible says in Psalm 24:1-3 (NKJV): *"The earth is the Lord's, and all its fullness, the world and those who dwell therein. For He has founded it upon the seas, and established it upon the waters. Who may ascend into the hill of the Lord? Or who may stand in His holy place?"*

Clearly this Scripture reveals that the earth belongs to the Lord, the fullness of it, the world and those who dwell in it. It doesn't belong to the devil. The Lord has given humankind dominion to rule over all the earth after the likeness and in the image of God. Man was created to rule over the earth with the same god-like authority that the Lord rules over all things.

Heaven's Spiritual Representatives

Humans were literally given the lordship, to be the lords of the earth. Even Jesus says truthfully in John 10:34, speaking to the unbelieving Jews about what was written in the Law, *"Is it not written in your own Law, 'I have said you are "gods"'?"* Clearly, Jesus makes no mistake of our spiritual position, DNA, and supernatural genetics and identity as spiritual representatives of God on earth to rule with god-like dominion in this natural domain.

God has appointed man and given him dominion over the works of His creation and placed everything under their authority, or feet. However when sin entered, that opened the door for the unseen enemy, the devil, to influence and deceive those in power. Thank God for Jesus who came to destroy the works, powers, and influence of the devil in the first century. God needed to reconcile what was lost and redeem His people back to Him. He loved the world so much that He had to send His Son to bring reformation, change, and eternal life (read John 3:16).

You can see that the only weapon and strategy that works for the enemy is to blind the minds of those who will not adhere to the Gospel. In other words, satan blinds the minds of unbelievers. I'm not referring to their actual eyesight or natural physical sight, but to blind them from understanding, comprehending, and embracing the Truth that shines in darkness. The enemy wants to keep people blinded to the truth of God's Word.

The devil wants people to remain in his domain of darkness. In other words, the enemy wants people to remain ignorant of their destiny, blinded from the truth of God's Word and His supernatural realities, and for them to walk in doom and gloom. That's why it's imperative for believers to discern the works of the enemy. One of the works of the enemy is deception! He uses deception to manipulate by controlling the uninformed, ignored, and unheeded. Humankind has too long been hoodwinked and bamboozled.

Don't Get Duped by the Enemy

What does the word "bamboozled" mean? It means "to be deceived by underhanded methods, to dupe, hoodwink, confuse, frustrate, or throw off thoroughly." Today, the only way satan can gain access and power in the world system is if it is given to him by worldly, rebellious, ignorant, and demonically influenced people who are in power and authority in those seats. Satan likes to play mind games, which is one of his wartime strategies.

Don't get duped by the enemy in this season. Stand on guard and be alert! Empower yourself with the necessary spiritual tools, resources, and leadership that can protect you from the wiles of the devil. The unseen war is after not only your soul (mind, will, and emotions) but after your decision-making process as well. We must know there are two battlefronts that we are engaged in—the *natural* and the *spiritual*. Both kingdoms are simultaneously operating and engaging.

The natural kingdom is made up of people in power and authority as a civilization on earth.

In addition to the natural kingdom of this world, there are also two spiritual kingdoms: God's spiritual Kingdom and satan's spiritual kingdom. All people are living in the natural kingdom and one or the other spiritual kingdoms. The satanic kingdom consists of satan, his demons, and rebellious and sinful people who are blinded to God's Word. Carnality, flesh, sin, and worldly lusts are driving demonic forces at work in the world system today. Those in this kingdom are forces of evil.

On the other hand, God's Kingdom is the very opposite and consists of God the Father, Jesus Christ, and the Holy Spirit, angelic spiritual beings, and righteous, faithful, loving, and obedient men and women submitted totally to the lordship of Jesus and to God's Word. Those occupying this eternal kingdom are forces of good. I want to be clear that the Kingdom of God is not the church and the church is not the Kingdom of God. They are two separate entities.

Kingdom Power

However, the church, which is the *ekklesia*, functions in Kingdom power and authority through the Holy Spirit. The Kingdom of God operates through the church, which is the body of believers. Matthew 16:18-19 (ESV) confirms: *"And I tell you, you are Peter, and on this rock I will build my church, and the gates of hell* [Hades] *shall not prevail against it. I will give you the keys of the kingdom of heaven, and whatever you bind on earth shall be bound in heaven, and whatever you loose on earth shall be loosed in heaven."* The church and the kingdom are working in unison, but are not one and the same. The church possesses the Kingdom and uses the keys of authority and power to push back darkness and disable demonic powers.

In ancient times, one method to gain control of the enemy was to control the gates and conquer the city. Genesis 22:17 (ESV) speaks of the promise of Abraham's blessing from God where it says, *"your offspring shall possess the gate of his enemies."* Jesus is the greater Abraham in the New Testament who promises to build His church and declared emphatically that, *"the gates of Hades will not overcome it"* (Matthew 16:18). Having an understanding of the term "gates" biblically and why rulers, prophets, and political leaders met at the gates to receive counsel is important.

Jesus was basically declaring that all demonic plots, plans, and evil works of satan himself will never defeat or prevail against the church. The strategy of the enemy and plans of hell is to control the gates. But! Jesus gave us the keys to the Kingdom. We are to become gatekeepers and watchmen through prayer to guard and protect what God has given us stewardship over.

The keys of the Kingdom allow believers to permit and prohibit things to happen on earth under God's heavenly supervision, delegation, and earthly jurisdiction (domain). The church prevails over the works and powers of hell. The invisible war that is going on in the unseen realm is against the power of Jesus' church. Jesus' spiritual warfare strategy is to empower the Body of Christ to use the power, access, and authority given to them by Jesus in every generation. The unseen war is between the power of darkness and death and power of light and life.

Possessing the gates of our enemy will dismantle, disarm, and defeat the works of the enemy that comes to steal, kill, and destroy. The keys of the Kingdom are not natural keys but spiritual and symbolic representing the authority and power by God to His people to rule on earth as the church by governing and addressing the judicial and spiritual affairs of Heaven. It's all about knowing what you possess and have access to spiritually. The gates of hades are the satanic strategy of hell that ultimately bring destruction and death. This is binding and loosing power through the church of Jesus Christ.

A WARRIOR BRIDE OF CHRIST

I believe that God is raising up warriors and a family army that will contend daily for the survival and breakthroughs for destiny of the church. We are more than conquerors in Christ Jesus. These conquering warriors of God's army will disarm the plans of the enemy and he will be defeated once and for all in life.

Keep in mind and know for certain through biblical truth that our Lord Jesus is the Head of His church and He *"disarmed the powers and authorities, he made a public spectacle of them, triumphing over them by the cross"* (Colossians 2:15). This is still our mandate today as the Body of Christ is to do the same spiritually speaking. You have been given the power and delegated authority to disarm the powers of the enemy by discharging the supernatural power of God through the Holy Spirit.

The plan of the devil is the steal, kill, and destroy Jesus' assignment on earth and to prevent Him from fulfilling His Father's will on earth. In Matthew 16:18, Jesus talks about the gates of hell and the keys to bind and loose while referencing His soon-impending death on the cross, knowing that He would be crucified and buried and would be later raised from the dead on the third day to build His church. Matthew 28:18-20 reveals the power given to Jesus when He said to His disciples:

> *All authority in heaven and on earth has been given to me.*
> *Therefore go and make disciples of all nations, baptizing*
> *them in the name of the Father and of the Son and of the*

Holy Spirit, and teaching them to obey everything I have commanded you. And surely I am with you always, to the very end of the age.

We must understand that satan does possess the power of death, and he will continue to use that power in attempts to destroy Jesus' church today. That's why Jesus was emphasized and referenced His death, burial, and resurrection that would in fact dismantle the powers of death and hell that could not hold Him. Death would not hold Him in the grave, and the church would not die either—rather because of Jesus' sacrifice and power over the spiritual realm, He would build the church and it will and survive and thrive in the face of unseen warfare by the enemy.

Clearly, Jesus was declaring that death has no power to hold the Lord's people hostage and captive. The gates of hell can be breached and its hell-bound gates are not strong enough to over-power, prevail, and imprison God's people, the church. Jesus our Lord has conquered death once and for all as King (Romans 8:2; Acts 2:24). And because *"Death no longer has dominion over Him"* (Romans 6:9 NKJV), it is no longer master over those who belong to Him.

It is great to know that in this unseen war that the invisible Kingdom of God and power through the church will never fail, though future generations would succumb to the power of natural death, yet other generations after will arise to perpetuate the glorious church victoriously. We have to know that Jesus promises that His church, the "called out," will prevail no matter what: *"Yet a little while and the world will see me no more, but you will see me. Because I live, you also will live"* (John 14:19 ESV).

The Church of Jesus—the called out ones—will engage in unseen warfare against the powers of hell and will prevail to continue Jesus' mission on earth as He has commanded. Believers have been liberated from the devil through Jesus Christ and are overcomers and victors in this unseen war raging against them daily.

Before we can go into more in-depth topics on rules of engagement as it pertains to spiritual warfare to discern, disarm, and defeat the works of the devil, we must first have a clear understanding who, what, why, where, and how this invisible war began. We have to ask ourselves, where does this invisible battle rage? The devil's purpose is to maintain full control of the kingdoms of this world. He wants to keep control and not allow it to be under the power and authority of God.

THE ORIGIN OF SPIRITUAL BATTLE

In addition to demonic attacks on the church as a whole, spiritual warfare is raging within the hearts, minds, and souls of individual men and women. As mentioned before, the devil comes to blind the minds of unbelievers and attacks God's people in the areas of prayer, worship, reading the Word of God, their purpose, calling, identity, and their God-given destiny.

How did this unseen war begin? The invisible war was initiated in Heaven with lucifer who was created by the Lord as a beautiful angel and was part of God's Kingdom. Lucifer wanted to be like God and take over the Lord's Kingdom. Isaiah 14:12-15 speaks of it:

> *How you have fallen from heaven, morning star, son of the dawn! You have been cast down to the earth, you who once laid low the nations! You said in your heart, "I will ascend to the heavens; I will raise my throne above the stars of God; I will sit enthroned on the mount of assembly, on the utmost heights of Mount Zaphon. I will ascend above the tops of the clouds; I will make myself like the Most High." But you*

are brought down to the realm of the dead, to the depths of the pit.

The rebellious group of angels later called demons follow lucifer's prideful movement against God. Lucifer and his angelic rebels were ousted from Heaven by the Lord. Later, they decided to set up their own kingdom on earth. Satan began to take on different names after losing his heavenly name and identity after being evicted from Heaven to earth. The Book of Revelation clearly explains where the invisible battle began—in Heaven.

Then war broke out in heaven. Michael and his angels fought against the dragon, and the dragon and his angels fought back. But he was not strong enough, and they lost their place in heaven. The great dragon was hurled down— that ancient serpent called the devil, or Satan, who leads the whole world astray. He was hurled to the earth, and his angels with him (Revelation 12:7-9).

The war in Heaven was between Michael and his angelic host against the dragon (satan) and his angels. Lucifer became known as satan and the angels that followed him in rebellion are known as demon spirits. Demon spirits (fallen angels) can gain access to people's lives to manipulate, control, and torment humans who are under satan's rule and command.

Also, they gain legal access through ungodly humans who are demonically influenced and motivated to perform acts of pure wickedness and evil. Satan commands his demons to perform demonic activities on his behalf in his kingdom of darkness. He oftentimes combines these powerful dark forces with the flesh and the world to war against the human will.

THE WAR OVER SIN

Lastly, we must understand the purpose or reason behind the spiritual battle. You are the most lethal threat against the powers of darkness. You were created in the image of God and for the glory of the Lord (read Genesis 2). The unseen war against humankind began with the first temptation in the garden of Eden (read Genesis 3). Through the serpent in the Garden, satan tempted Adam and Eve, which caused them to sin. This ultimately resulted in all humans inheriting the sin nature: *"Therefore, just as sin entered the world through one man, and death through sin, and in this way death came to all people, because all sinned"* (Romans 5:12).

Furthermore, God said, *"And I will put enmity between you and the woman, and between your offspring and hers; he will crush your head, and you will strike his heel"* (Genesis 3:15) We can clearly see by this Scripture the unseen war between man and the forces of evil. However, it is through the Seed of the woman that the forces of good represented by the Lord Jesus Christ will crush the evil war strategy of the devil. Adam and Eve's sin of disobedience to God's commands after being tempted by satan caused humankind to inherit the sin nature.

Due to sin, humankind was separated from the Lord and condemned to death. However, the Father always had a plan to reconcile His children to Him. His love for humans is so immense that He sent His Son into the world, not to condemn it, but that the world, through His Son Jesus Christ, might be saved (see John 3:16-17). Our confession and repentance of sin through faith in Jesus allows men and women to be freed from the power of the enemy. Jesus' death and resurrection not only defeated the works of the unseen enemy, but first resulted in our salvation from sin.

Someone may ask, "If satan is defeated by Jesus, then why are we still engaging in warfare? Why does this invisible war still rage today?" We must understand that after any war there will still be some level of resistance from radical troops who will not concede to defeat and will relentlessly fight until they are subdued and forced to give up. Although Jesus defeated the enemy, there are still occupying forces of the enemy who will not leave the area freely. When we fully understand spiritual warfare at the basic level, then we have the advantage over the enemy and are able to properly address these evil powers head-on.

Today, we must understand that it has always been and will continue to be the enemy's plan to keep people in bondage to sin and to reign havoc in our lives. The raging war is intense one to overcome the deceptive methods of the devil who loves to entice people into lustful, sinful desires and living. Satan's primary aim is to tempt people through their minds, will, and emotions (soul) which rightfully belong to the Lord.

The enemy is not going to give up easily or freely, his tactics and plans are to directly and indirectly thwart the Lord's plan and purpose for His people. The unseen warfare is a continuum of the war in Heaven, but now on earth through the world system. The spiritual conflict that is raging will continue until the final battle and victory by the Lord's return. Understanding basic training as soldier in the army of God and the root cause of this invisible battle will bring you into spiritual warfare 101.

Chapter 3

SPIRITUAL WARFARE 101

For though we walk in the flesh, we do not war according to the flesh. For the weapons of our warfare are not carnal but mighty in God for pulling down strongholds (2 Corinthians 10:3-4 NKJV).

One early Monday morning a young man was out walking his dog. As he went along the sidewalk entering the park area, he noticed a table with a large sign on it. The sign stated: "Register today to see the world for free. Housing allowance, lodging, food, college tuition, and everything is provided." In fact, the sign stated that he would be paid a salary, too. This offer sounded promising and too good to be true to pass up. He went over to the table and signed his name on the registration form, excited about the benefits. To his surprise, he was suddenly given a large rifle, a military uniform, and equipment.

Unfortunately, the boy did not realize what he signed up for and what was expected of him. He was excited about the benefits but didn't realize that his life would be on the line as sooner or later he would have to go to war with an enemy whose sole purpose was to see him defeated.

SALVATION STARTS THE WAR

Likewise, many Christian believers today give their lives to the Lord Jesus Christ after receiving an amazing invitation from Him to be their Lord and Savior. However, after experiencing the bliss of abundant love, joy, peace, and acceptance, they were surprised to find they too have an enemy. Perhaps they expected to live a perfect life with no problems or challenges to face. We must understand that salvation doesn't end the battle that believers face.

Like the young man who was excited about all the benefits advertised on the sign, many believers don't know there is a real enemy that automatically hates you because you are a child of the living God and have been drafted and engrafted into His Kingdom. I must say that this young man didn't expect to be given weapons to defend himself right away—just like believers don't realize that at conversion they are given spiritual weapons to win every battle.

God gives us the necessary spiritual weaponry and knowledge as it pertains to spiritual warfare and the real unseen enemy we may face daily. Keep in mind that when you accepted Jesus as your Savior, you also accepted satan as your enemy. That's part of the deal. In other words, you were transferred from the kingdom of darkness into the Kingdom of light, you broke rank and departed from the enemy's army and joined God's army! One of the revengeful plots of the enemy when trying to get back at the Lord is to start attacking God's children—you and me!

Because you are made in God's image and after His likeness, and because you are now a born-again believer, you are in the midst of a war you didn't ask for, initiate, want, or understand. Also, the battle seems impossible to overcome and win. The questions that come to your mind may include:

- What do I do now?

- How can I prepare for what is to come?
- What are my options to safeguard myself?
- How long will this warfare or war last?
- Where can I receive instant combat training for this level of spiritual warfare?
- What am I up against daily?
- How can I discern, disarm, and defeat the works of the enemy in my life?

Let me be clear that the notion or idea of spiritual warfare following salvation isn't anything new. In the Word of God, there are instances throughout the Old Testament of satan resisting and opposing God even though his plans always come to nothing in the end. However, if his agenda is possibly able to cause the slightest delay or wrinkle in the plan of God, then the enemy has the advantage.

Spiritual warfare isn't a favorite subject of believers to address, but it's necessary and essential for spiritual victory, longevity, prosperity, sanity, and divine breakthrough for all Spirit-filled believers ready for war in this season. When you think about warfare, what comes to your mind? What is warfare? And why does the Bible make reference of it as it pertains to the life of believers? Oftentimes many Christian believers are unaware of spiritual warfare activities happening in and around them. The insights and teachings contained in this book lead you to understanding the unseen war and answers to all your questions about spiritual warfare.

It's Not a Natural Battle

Have you ever wondered or thought to yourself why unusual or unnecessary things occur seasonally, periodically, annually, weekly, monthly, or even daily? We must understand the unseen threat that the enemy poses against born-again believers. The fight we are facing as believers is not a natural battle. It's a spiritual one. Moreover, the Bible declares in Second Corinthians 10:3-4, *"For though we live in the world, we do not wage war as the world does. The weapons we fight with are not the weapons of the world...."*

In other words, even though we live in the world, we don't wage war like the world does. The war we fight is a spiritual war and the weapons we fight with are spiritual weapons. The weapons the Lord has given us are spiritual and can disarm and destroy demonic weapons of mass destruction against the Body of Christ. In addition, these weapons of God can defeat the weapons of the devil.

When it comes to understanding spiritual warfare, there are two errors that are equally prevalent in the Body of Christ. Some overemphasize or underemphasize this topic. I have witnessed during years in ministry that some people seem to blame everything on the devil. But there are things the devil and his demon accomplices haven't caused to happen. Therefore, I always say that everything bad is not always because of demons—bad things may be the result of the person's decisions. Bad or unwise decisions on our part isn't something the devil made us do.

We can't over-spiritualize spiritual warfare and blame every sin, every conflict, and every problem on demons that need to be driven out. What do I mean by overemphasizing spiritual warfare? When someone's car breaks down, that doesn't mean it was a result of demons. It may be the result that the person didn't maintain it properly.

On the other hand, some believers underestimate the power of demons and the effects of spiritual warfare that they completely ignore the spiritual realm and the fact that the Word of God says that our conflicts and battles are against spiritual powers of evil. The key to successful spiritual warfare is finding the biblical balance. Jesus sometimes cast demons out of people; other times He healed people with no mention of the demonic. Apostle Paul instructs believers to wage war against the sin within themselves (Romans 6) and warns them to resist the devil's schemes (Ephesians 6:10-18).

DISCERNING TEMPTATIONS

Jesus Christ is the ultimate example of resisting temptation and rebuking satan when it comes to personal spiritual warfare. Jesus discerned the enemy speaking through Peter in Matthew 16:23, *"Jesus turned and said to Peter, "Get behind me, Satan! You are a stumbling block to me; you do not have in mind the concerns of God, but merely human concerns."*

And in Matthew 4 we see how our Lord Jesus handled direct attacks from satan himself when He was in the wilderness fasting and praying to the Father. Jesus released a direct command, *"Away from me, Satan! For it is written: 'Worship the Lord your God, and serve him only.' Then the devil left him, and angels came and ministered to him"* (Matthew 4:10-11).

You don't have to be afraid of the devil's temptation if you apply the Word of God daily in your life and the power of the name of Jesus. The Word of God is the most powerful, lethal weapon against the temptations and strategies of the enemy—the devil. I love what Psalm 119:11 declares: *"I have hidden your word in my heart that I might not sin against you."*

The enemy doesn't have legal right to run rampant in your life or live in your spiritual atmosphere unless you give him legal authority, access, or an open invitation to do so through unrepented sin, rebellion, unforgiveness, ignorance, and illegal soul ties (relationships) that God hasn't ordained. We will talk about soul ties in the last chapter.

The day-to-day struggles we often may face could be a result of unseen demonic entities working against us to keep us from fulfilling our prophetic purpose and destiny in our generation. The enemy is threatened by those who know their God and will do great exploits in His name. God wants us to gain a deeper understanding of spiritual warfare and its negative impact on our daily lives.

It's time to fight back and safeguard yourself with the biblical knowledge and authority that Jesus has given you through the Holy Spirit to live day-to-day victoriously. Knowing and walking fully in your spiritual authority allows you to discern, disarm, and destroy the destructive, divisive, and demonic powers of the enemy.

The hostility the enemy has against you is because of what God has given to you. Satan is trying to rule in the place that God has given to humankind to rule in Genesis chapter 1. Satan wants to destroy and defame what God has placed in our power to control, rule, and maintain. God wants us to occupy the earth until He comes again.

In other words, take care of God's business on earth while resisting the enemy with the authority and power we possess. The enemy can only win when we wave the white flag of surrender to his attacks and plans. Don't throw in the towel in the boxing ring of life when you are knocked down by the brutal spiritual hits of the enemy. You were built to last and to bounce back.

The spiritual battle we face daily is as real as the devil himself. Understanding basic training and the unseen war from a spiritual perspective will assist you in spiritual warfare. Spiritual warfare 101 is knowing the foundation and fundamentals of war both naturally and spiritually. Knowing the Word of God and the power of Jesus' name must be used by true believers of Christ who possess the authority and power of Jesus in the Holy Spirit.

ACCESSING AND POSSESSING THE POWER TO COMMAND

A word of caution concerning spiritual warfare is in order. The name of Jesus Christ is not some buzzword, tagline, or magical incantation that causes demons to flee from us. Why? Because the seven sons of Sceva are prime examples of what can possibly happen to someone who presumes and operates in an authority they were not legally given (Acts 19:13-16).

The spiritual realm operates in an orderly system. In addition, the spiritual dimension is structured so that demon spirits recognize spiritual authority in a hierarchal manner. Anything illegal or illicit is grounds to be confronted and addressed. The seven sons of Sceva knew Jesus' spiritual authority, power, and capabilities as well as apostle Paul's authority and power through the message he preached of Jesus and with apostolic legal authority as God's bondservant.

Therefore, loosely and ignorantly saying the words, "The Lord rebukes you!" doesn't mean anything if you haven't been given authority by God to say it. The enemy only responds to those who have spiritual authority. For example, the archangel Michael did not rebuke satan in his own power but stated, "The Lord rebuke you!" (see Jude 1:9). That's why we do everything in the name of Jesus. In other words, in the power and authority of the Name that is above all names.

Believers can only defeat the enemy in the power and authority of Jesus Christ who is the Word of God. When we start speaking to the enemy, the devil, we run the risk of being deceived or led astray as Eve was in the Garden (see Genesis 3:1-7).

Our primary focus should be on the Lord and not going around chasing demons. I know many deliverance and spiritual warfare ministers who blindly and ignorantly go on witch hunts looking for devils to cast out. Jesus never did that—and He's our prime example for spiritual warfare and deliverance. Oftentimes, demonic manifestation would happen when Jesus showed up because He is the Word of God and carries the Spirit of God being God in the flesh.

Simply, we must rely solely on God's power, not our own in spiritual warfare 101. We draw on the power of Scripture—the Word of God is the Spirit's sword, which is a piece of the armor of God. We pray and fast in perseverance and holiness, making our appeal to Heaven to see supernatural breakthroughs, healing, and deliverance. We must stand firm (Ephesians 6:13-14); we submit to God; we resist the devil's work (James 4:7), knowing that the God of the angel armies is our overall Protector. *"Truly he is my rock and my salvation; he is my fortress, I will never be shaken"* (Psalm 62:2).

WHO IS THE REAL ENEMY?

Furthermore, it's vitally important to know in spiritual warfare 101 that satan and his demons exist. To deny the existence of satan and his demons is a flat rejection of the Bible's divine inspiration, revelation, and truth. In the Word of God there is a prepared place of eternal fire for *"the devil and his angels"* (Matthew 25:41).

Moreover, the Bible is clear about who the enemy is. Satan, the adversary; he is the devil, our accuser—the enemy of God and humanity. He is the enemy, serpent, dragon, the always-tempting one, deceiver, the father of lies, a murderer from the beginning, ruler of this world, and prince of the power of the air (see 1 Peter 5:8; Matthew 13:25; Revelation 12:10; Romans 16:20; Revelation 20:2; Matthew 4:3; 1 Thessalonians 3:5; John 8:44; 12:31; Ephesians 2:2).

And he is not alone in his evil schemes (Matthew 25:41). These created beings are subject to the sovereignty of God, exercise only limited authority, are fallen and condemned, and will ultimately be defeated by the Lord (see 2 Peter 2:4; Jude 6; Hebrews 2:16; 1 Corinthians 15:24-25). They will suffer eternal punishment (Matthew 25:41).

When approaching spiritual warfare engagement, we must understand it from a spiritual sense and aspect, not carnally. Logically and scripturally speaking, we don't wage war in a carnal, fleshly, worldly, and humanistic way but through spiritual intelligence, weapons, and supernatural power through the Holy Spirit, the Word of God who equips, empowers, and educates us on the spiritual rules of engagement pertaining to spiritual warfare strategies against the invisible forces of the enemy.

Most Christian believers don't speak on the topic of spiritual warfare because they were never taught about it. Or they would rather avoid confrontational issues such as this. Or they believe that God will cover them, so they don't need to do anything. Spiritual warfare 101 is understanding the basics of it biblically and spiritually and knowing how to engage in spiritual battles or warlike combats with the power of God through the Holy Spirit.

In addition, having the proper training and knowledge through seasoned leaders and the Holy Spirit allows you to outwit the enemy while properly handling the Word of God. We must understand basic terms, definitions, principles, and operation of war to conquer the enemy for Kingdom advancement.

MENTAL ADVANTAGE OVER THE ENEMY

I discovered that one of the advantages of gaining a thorough understanding of spiritual warfare, deliverance, the devil, demons, and his kingdom better equipped me to discern the works of the enemy. Researching and reading reliable and sound biblical resources on the topic, I believe wholeheartedly that I am now more knowledgeable about spiritual warfare. When I used to play football, there was a saying that the sports performance is 90 percent mental and 10 percent physical.

However, I beg to differ. I believe that it's 100 percent mental. Why? Because our thoughts influence our actions, and our actions influence our thoughts. That being said, spiritually speaking, to defeat the enemy we must be 100 percent mentally prepared to apply the knowledge, intelligence, and wisdom of God in spiritual warfare battles. Most war strategies and tactics, in my opinion, are first thought out before they are ever executed or implemented physically. The rules of engagement in spiritual warfare are 100 percent having the mind of Christ, the Word of God, and being Holy Spirit-led to have the upper hand against the enemy.

Keep in mind, the enemy is after your belief system. He is after your faith in God. He is after your mind, which is the battlefront of your decisions. I always say that "The greatest form of spiritual warfare is when the enemy counsels your mind." In other words, the war strategies of the enemy against God's people are mind games which are weapons of warfare against you!

There is a difference between war and warfare. What is the difference between the two words? As nouns the difference between war and warfare is that *war* is large-scale, armed conflict between a particular country, countries, or between national, ethnic, or other sizeable groups, usually involving the engagement of military forces. While on the other hand, *warfare* is the waging of war or armed conflict against an enemy (according to wikidiff.com/war/warfare).

What is spiritual warfare? Spiritual warfare, according to Wikipedia, "is the Christian concept of fighting against the work of preternatural evil forces. It is based on the biblical belief in evil spirits, or demons, that are said to intervene in human affairs in various ways. Although spiritual warfare is a prominent feature of neo-charismatic churches, various Christian groups have adopted practices to repel such forces, as based on their doctrine of Christian demonology, too."

SPIRITUAL WARFARE FROM GOD'S PERSPECTIVE

I must say this before we get into other things on the topic of spiritual warfare. The subject of spiritual warfare must be viewed and studied within the context of the Lord's divine purpose and redemptive plan to save humankind. The parable of the sower and the tares among the wheat in the Book of Matthew chapter 13, which both parables speaks of kingdom advancement and growth through planting the Word of God.

In addition, both parables are a depiction of conflict or warfare between the two kingdoms with the battle centering on the redemptive plan of the Lord for humanity. As you grow in your understanding of unseen warfare, you will be prepared to engage the system of this world and fighting for the souls of men and women, boys and girls everywhere. This is the main purpose of possessing authority over the devil, which was given to the Christ's disciples before they were commissioned to share the Good News with all nations (Matthew 28:18-20).

Satan and his demonic hosts will rage war against you as you seek God's Kingdom first and win men and women to Christ through the Gospel, bringing them under the rulership and reign of the King and His Kingdom. As you employ the Word of God, the scriptural strategies to spiritual warfare will assist you in challenging and disarming principalities and powers who rule over individual lives, cities, communities, regions, nations, and areas of the world. That is why prayer shouldn't be taken lightly and we must daily commune with God in prayer to be led of God's Holy Spirit to be successful in spiritual battles.

Prayer is a common form of spiritual warfare among Christians. Other practices may include deliverance, casting or driving out demon spirits, the laying on of hands, fasting with prayer, praise and worship, prophetic intercession, binding and loosing through spiritual delegated authority and speaking prophetic decrees, declarations, proclamations and judgments, and anointing with oil.

Before we understand anything else in this book about spiritual warfare, we have to know the definition of it. Spiritual warfare from a Christian perspective:

> Is the cosmic war of good versus evil: its battles are fought daily between God and Satan; between the Church of Jesus Christ—the *ekklesia*—and the world system ruled by our spiritual enemy; and within every child of God, between the Holy Spirit and the lusts of the carnal flesh. The clear meanings of good and evil, as defined by God rather than man, are revealed within the verses of the Holy Bible and the life of Jesus Christ.[1]

I love how Billy Graham defines and explain the reality of spiritual warfare in his book *Angels*:

> We live in a perpetual battlefield.... The wars among the nations on earth are mere popgun affairs compared to the fierceness of battle in the spiritual unseen world. This invisible spiritual conflict is waged around us incessantly and unremittingly. Where the Lord works, Satan's forces hinder; where angel beings carry out divine directives, the devils rage. All this comes about because the powers of darkness press their counterattack to recapture the ground held for the glory of God....

It's always been in the plan of satan (formerly known as lucifer) since his fall both night and day, the master craftsman of the devices of darkness and wickedness continues tirelessly to undermine God's redemptive plan of the ages.

> We can find inscribed on the pages of human history the consequences of the wickedness that the devil has brought into fruition by his evil powers of darkness when he is in power. The devil will never bend an inch, nor will he stop in his pursuit to stop the plan of God to redeem the "cosmos" from his control.[2]

THE DIFFERENCE BETWEEN WAR AND WARFARE

As I stated before that there is a difference between war and warfare. We see many times throughout the Old Testament of God's people going to war. There are times to engage in spiritual war and in the natural the military are ordered to go to war to defend their country, nation, and people from opposing armies. God is the Commander and Chief of the host of angelic armies. He is the God of war who understands warfare and we must understand it biblically.

Always keep in mind that you were born into war. This may not sound like the good news of the Gospel, however you are part of a great awakening that will bring about breakthrough when you defeat the enemy's works in this battle. I love what the late C. Peter Wagner stated in a message I heard online when he stated, "For 2,000 years the kingdom of God has been advancing with force, and God's plan is for this advance to continue with increasing vigor until Jesus returns. Satan knows his time is getting shorter, but he certainly does not intend to go quietly. For the church, this means war!"

We as Christian believers can't talk about spiritual warfare and war if we don't understand what the Bible says about it. War is fought for the liberation of those who are bound, oppressed, and held hostage against their will. There are times where God Himself declares war on His enemies.

What does the Word of God say about war?

When it comes to war, some make the mistake of reading and applying what it says in Exodus 20:13, *"You shall not kill,"* to killing someone in war. However, the Hebrew word literally means "the intentional, premeditated killing of another person with malice; murder." There are times when the Lord commanded His people to go to war with other nations (1 Samuel 15:3; Joshua 4:13).

Moreover, the Lord would also order the penalty of death or death sentencing to those who have committed several crimes against each other (Exodus 21:12, 15; 22:19; Leviticus 20:11). We have to understand that there are some circumstances that the Lord doesn't oppose killing, but He does oppose murder. When human soldiers in the military are deployed into war, it's never a good thing. Even prepared soldiers realize war is a life or death situation and must be taken seriously. They go to war to defend their nation and the people they are sent to protect. They are sacrificing their lives for many. At times war is necessary and inevitable.

In other words, war isn't a good thing, but sometimes it is a necessary thing. In a world filled with sinful people (Romans 3:10-18), war is inevitable. The Bible cites measures to prevent sinful people from causing insurmountable harm to the innocent, one being going to war. Keep in mind that Jesus was not a pacifist. It's biblically incorrect to believe and say that the Lord never supports war. With today's society and world system filled with wickedness and evil individuals, there are times when war is the only option to prevent even greater evil from spreading and influencing others.

If Hitler had not been defeated by World War II, many more millions of innocent people would have been killed by his dictatorship. Even today's global and national terrorists who pose a serious threat to their own people and other nations must face the consequences. If the United States didn't declare war on terroristic dictators and evil tyrants, millions of people would be walking in fear and even killed worldwide. There are times to declare war! And there are times to call for ceasefire and peace. Jesus is the Prince of Peace. God will give us the rules of engagement when and how to defeat our enemy!

> *Therefore submit to God. Resist the devil and he will flee from you. Draw near to God and He will draw near to you. Cleanse your hands, you sinners; and purify your hearts, you double-minded* (James 4:7-8 NKJV).

Every day there is some kind of warfare, argument, or civil rivalry happening between people, places, and things. As an African American leader in the Body of Christ, I am grateful for the American Civil War. If the American Civil War had not been fought, how much longer would African Americans have had to suffer as slaves? War is a terrible thing. Some wars are more "just" than others, but war is always the result of sin (Romans 3:10-18).

At the same time, Ecclesiastes 3:8 declares, *"There is...a time to love and a time to hate, a time for war and a time for peace."* In war there are real weapons and real lives that are at stake. Soldiers are not fighting with plastic knives and water guns. It's heavy-duty machinery and weaponry of war. God understands war and warfare and has specific "warring angels" to protect, defend, and help His people.

In the Old Testament, the Lord commanded the children of Israel to *"Take vengeance on the Midianites for the Israelites"* (Numbers 31:2). There were also times when the Lord would order the Israelites to utterly destroy their enemies (Hittites, Amorites, Canaanites, Perizzites, Hivites, and the Jebusites). Deuteronomy 20:16-17 says, *"However, in the cities of the nations the LORD your God is giving you as an inheritance, do not leave alive anything that breathes. Completely destroy them...as the LORD your God has commanded you."*

Furthermore, we can see again the Lord giving command to war against His enemies in First Samuel 15:18 where it says, *"Go and completely destroy those wicked people, the Amalekites; make war against them until you have wiped them out."* Obviously, God is not against all war. I am also reminded of the story of the Lord giving King David instructions to engage in warfare against the Philistines. God will activate the rules of engagement when He sees fit. The Lord knows the weakness of the enemy.

SEEK WISDOM IN WARFARE

Note that David couldn't pursue the enemy on his own terms but needed the wisdom and strategy of the Lord. When we try to fight an unseen battle and enemy in our own strength and human wisdom, we will lose on the battlefield. David inquired of the Lord *first* before declaring war against those who came to destroy him. We can clearly see in Second Samuel 5:18-25 what was happening:

> *Now the Philistines had come and spread out in the Valley of Rephaim; so David inquired of the LORD, "Shall I go and attack the Philistines? Will you deliver them into my hands?" The LORD answered him, "Go, for I will surely deliver the Philistines into your hands." So David went to Baal Perazim, and there he defeated them. He said, "As*

waters break out, the LORD has broken out against my enemies before me." So that place was called Baal Perazim. The Philistines abandoned their idols there, and David and his men carried them off. Once more the Philistines came up and spread out in the Valley of Rephaim; so David inquired of the LORD, and he answered, "Do not go straight up, but circle around behind them and attack them in front of the poplar trees. As soon as you hear the sound of marching in the tops of the poplar trees, move quickly, because that will mean the LORD has gone out in front of you to strike the Philistine army." So David did as the LORD commanded him, and he struck down the Philistines all the way from Gibeon to Gezer.

As you can see, David was given the rules of engagement by the Lord to outwit the Philistine attack. God told David that He would deliver them into his hands when he asked the Father, the God of war! Keep in mind that David asked God if He would deliver the enemy into his hand. Furthermore, David knew that without the wisdom of God it would be impossible to receive divine breakthrough.

How many battles have we lost because we didn't seek the Lord's counsel and wisdom? How many spiritual conflicts could have been avoided if we would first seek the Lord's wisdom in the matter? Breakthrough in warfare only comes when we seek the Lord of the breakthrough! God helped David defeat his enemies. The Bible clearly reveals to us in Second Samuel 5 that God's breakout against the Philistines was like water breaking out of its boundaries in Baal Perazim, the place where the battle was fought.

In addition, David removed the idols that the Philistines abandoned and later he inquired of the Lord when he came to the

Valley of Rephaim, which means "giants" in Hebrew. David, of course, was familiar with slaying giants as he did so when he was a shepherd boy. Now King David was facing a gigantic Philistine army in the Valley of Rephaim. The same God who anointed and equipped David to have victory over the Philistine's giant warrior and champion Goliath, gave by His strong arm victory against a large army. David didn't take matters into his own hands, again he asked for the Lord's instructions and wisdom.

The Bible reveals that God gave David a different rule of engagement against the enemy the second time around. The Lord says, *"Do not go straight up, but circle around behind them and attack them in front of the poplar trees. As soon as you hear the sound of marching in the tops of the poplar trees, move quickly, because that will mean the LORD has gone out in front of you to strike the Philistine army."*

INQUIRE OF THE LORD

Before I talk about the rules of spiritual engagement, I want to draw your attention to David as leader, king, and protector of God's people. A true leader and believer of God will never make decisions without first seeking God's wisdom. The Bible says in Proverbs 9:9-11, *"Instruct the wise and they will be wiser still; teach the righteous and they will add to their learning. The fear of the LORD is the beginning of wisdom, and knowledge of the Holy One is understanding. For through wisdom your days will be many, and years will be added to your life."*

Godly kings, warriors, soldiers, and leaders don't foolishly engage in battle or anything else without the Holy Spirit directives, insight, and wisdom. David, one of the greatest kings, sought the wisdom of God nine times. As you read and study about them, you will see the type of leader God had chosen to rule over Israel. He was a man after God's own heart and a man of war who *"have shed blood"* (read 1 Chronicles 28:3). The following are the Bible references to read and study on your own time:

- David's 1st Inquiry—1 Samuel 23:1-3
- David's 2nd Inquiry—1 Samuel 23:4-5
- David's 3rd Inquiry—1 Samuel 23:10-11
- David's 4th Inquiry—1 Samuel 23:12-14
- David's 5th Inquiry—1 Samuel 30:8-9
- David's 6th Inquiry—2 Samuel 2:1-2
- David's 7th Inquiry—2 Samuel 5:17-21
- David's 8th Inquiry—2 Samuel 5:22-25
- David's 9th Inquiry—2 Samuel 21:1

We can see the importance of inquiring of the Lord in prayer each and every day, especially when we have an unseen evil lurking in darkness. God will give us the ability to overcome personal struggles, proclivities, weaknesses, and strongholds that attack our minds. You can fight back and overcome it every time. No one wants to get into a spiritual altercation, conflict, or battle with anyone, especially those we love.

However, we have to discern what's the motive and who's behind the attack to trigger a negative response. Be alert and smart! Don't allow to the enemy to get the best of you. Take the high road, it's worth it.

In a society plagued by sin, evil, jealousy, lust for power, wickedness, and hatred (Romans 3:10-18), war is inevitable. I believe that we should not desire war; neither should believers resist, oppose, or fight against those God has placed in authority over us in government (Romans 13:1-4; 1 Peter 2:17). We should be always praying for leadership, remembering that no one is perfect.

During times of war it is important to pray for the safety of our men and women in the military, praying for quick resolution to conflicts, praying for godly wisdom for our leadership, and praying for everyone involved on both sides of war and any conflict (Philippians 4:6-7).

The Bible speaks of spiritual warfare in many places, but most directly in Ephesians 6:12 (KJV), where Paul speaks of putting on the full armor of God: *"For we wrestle not against flesh and blood, but against principalities, against powers, against the rulers of the darkness of this world, against spiritual wickedness in high places."* In a broader sense of the terms "armed forces" and "military" are often treated as synonymous, although in technical usage a distinction is sometimes made in which a country's armed forces may include both its military and other paramilitary forces.

There are various forms of irregular military forces not belonging to a recognized state; though they share many attributes of regular military forces, they are less often referred to as simply "military." Spiritual warfare exists in the unseen, supernatural dimension where God is all-powerful and satan is in revolt. As any believer soon will discover in their Christian walk and journey, although spiritual warfare is unseen, it's absolutely real and confrontation is inevitable.

Spiritual warfare are the battles we face with the devil, the world, and the old sinful nature. The following highlights the battles that we face every day. There are four insights into winning the spiritual battles in our lives. Keep each one in mind or memorize them while in your Spiritual Warfare 101 training:

1. There are three main enemies:

- The devil (1 Peter 5:8).
- The world system and influence (1 John 2:15-17).
- The flesh or the old sin nature (1 Peter 2:11).

2. There are two main battle fronts:

- Personal holiness (1 Peter 1:13-16).
- Personal witness (Matthew 28:19-20).

3. We have four main weapons:

- The armor of God (Ephesians 6:11,13).
- The Word of God (Ephesians 6:17).
- Holy Spirit anointing (1 John 2:27; Acts 1:8).
- Angelic assistance (Psalm 34:7; Hebrews 1:14).

4. There are three institutions and domains:

- God's government, heavenly domain, and the sovereign sphere (Psalm 24:1-3, 33:13; Philippians 3:20; Hebrews 12:22-24).
- The earthly domain and sphere of believers for rulership as king-priests (Genesis 1:26; Psalm 8:6; Psalm 115:16; Revelation 5:10).
- The Church—the *Ekklesia*—assembled body of believers (Matthew 16:18, 18:17; 1 Corinthians 12:27; Ephesians 1:22, 2:19-22; Colossians 1:18).

RULES OF ENGAGEMENT

We hear the term rules of engagement as it pertains to warfare. But do we truly understand its meaning in war? In spiritual warfare we must be able to fully grasp this concept to know what are our limitations, rights, and what we have at our disposal spiritually speaking. I believe that to discern, disarm, defeat, and destroy the works of the enemy, it's imperative to understand the rules of engagement (ROE).

However, since we are speaking about spiritual warfare, combat, battle, or conflict in a spiritual sense and perspective, I will use the phrase: *Rules of Spiritual Engagement* (ROSE).

The definition of rules of engagement from the Oxford Dictionary: "A directive issued by a military authority specifying the circumstances and limitations under which forces will engage in combat with the enemy. Rules of engagement (ROE) by definition is: whereas the mandate primarily contains clear instructions regarding the objectives and main tasks of the national contingent, ROE contain precise and classified prescriptions on exactly when (use of force) and how (degree of force) military armed forces may employ force against the Enemy while performing tasks towards stated mission objectives."

Also, it's defined as "the internal rules or directives among military forces (including individuals) that define the circumstances, conditions, degree, and manner in which the use of force, or actions which might be construed as provocative, may be applied. They provide authorization for and/or limits on, among other things, the use of force and the employment of certain specific capabilities. In some nations, ROE has the status of guidance to military forces, while in other nations, ROE is lawful commands. Rules of engagement do not normally dictate how a result is to be achieved, but will indicate what measures may be unacceptable."

While rules of engagement (ROE) are used in both domestic and international operations by some militaries, ROE are not used for domestic operations in the United States. Instead, the use of force by the U.S. military in such situations is governed by Rules for the Use of Force (RUF). Simply, the rules of engagement are the orders that soldiers fighting in war are given about what they can and cannot do. If a soldier in the natural violates this order, it is considered excessive abuse of power.

We are given directive orders and commands by the Lord through the Holy Spirit to engage in spiritual warfare battles. Jesus has given us all the power needed to combat evil powers. The rules of spiritual engagement (ROSE) for the believer is to never abuse the delegated authority and power of God given to you.

In the natural the military has rules, guidelines, and protocols as it pertains to use of force and the degree of force meaning how much. In rules of spiritual engagement (ROSE), as believers we should know when to use the power of God to defeat the enemy and how much spiritual force is needed to ward him off.

There are times when I am under spiritual attack for a season, and the Lord would have me fast and pray longer, decree and declare the Word of God for several days, pray in the spirit with worship targeting areas under demonic attacks, and ask God for angelic assistance. There will be times of intensity when the proper rules of spiritual engagement are to be deployed against the unseen enemy.

NOTES

1. Robert Sims, "What is spiritual warfare?"; Battle Focused Ministries, November 11, 2008; http://www.battlefocused .org/articles/what-is-spiritual-warfare/#:~:text=From%20a% 20Christian%20perspective%2C%20spiritual%20warfare% 20is%20the,Spirit%20and%20the%20lusts%20of%20the% 20carnal%20flesh; accessed November 12, 2020.

2. Ibid.

Chapter 4

ARMED AND DANGEROUS

You are of God, little children, and have overcome them, because He who is in you is greater than he who is in the world (1 John 4:4 NKJV).

This is a time to be strong in the Lord and His supernatural power. God wants His people to be supernaturally armed and dangerous in the Holy Spirit against the enemy. Greater is He who is in you than those who are in the world. You have an advantage over those who are separate from God and living in darkness. When you have the Lord on your side, which is the winning side of this battle, you are unstoppable and unconquering! You will receive divine boldness, courage, and unflinching stance and faith in times of warfare.

As we engage in spiritual warfare, I must remind you not to focus on satan or his demons and don't fear what they can do to you. Do not search for every demon behind every bush. We must have balance during spiritual warfare. To be armed and dangerous in the Holy Spirit against the evil one in this invisible conflict, we must know the answers to the following three questions:

1. What is the difference between deliverance and a spiritual warfare victory?
2. What is an offensive and defensive warfare?
3. What is satan's trio (weapons used against believers) in spiritual warfare?

When we can understand and answer these questions, we will become Holy Spirit-filled lethal threats against the dark powers of the devil. Let's discuss the answers to these three important questions.

In understanding the rules of engagement to discern, disarm, and destroy the works of the enemy, we must first know the difference between *spiritual warfare* and *deliverance*. Spiritual warfare is the act of overcoming, resisting, disarming, and defeating the lies of the enemy that comes in the form of deception, temptation, and accusations that he releases toward God's people. Deliverance on the other hand is addressing demonic hindrances and bondages by rescuing or liberating yourself or someone from the enemy's stranglehold. As we look at the difference between the two, you will understand what this book is all about.

This book is not about deliverance through casting out demon spirits, unearthing legal grounds established, and demolishing strongholds, or offensive spiritual warfare. The enemy's three primary weapons against believers perpetuates an ongoing spiritual battle struggle. Spiritual warfare primarily focuses on three key attacks from the devil at God's people:

1. Deception
2. Temptation
3. Accusation

According to the Merriam-Webster Dictionary, "deception" or "deceit" means: "the act of causing someone to accept as true or valid what is false or invalid; the act of deceiving; resorting to falsehood; the quality of being dishonest or misleading; the quality of being dishonest or misleading." This is what the devil does with the truth of God's Word in spiritual warfare by tricking people. Revelation 12:9 says, *"The great dragon was hurled down—that ancient serpent called the devil, or Satan, who leads the whole world astray. He was hurled to the earth, and his angels with him."*

Also according to the Merriam-Webster Dictionary, "temptation" means: "the act of tempting or the state of being tempted especially to evil; a cause or occasion of enticement." This is the devil's sole purpose, to entice God's people into acting in opposition to God's will, or tempting them to sin. Satan is the enemy of our salvation. He is the tempter! Matthew 4:3 (NKJV) says, *"Now when the tempter came to Him, he said, "If you are the Son of God, command that these stones become bread."* Temptation often follows deception. Eve was tempted by satan who enticed her to sin and disobey God's command not to eat fruit from the forbidden tree. She was deceived, the Bible says, tricked into believing satan's lie rather than God's truth.

And again according to the Merriam-Webster Dictionary, "accusation" means "a charge of wrongdoing; the act of accusing someone; the state or fact of being accused." This is another wicked plan of the enemy to falsely accuse God's people; satan is known as *"the accuser of our brothers and sisters who accuses them before our God day and night"* according to Revelation 12:10. One of the devil's plans is to accuse us of our sins before the Father. He really doesn't want the Lord to forgive you and extend His grace to you. Jesus says in John 8, *"The devil was a murderer from the beginning. He has never been truthful. He doesn't know what the truth is. Whenever he tells a lie, he's doing what comes naturally to him. He's a liar and the father of lies"* (John 8:44 GW).

Oftentimes we fight spiritual battles on the defensive and forget how to fight offensively. God wants you to know the difference and fight effectively both offensively and defensively. When I played collegiate football, I played both defensively and offensively. My primary position was as a wide receiver who was defended by a defensive back or cornerback. Their job was to prevent me from catching the ball. However, I was athletically flexible enough to also play the defensive back position, blocking wide receivers from catching the ball.

As a defensive back, one of my goals was to intercept the ball. Having the ability and knowledge to play both positions gave me the upper advantage because I could think offensively and defensively, which made me an all-round athlete. Likewise in spiritual warfare, we should be able to fight and spar defensively and offensively keep the enemy from deceiving, tempting, and making false accusations against us.

As soldiers in God's army, our position in battle is to defensively guard ourselves against demonic or satanic plans, schemes, tactics, and strategies. Moreover, our offensive position as warriors of God is tearing down demonic fortresses, strongholds, and doctrines of the devil that has formed in our minds or someone's mind through deception and accusations. I think about Jeremiah the prophet's assignment: *"Today I appoint you to stand up against nations and kingdoms. Some you must uproot and tear down, destroy and overthrow. Others you must build up and plant"* (Jeremiah 1:10 New Living Translation).

Jeremiah was given both an offensive and defensive prophetic mandate assignment for the nations and the kingdoms of this world. He was to:

1. Tear down
2. Destroy
3. Overthrow
4. Build
5. Plant

God will continue to appoint prophetic voices and leaders in every generation with this battle-ax prophetic assignment to advance the Kingdom of God in the nations of the world. Dealing victoriously with deception, temptation, and accusation from the enemy will only happen when you wear the whole armor of God. You can overcome him every time and win the battle.

RULES OF ENGAGEMENT ADVANTAGE

Understanding the enemy's tactics gives you the upper hand when you face any of satan's weapons. That's why it's imperative to have the Holy Spirit, discernment, and know the Word of God. This allows you to be armed and dangerous against the enemy every time he wants to pick a fight with you—because you know what he is after and what three weapons of attack he will use. Therefore, to truly know the rules of spiritual engagement is necessary that you can grow in knowing how to effectively use your spiritual tools to conquer satan's works.

The devil doesn't cause trouble for those who are not committed to God, but those who are. Those who are not committed to Christ are the devil's subjects (Colossians 1:13) and are committed to him (Ephesians 2:2). Only when a person turns away from the enemy and accepts Jesus as their Savior and make Him Lord over their lives is when satan opposes the person.

Keep in mind that the devil will not give up a fight easily and will do everything he can in his limited power to draw them back under his rule. He can't take their salvation away, but he can tempt them to live a sinful lifestyle as before—one of service to the devil. The Lord does not desire us to live life without Him or to revert to the old sin nature.

Jesus has defeated satan on the cross and has provided provision for us all to share in this victory. The Lord as a good Commander and Chief has equipped us with the necessary equipment needed to defeat satan and to protect ourselves (Ephesians 6:10-17; 2 Corinthians 10:35; Matthew 12:29). Believers must wear their supernatural armor of God to win spiritual battles. What soldier goes to battle without their armor and weapons? It doesn't make sense for them to engage in any type of combat without wearing protective gear. It says in Ephesians 6:10-13:

> *Finally, be strong in the Lord and in his mighty power. Put on the full armor of God, so that you can take your stand against the devil's schemes. For our struggle is not against flesh and blood, but against the rulers, against the authorities, against the powers of this dark world and against the spiritual forces of evil in the heavenly realms. Therefore put on the full armor of God, so that when the day of evil comes, you may be able to stand your ground, and after you have done everything, to stand.*

This passage of Scripture from Ephesians 6 teaches some crucial truths, including the fact that believers can only stand strong in the Lord's power—not our own. The apostle Paul opens by admonishing them to be strong in the Lord. Furthermore, it is the Lord's armor that overall protects us, and our spiritual conflict is ultimately against spiritual forces of evil in the world.

Ephesians 6:13-18 specifically describes six pieces that make up the whole armor of God. These are symbolically used to describe a literal armor that a soldier, knight, or warrior would wear in combat. It's interesting to note that six pieces protect the whole body of a person, and six is the number of man.

> *Therefore **put on the full armor of God**, so that when the day of evil comes, you may be able to stand your ground, and after you have done everything, to stand. Stand firm then, with the **belt of truth** buckled around your waist, with the **breastplate of righteousness** in place, and with your **feet fitted with the readiness** that comes from the Gospel of peace. In addition to all this, take up the **shield of faith**, with which you can extinguish all the flaming arrows of the evil one. Take the **helmet of salvation** and the **sword of the Spirit**, which is the word of God. And pray in the Spirit on all occasions with all kinds of prayers and requests. With this in mind, be alert and always keep on praying for all the Lord's people.*

PROTECTIVE SPIRITUAL ARMOR

God is Spirit, and what He provides for our protection is also spiritual. The text states that we are to put on the full armor of God, not just some of it. That way you can stand firm against all strategies of the devil. In the next chapter we will look at specifically what each piece of armor represents and what purpose they serve as we engage the realm of spiritual warfare.

The six pieces to God's armor are:

1. Belt of truth
2. Breastplate of righteousness
3. Shoes of the Gospel of peace
4. Shield of faith
5. Helmet of salvation
6. Sword of the Spirit

These six pieces of armor protect and arm us, making us supernaturally dangerous against the enemy. When he sees believers fully equipped, he knows they are ready to fight and win the war!

What do these six pieces of God's spiritual armor represent to the warrior in spiritual warfare? We are to know the truth, believe the truth, and speak the truth. In basic training in the natural, a soldier is educated about their equipment, what it is used for, and how to properly wear it as well. In addition, they are also trained in how to assemble, dissemble, discharge, recharge, and clean their weapons and armor. Maintenance and regular training are important when preparing for war. Knowing what weapons and armor the soldier has given you and the purpose for each is equally important. Out of these six pieces of the armor, five of them are used offensively and only one is used defensively.

What I am about to share is very important but simple to understand. Paul wrote this passage to the believers in Ephesus knowing that they understood physical warfare and knew what armor was needed to protect themselves and defeat the enemy. Likewise, the full armor of God in a spiritual sense provides protection and can defeat the enemy today. The early believers were admonished to be strong in the Lord and in His mighty power, and we have the same commission today as believers in our generation. Moreover, as the early believers were fully prepared and equipped with the whole supernatural armor of God for the troubles of their day, we too have that same spiritual access to the whole armor of God to live victoriously for Jesus Christ during times of crisis, turmoil, and war.

EFFECTIVE SUPERNATURAL ARMOR

I must say that because the armor of God worked powerfully for the early church believers and leadership, it will work just as effectively and powerfully for us now as it did then! There is no recall or defective equipment in God's armor. You don't have to worry about anything going wrong. He provides effective and powerful weapons for the Body of Christ to use today. There is no excuse to be unprepared and unarmed for battle. The battle is real—and it can be won through God and God alone.

The enemy's weapons may be formed against you, but they will not prosper. They are ineffective against believers who are strong in the Lord and in His power. I love what Isaiah 54:15-17 says about the blessing and protection that God's provides Zion, His people:

> *If anyone does attack you, it will not be my doing; whoever attacks you will surrender to you. "See, it is I who created the blacksmith who fans the coals into flame and forges a weapon fit for its work. And it is I who have created the destroyer to wreak havoc; no weapon forged against you will prevail, and you will refute every tongue that accuses you. This is the heritage of the servants of the Lord, and this is their vindication from me," declares the Lord.*

In other words, God is saying that He created the blacksmith who fans the coals into flames and forges weapons suitable and fit to work. However, it is the Lord who also created the destroyer who wreaks havoc—but his plans will fail. God will vindicate those who serve Him and will protect them from those who accuse, slander, or come to destroy them. Spiritual conflicts, battles, or warfare make up the smaller components of the bigger picture, so to speak. Wars are fought between opposition forces.

WARFARE POSITIONS

According to the Merriam-Webster Dictionary, "war" is defined as "battles involve combat between two persons, between factions, between armies and they consist of any type of extended contest, struggle, or controversy." We are to unapologetically preach, teach, and proclaim the Gospel no matter how much spiritual resistance we face daily from the enemy. You are more than a conqueror in Christ Jesus and this battle is not against you but against everything God created and stands for and that stand with Him.

We are not to waver in our faith; we are to trust God's promises no matter how strongly we are attacked. Our ultimate defense is the assurance we have of our salvation, an assurance that no spiritual force can take away. Our offensive weapon is the Word of God, which is the sword, not our own opinions and feelings. And we are to pray in the power and will of the Holy Spirit.

It's important to note that this spiritual unseen warfare is our portion as Christians whether we ask for it or not. But you are not alone in this battle. The Lord needs you to fulfill and carry out His will on earth. Your destiny and prophetic purpose are hanging in the balance, and you will win no matter what if you keep your faith and trust in God.

However, I want to share a little background about why the apostle Paul decided to use the Roman soldier's physical armor as a metaphor or analogy of God's spiritual armor. The supernatural armor of the Lord is an important biblical truth to comprehend and apply daily. It's about a real spiritual ongoing battle and a direct command from the Lord to put on the whole armor of God as protection from the enemy.

For believers to put on the armor of God really means to believe in all the blessings that Jesus accomplished for them (Ephesians 1–3) and to walk them out daily (Ephesians 4–5). In other words, it's basically living in the supernatural power of everything the Lord has fulfilled for us in every area of life even when we are faced with challenges. To put on the full supernatural armor of God is to apply the entire message of the Gospel to your life as a believer.

JESUS ALREADY WON THE BATTLE

To put on God's armor is not primarily about a spiritual warfare technique or zeroing in on darkness, the devil, and evil. It's about the full expression of our sole reliance on God's supernatural blessing, provision, protection, and ultimately what He has already done through Jesus Christ. Our victory in spiritual warfare has already been secured at the cross of Christ and the blood that He shed there (Revelation 12:11).

One of the primary ways we can overcome challenges and have victory in our lives is found in Revelation chapter 12. This passage of Scripture speaks about the war in Heaven when satan and his demons were evicted from Heaven. The Bible says in Revelation 12:10-12:

> *Then I heard a loud voice in heaven say: "Now have come the salvation and the power and the kingdom of our God, and the authority of his Messiah. For the accuser of our brothers and sisters, who accuses them before our God day and night, has been hurled down. They triumphed over him by the blood of the Lamb and by the word of their testimony; they did not love their lives so much as to shrink from death. Therefore rejoice, you heavens and you who dwell in them! But woe to the earth and the sea, because the devil has gone down to you! He is filled with fury, because he knows that his time is short."*

It's clear that they knew that they have only a short time. The only way we can conquer the devil is by Jesus' atonement of His blood and also by the word that we speak out of our mouths as a testimony. What does the Bible say about the power of testimony? Second Timothy 1:8 gives the answer: *"So do not be ashamed of the testimony about our Lord or of me his prisoner. Rather, join with me in suffering for the gospel, by the power of God."*

In other words, we share in His suffering for the Gospel's sake and we are not to be ashamed. We overcome sin and evil by our testimony when we speak of God's saving grace, supernatural power, breakthrough, and faith in what God has already done through Jesus' death, burial, resurrection, and ascension. The enemy is not only after your salvation but wants to steal your joy, peace, and righteousness in the Holy Spirit. He wants to make your life a living hell on earth. But God wants through Jesus to give you life and for you to enjoy it here and now on earth.

In other words, God wants you to experience Heaven on earth. Don't allow the devil to steal your testimony in what He has done for you. We only overcome the devil in spiritual warfare battles when we understand and use the power of Jesus' shed blood, the power in His name, and the power of our testimony as witnesses. It is also important to know that misunderstanding the purpose of the whole armor of God can lead to confusion because the life of a Christian believer is a life called to war.

If this teaching in Ephesians 6 is taken out of context and misapplied, it can become a distraction from its premise and revelation of Jesus. Let's look at why the apostle Paul spoke about the whole armor of God and use this term as it relates to war, soldiers, and warfare.

THE POWER OF THE GOSPEL

One of the greatest awakenings in early church history occurred in Ephesus. Within two years the Gospel spread like wildfire in the entire region of Asia Minor where unprecedented miracles broke out to confirm the message of Jesus. As a result, the Gospel toppled pagan worship of Roman gods and many started to burn their possessions, stop their pagan practices, and discarded their magic scrolls to follow after Jesus instead.

The power of the Gospel message created a cause and effect through Paul's preaching to the Ephesians. But keep in mind that it wasn't Paul in his natural strength who conquered the Roman Empire—it was the power of the Gospel and boldness and perseverance of Paul's apostolic mission to reach each person for Christ.

The power of the Gospel transformed the pagan and idol worshipping culture in the region without a direct political campaign, budget, or involvement. It was through the raw power of the Gospel of Jesus, which included Paul's understanding of equipping himself with the full armor of God to fulfill such a difficult task. Paul needed the strength, stability, and power of God to stand against all the strategies of the enemy. Paul put into practice what he preached.

Paul wanted to encourage the Ephesians in times of spiritual warfare engagement, which only can come from accessing and wearing God's full armor. The whole armor of God is mentioned in chapter 6, the last chapter of the apostle Paul's letter to the church in Ephesus.

Before we can understand Ephesians chapter 6, we have to first understand Ephesians chapters 1 through 5, which later will make sense why Paul starts Ephesians chapter 6 with the word "Finally." Paul was making his closing remarks to them. Basically, he was building up to his final thought and point from the previous five chapters. Ephesians 6:10-11 says, *"Finally, be strong in the Lord and in his mighty power. Put on the full armor of God, so that you can take your stand against the devil's schemes."*

- Ephesians chapters 1–3 reveal our position in Christ as believers by describing how we are seated in heavenly places with Christ.

- Ephesians chapters 1–4 reveal how we as believers should walk and live out our lives daily as followers of Christ, as Christians.

- Ephesians chapter 6 is the conclusion that explains and reveals how our posture should be as we are to stand even in the face of opposition, resistance, and challenges.

I want to stop and share the overall point as it pertains to spiritual warfare. You are not fighting a war in vain. There is a spiritual blessing involved as well. When a military army defeats the enemy or opposition, there are blessings that come with it. They receive the spoils and possessions of that country, state, or place they just have conquered. On the other hand, in a spiritual war, the enemy's plan is to steal and keep for his own gain your spiritual blessings. He wants to prevent you from keeping what God has promised you.

There are supernatural blessings you receive when you stand strong in the Lord and in the power of His might. Ephesians 1:3-14 reveals twelve spiritual blessings from the Lord. They are linked to God's supernatural armor in Ephesians chapter 6. When you arm yourself with the full armor of the Lord, you will receive all the spiritual blessings associated with the armor, which God has already blessed you with (Ephesians 1:3).

THE BATTLE'S SPIRITUAL BLESSINGS

In Ephesians 1, Paul describes the method the Lord has blessed you with that will make wearing God's full armor an honor. Ephesians 1:3-14 tells us:

Praise be to the God and Father of our Lord Jesus Christ, who has blessed us in the heavenly realms with every spiritual blessing in Christ. For he chose us in him before the creation of the world to be holy and blameless in his sight. In love he predestined us for adoption to sonship through Jesus Christ, in accordance with his pleasure and will—to the praise of his glorious grace, which he has freely given us in the One he loves. In him we have redemption through his blood, the forgiveness of sins, in accordance with the riches of God's grace that he lavished on us. With all wisdom and understanding, he made known to us the mystery of his will according to his good pleasure, which he purposed in Christ, to be put into effect when the times reach their fulfillment— to bring unity to all things in heaven and on earth under Christ. In him we were also chosen, having been predestined according to the plan of him who works out everything in conformity with the purpose of his will, in order that we, who were the first to put our hope in Christ, might be for the praise of his glory. And you also were included in Christ when you heard the message of truth, the gospel of your salvation. When you believed, you were marked in him with a seal, the promised Holy Spirit, who is a deposit guaranteeing our inheritance until the redemption of those who are God's possession—to the praise of his glory.

The following are the twelve spiritual blessings Paul speaks about in Ephesians 1:3-14:

1. Blessed with every spiritual blessing from Jesus Christ in the heavenly realm (vs. 3).

2. Chosen by Jesus Christ before the creation of the world to be holy and blameless (vs .4).

3. In Christ's love, you were already predestined (vs. 5).

4. Receive spiritual adoption as His children through Jesus Christ (vs. 5).

5. Accepted in the Beloved (vs. 6).

6. Receive redemption through Christ's blood, according to the riches of His grace (vs. 7).

7. Receive forgiveness of your sins (vs. 7).

8. Receive spiritual understanding, godly wisdom, mysteries of God's will according to His will (vss. 8-9).

9. Be given an inheritance (vs. 11).

10. Bring glory, praise, and honor to the Lord (vs. 12).

11. Receive the promise of the Lord—the Holy Spirit (vs. 13).

12. Receive a guaranteed inheritance until your redemption is fulfilled as God's possession (vs. 14).

Again, to receive every spiritual blessing of Jesus Christ, we must put on the full armor to understand the blessings that come with it. Every piece of God's armor must be worn, not one missing piece. Each piece of armor outlined in Ephesians 6 serves a distinct purpose to guard us, so it is necessary to put the whole armor on, not some.

FULLY ARMORED AND EQUIPPED

Can you imagine a football player not wearing his helmet during a game? He could experience serious ramifications and injuries. Wearing God's full armor protects you when you face fear, guilt, doubt, unbelief, shame, temptation, and other devilish attacks that the enemy sends toward you to test your faith in God's power.

Believers are to stand strong against slander, lies, false accusations, and persecution by the unseen enemy by believing in God's

Word concerning you. The ongoing spiritual battle is real and cannot be ignored; however, God's supernatural armor and mighty weapons have already been forged and given to you so you can stand firm in faith against anything that comes your direction from the enemy.

I believe that effective spiritual warfare should be God-centered, not satan-centered. In other words, the reason why we are engaged in spiritual warfare in the first place is that the Word of God is focused on the Lord and what Jesus Christ has done for you.

In the first century, Jesus and His apostles in the New Testament didn't give their attention to the devil. We are not to give our attention to him either. However, we should not be ignorant of what the enemy is capable of and his tactics. As we to focus primarily on the Lord and on what the Lord Jesus Christ has already done for us.

The supernatural power in spiritual warfare is laced in the cross of Christ at Calvary and His atonement of the blood that was shed there for our sin. We disarm the enemy in knowing and overcoming him by the blood of the Lamb. Putting on the full armor of God disarms the enemy. As believers, putting on the full armor of God daily assists in overcoming day-to-day struggles we experience, which will ultimately disarm, disable, and defeat the enemy just like Jesus did at the cross.

Colossians 2:13-15 (NLT) says emphatically, *"You were dead because of your sins and because your sinful nature was not yet cut away. Then God made you alive with Christ, for he forgave all our sins. He canceled the record of the charges against us and took it away by nailing it to the cross. In this way, he disarmed the spiritual rulers and authorities. He shamed them publicly by his victory over them on the cross."*

The rulers of darkness and powers are put to shame as they are reminded of what happened at the finished work of the cross. The powerful words of Jesus, "It is finished," solidified the victory once and for all who believe on Him. Sin and death have no victory over God's people when you are divinely protected and fully armored. Keep in mind, before we go into the different pieces of the armor of God, what spiritual warfare is not. Spiritual warfare is not asking the Father to remove your sin, when we know Jesus already accomplished that on the cross.

STAND YOUR GROUND, SOLDIER!

Standing in the midst of daily challenges and struggles is having confidence in Christ and being transformed daily in applying the Word of God because of what He has already done and being the image of Christ on earth. The spiritual warfare Jesus experienced throughout His life and ministry on earth is no different from what you will continue to face by the enemy. Jesus died on the cross of Calvary for the penalty of sin and the power of sin to control our lives.

The way you stand strong and firm in God is to possess faith in believing what Jesus said and not turning back to the old way of living or sin nature. You put off the old garment of the enemy and put on the whole armor of God by being renewed in the spirit of your mind, and putting on the new (read Ephesians 4). Ephesians 6 is an accurate explanation of the full armor of God. However, it is not the only scriptural reference of God's supernatural armor. The Word of God mentions it in several difference places:

- Isaiah 59:17 speaks of the Lord putting on two of the pieces of the armor we see in Ephesians 6: righteousness as a breastplate and a helmet of salvation on His head.
- Romans 13:12 speaks of the armor of light.
- First Thessalonians 5:8 speaks of two pieces of God's armor: the breastplate of faith and love, and the helmet of the hope of salvation.

- Ephesians 6:10-18 speaks of six pieces of the armor of God.

It's important to understand God's armor for every believer is not so much about the metaphor or analogy of the armor but what each part of the armor does. It serves no purpose to just understand the importance of the armor without knowing what each part can do.

The primary significance of the armor of God is in the power and the reality of the spiritual weapons God has given us. The importance of each piece of the armor and what each represents can help us stand against all evil strategies of the devil.

PART TWO

DISARMING THE WORKS OF THE ENEMY

Chapter 5

THE SUPERNATURAL ARMOR OF GOD

A final word: Be strong in the Lord and in his mighty power. Put on all of God's armor so that you will be able to stand firm against all strategies of the devil. For we are not fighting against flesh-and-blood enemies, but against evil rulers and authorities of the unseen world, against mighty powers in this dark world, and against evil spirits in the heavenly places. Therefore, put on every piece of God's armor so you will be able to resist the enemy in the time of evil. Then after the battle you will still be standing firm (Ephesians 6:10-13 NLT).

The armor of God we are given is God's very own armor. It's the armor that He actually wears Himself. How powerful is that! The Lord provides you His spiritual armor to stand against the enemy—the devil.

Let's examine and break down briefly what the apostle Paul is saying in Ephesians 6:10-13 to gain a clearer picture and revelation of God's armor and how we are to offensively and defensively use each piece to discern, disarm, and defeat the works of the devil in our personal lives spiritually. One thing to note is that this armor is not made by human hands—it's made by God. Meaning that when we stand strong in God and in His power, we are not standing in our human strength, will, and power but in God's supernatural strength, power, and will.

SUPERNATURALLY SUITED

Some say there are seven pieces of the armor of God, the seventh is praying at all times in the Spirit. Of course prayer and worship are very important while engaged in spiritual warfare to stand against attacks of the enemy. But prayer is not connected to a piece of armor as described in Ephesians 6. I would go so far as to say that it's more accurate to note that praying in the Spirit is an activity that flows out of putting on God's armor fully. Praying in the Spirit is not technically one of the pieces of the armor of God.

Why is there still spiritual conflict if the war is already won? The main reason is that the Lord is still advancing His Kingdom and building His church in every place on earth. For every new believer, God's Kingdom continues to grow.

In a broken and fallen world, the enemy—the devil and his princes—are still given access to roam about like a roaring lion. You may find day-to-day or seasonal struggles insurmountable at times, and you pray that the Lord Jesus would come now rather than soon. But since He has not come yet, I believe that means there are more and more people who need salvation.

This is why the spiritual battle rages on, even though victory is already the Lord's. So, to fight and win your daily conflicts, you need to place upon yourself the supernatural armor of God. The greatest deception of the enemy is to convince the world that he doesn't exist and not to believe in evil spirits, demons, the devil, and spiritual warfare.

However on the contrary, the people who are deceived are often the same people who love horror movies that capitalize on the imagery of what these unseen beings are like and capable of doing. Unfortunately, these people may be the devil's puppets in his ongoing war throughout history. The war is for your soul; and only you can decide to win the war with God's supernatural help and guidance. The end of the war is decided upon you cooperating with God's Word.

Now, let's examine each piece of God's armor in more detail and its purpose.

1. Belt of Truth

"Standing firm then, with the belt of truth buckled around your waist..." (Ephesians 6:14).

What is the belt in God's supernatural armor? The *belt of truth* is the first piece mentioned in Ephesians 6. Bible scholars believe and exclaim that the belt of truth is the piece that holds all the pieces of God's armor together. The New American Standard Bible 1995 edition uses the term or phrase *"having girded your loins with truth."* The word "loin" is uncommonly used in our modern-day vernacular. Basically, the loins reference the lower back, including the crotch area. During ancient times, men would wear long, blood-red military cloaks or robes that would be a distraction and get in the way of fighting or working, so the soldier wrapped up the long, draping material with a belt.

Because the devil is the father of lies according to John 8:44, truth is needed when dealing with the evil one. Truth is the opposite of a lie. The Roman soldiers wore a belt known as the balteus or cingulum. Their belt was the most important and critical piece of their armor because it held their armor securely together.

Belts today hold up pants or skirts or are worn around dresses as an accessory. Modern-day soldiers and police officers have a belt that holds in place their weapons and other needed accessories. Spiritually speaking, the truth is what holds our spiritual armor in place. Without the truth we cannot discern the enemy's deceptions and demonic works, tactics, and strategies. Without truth we are defenseless against this unseen enemy. The belt of truth holds the sword of the Spirit, necessary when engaged in this invisible war.

Keep in mind that we are "seen" targets in an unseen warfare. We are visible targets in an invisible war that the enemy rages against us daily. That is why the belt of truth is imperative for us to wear so that we are not confused, deceived, or manipulated by the evil one. One of the reasons the enemy can deceive a believer is by playing on our intelligence through ignorance.

If you don't possess truth, then you will fall for anything that the enemy throws your way—anything that may appear, sound, or feel like the truth but is simply a decoy, distraction, and destructive deception. Jesus is the Truth, and He is also the Word. John 1:14 (NKJV) says, *"And the Word became flesh and dwelt among us, and we beheld His glory, the glory as of the only begotten of the Father, full of grace and truth."*

Sanctified by Truth

Likewise, to affirm that the Word of God is truth, Jesus earnestly prayed for His disciples on the night of His betrayal, *"Sanctify them by Your truth. Your word is truth"* (John 17:17 NKJV). When it comes to the belt of truth, we also need to know that Jesus declares of Himself in John 14:6 (NKJV), *"I am the way, the truth, and the life. No one comes to the Father except through Me."* To put on the belt of truth is to put our full faith and trust in God's truth and believe what He says.

In other words, we are to value the Word of the Lord as total truth and believe it over any lies that the accuser might whisper in our ear. Will you believe the truth about what the Lord says about you, your destiny, and future—or will you believe the lies of the enemy, the deceiver? When you wrap yourself with the truth of God's Word, you are covering yourself with the Spirit of truth, guarding yourself against demonic deception and defending truth no matter what.

Putting on the truth belt means deciding to trust in what the Father has accomplished for you thus far, regardless how you feel at the moment. Your belt is used to help you engage in spiritual warfare with freedom as you fight against the enemy. In addition, as the belt allows freedom to fight, so the truth makes us free. Through the Holy Spirit truth in God's Word is applied in our lives and hearts, for the Lord is called the *"Spirit of truth"* (John 14:17; 15:26).

The enemy is the very opposite. His demons carry the belt of lies or deception as their armor. Satan is a liar (John 8:44) and he works deceit and counterfeits to get God's people to walk in fear and be defeated. The enemy's battle plan is to be untruthful (Acts 5:3) and uses lies to gain legal access to us when we disobey God's rules of engagement. Therefore, we must stand our ground and stand firm against anything not 100 percent truthful, honest, and earnest in us or in others.

How to Apply the Belt of Truth

- Study the Word of God to understand the whole truth of it, not for your own specific reason or justification.

- Pursue the whole counsel and wisdom of God to know the truth that frees you.
- Pray God's Word and use the Word of truth as a template to guide your request, prayer petitions, and supplications before God.
- Memorize, meditate on, and write devotional Scriptures verses to apply daily to deal with spiritual warfare and deception.

2. BREASTPLATE OF RIGHTEOUSNESS

"...With the breastplate of righteousness in place..." (Ephesians 6:14).

The breastplate on a Roman soldier is one of the important pieces of the armor. In the Greek and early Roman days, a breastplate was created with a solid piece of metal, fashioned and formed in the shape of a man's chest with a second piece of fitted metal across their back. The front and the back piece of the breastplate was put on as a vest. Like a police officer's bulletproof vest that not only covers the chest area but also their back.

During the time of Jesus, the soldiers' breastplate was done away with because it was so very heavy. When a soldier fell wearing it, he became helpless because he couldn't get up, he was like an upside down turtle. Roman soldiers in Jesus' era wore chain mail armor and/or a leather coat, which had long flaps of metal protection clinging down in layers, like a contemporary flak jacket. This type of upper-body armor gave the soldier flexibility and movement that serves as better protection than a traditional breastplate.

Opposing enemies would grasp each other's left forearms and with their right hand they stabbed at each other trying to find an opening in the armor. Likewise, our enemy is looking for a crack in our armor. In other words, he is looking for an opportunity to expose us and challenge our righteousness in Christ.

The enemy will test our faith in God. He will challenge our righteousness in Christ by looking for places in our lives where he can attack. Satan, like a physical enemy soldier, is trying to grasp us and attack our vulnerable areas. He knows our weaknesses and our weak spots.

The breastplate protects all the vital organs of a soldier, especially the heart. Without the breastplate, a soldier could be easily killed by a single blow to their abdominal or torso area. However, with the breastplate the same attack by the enemy could be deflected by the armor. So how does righteousness become like a protective breastplate when it comes to spiritual conflict? God is pure righteousness (Psalms 48; 119:137; 145:17).

Righteous Battle

God is also called, *"The Lord our Righteousness"* (Jeremiah 23:6 NKJV). We must understand that at the time of our salvation our sins are transferred over to Jesus and His perfect righteousness was imparted into us. To have righteousness means to be made right. The Word of God says of righteousness: *"God made him* [Jesus] *who had no sin to be sin for us, so that in him we might become the righteousness of God"* (2 Corinthians 5:21). There is also the "righteous acts of the saints" that the Scripture refers to, which is the righteousness that the Lord carries out through us all (Revelation 19:8). We must guard our hearts daily in this spiritual battle because both varieties of righteousness protect the heart.

It is imperative to clothe ourselves with the breastplate of righteousness of Christ, which is the fullness but also the ongoing righteousness that we obtain as a response to God's gift. The unseen enemy will attack areas of weakness that he uses to defeat us over and over by besetting sin.

Roman soldiers would make sure their breastplate armor was secure, sound, and in perfect condition before the war began. Likewise, we believers must, spiritually speaking, make sure there are no areas in our lives—such as our thoughts, appetites, priorities, agendas, and motives—that can be used by the enemy to defeat us. The devil doesn't care how large or small the cracks in our armor are—he will use each one against you in battle. There should be no cracks in our armor that the enemy can use to jab you and make you fall. We must close up every crack with the blood of Jesus.

Keep in mind that the devil will make attempts of all kinds, whether past or present, to get us to be involved in sinful entanglements. However, righteousness protects us from them all. Obedience to the Lord is a protective armor over our hearts so we are not wounded by sin in a spiritual battle. We must put faith in God's daily provision, not trusting or relying on our own good works or righteousness. God desires that *His* righteousness shines like a beacon of light through us, and for us to embrace His holiness (another word for righteousness) as ours "in Christ." Satan uses our sin as a weapon to defeat us.

Soldiers' backs in Jesus' time were not covered or protected like the earlier Roman soldiers. Just their front was protected and covered. So soldiers of Christ must not retreat or turn their backs on our enemy—only move ahead in victory. The Bible says in Romans 3:23-24, *"For all have sinned and fall short of the glory of God, and all are justified freely by his grace through the redemption that came by Christ Jesus."*

The armor that the apostle Paul refers to in Ephesians always refers back to Jesus Christ. Because we have all sinned, we all need to be given righteousness as a gift; and like all gifts given from God to us, we should value, accept, and use it.

How to Apply the Breastplate of Righteousness

- Secure your faith in God and guard your heart from the enemy's temptations to sin.

- Obey God's instructions by the Holy Spirit. If there is an area of weakness in your life that's challenging, find church leadership and/or those who will cover and provide biblical accountability. Seek people who can assist you to walk in holiness, righteous living, and fulfill God's will for your life.

- Find and ask trusted people to pray for you if you are struggling with obedience and having sin issues. All believers struggle, but we are not meant to struggle alone. We become easy, visible targets for the devil when we don't obey the Lord.

- Be open, honest, and transparent with those you are accountable to. Daily read the Word of God and be righteous and obedient to God through learning about biblical characters and ordinary men and women like you.

3. SHOES—READINESS OF THE GOSPEL OF PEACE

"...and with your feet fitted with the readiness that comes from the gospel of peace" (Ephesians 6:15).

In Paul's time, soldiers' shoes were held on with leather straps tied around their feet and ankles, completely covering their feet, ankles, and lower legs providing protection. Soldiers wearing this type of sandal boot allowed them to move quickly in combat. They were tough, sturdy, dependable, and waterproof.

Soldiers traveling on foot would encounter rough, rocky, and unstable landscapes while in the throes of battle; therefore, failure on the soldiers' part to properly maintain their sandal boots to protect their feet and provide balance and stability would suffer defeat.

Likewise, we must stand firm on the Word of God and must be always ready in season and out of season. God desires us to keep our balance and footing in the things of Him. In addition, we should be sure and ready for any attack that the enemy brings. When there is readiness, we are prepared to walk out our faith and commitment—standing on a firm or sure foundation of God's Word.

Warfare Readiness

The Bible says in First Peter 3:15 (ESV), *"But in your hearts honor Christ the Lord as holy, always being prepared to make a defense to anyone who asks you for a reason for the hope that is in you; yet do it with gentleness and respect."* This passage of Scripture means that we must be prepared or ready to take the message of the Gospel of peace to anyone who asks about our hope. We must be prepared to share the Gospel of peace to anyone at any time to those who need to hear it.

We are ambassadors of Christ and the light of the world and salt of the earth. God chose to reconcile us to Himself through His Son Christ Jesus (2 Corinthians 5:18). The shoes of peace are available because of what Jesus the Prince of Peace accomplished on the cross.

The Good News is that the sin that separated people from the Lord has been paid for through the shed blood of Jesus on the cross. The gracious gift of God is given through faith in Christ, which brings the peace of God through reconciliation that brings the peace of God to all who believe. Jesus is our Peace and He is peace (Ephesians 2:13-14; John 14:17), and as believers we have peace in Christ.

Christ provides peace through the Father (Romans 5:1), the peace of God (read Philippians 4:6-9; Romans 16:20; Proverbs 16:7). Wearing the sandals of peace is to walk in the peace of God and peace with God through Christ and to have peace with all people as the Bible says, *"If it is possible, as far as it depends on you, live at peace with everyone"* (Romans 12:18).

It's clear that Paul the apostle is implying here that peace may not always be possible at times in our Christian journey; however, it should be our desire to do so as believers of Christ. We should be peacemakers and keepers, not troublemakers! Paul is basically saying, "If it is up to you, do your best to preserve peace."

Another unseen plot and strategy of the enemy is to create chaos, confusion, dissention, turmoil, division, disorder, and ongoing disagreement in our daily lives. Then he comes along and offers false hope, peace, and fulfillment through sin and addictions such as sex, drugs, alcohol, greed, compromise, etc. God wants the opposite for you—righteousness, peace, joy, and freedom. Peace is an attribute of the Lord's very person and character (Galatians 5:22).

In Greek, peace is defined as having wholeness or oneness. The enemy is after our peace, which is why the Lord wants us to enjoy life in His Kingdom. We must continually arm ourselves with the readiness of the Gospel of peace that comes through God's sure Word, which is our sure foundation. The gospel, which means the Good News, is the forgiveness of our sins and grants access to and oneness with the Lord through faith in Jesus Christ.

Oneness with the Father always produces peace. Throughout the Book of Ephesians we are repeatedly told to "stand firm" and to "stand." It is the devil's desire and plan to weaken our resolve, but the Gospel that provides peace equips God's people with a firm spiritual footing.

One of the easiest methods the devil uses to shake our faith and rattle us from standing firm is to tempt us to becoming overwhelmed with life's problems, burdens, and circumstances. He wants us to be confused and distracted from standing on God's promises and on His Word that brings peace in the midst of our storms. When we carry anxiousness and worry with us, we rob ourselves of God's peace. However, if we turn to Him, the Gospel of peace will keep our feet planted, anchored, and standing firm on the spiritual peace that passes all understanding in the natural.

How to Apply the Shoes of the Gospel of Peace

- Read and study God's Word by standing on what God has said in the Bible.
- Ask the Lord to remind you daily of His prophetic promises through His Gospel work on your behalf.
- Establish your identity in Christ through His Word and be secure in His work and strength, not in your own.
- Remove anything that distracts or steals your sense of security in Christ.
- Ground yourself in God's Word with Scriptures that establish your position in God's truth in your heart when the enemy comes to deceive you.

4. SHIELD OF FAITH

"In addition to all this, take up the shield of faith..." (Ephesians 6:16).

I really enjoyed the movie titled *300*. One of the things I like about this movie is the bloodred mantles, cloaks or robes, the swords, and mostly the amazing shields of the soldiers. In defense against fiery darts or an ambush, they would formulate a force shield by linking themselves together and placing the shield in front of them. It protected them from the disorganized barbarian enemy.

I also enjoy Marvel comic book movies in which Captain America uses his arm accessory, which is a shield that he throws at his enemies and like a boomerang it comes back to him. His shield is emblazoned with American patriotic colors—red, white, and blue. Captain America's shield protects him from all types of attacks. It is vitally important to him, as it is one with him.

Having the shield of faith is even more vitally important to believers. Second Corinthians 5:7 (NLT) says, *"For we live by believing and not by seeing."* Although the shield of faith is unseen naturally, it should be seen through us as a witness for others. Other should be able to see that we are believers of Christ.

A physical shield used in early Roman days was the size of a young boy or girl that covered most of a soldier's body. A soldier could move it to deflect arrows or swords, especially over the head, heart, and torso areas. At that time, Roman shields were made of wood or animal hides, which is why shields needed to be dipped in water before battle, as the enemy would oftentimes shoot long arrows with fiery tips.

Spiritually speaking, we soldiers in God's army need to be regularly dipped, soaked, and marinated in the water of the Word of God to be cleaned, revived, replenished, and fully functional—because *"faith comes by hearing, and hearing by the word of God"* (Romans 10:17 NKJV).

Our unseen enemy does not always attack directly! He will use any tactics and advances to win the battle no matter what. The shield of faith can protect you from devil's warfare tricks, tactics, and advances. Interestingly, the Roman soldiers in battle would also use their shields as portable stretchers to carry the wounded or deceased. This interesting metaphor for faith as a shield that apostle Paul describes shifts from the wardrobe to an accessory, as this piece of armor is not worn but held, like the sword of the Spirit.

Supernaturally Shielded by Faith

The shield of faith is what we are to "take up." Believers cannot raise up a physical shield that will protect us from the fiery darts of doubt, fear, unbelief, and deception by the enemy. But we can and should raise up our spiritual shields of faith daily.

Faith like a shield is an active piece of God's supernatural armor that shields us from spiritual attacks. We must understand that the devil comes to destroy our hope and diminish our convictions, but the shield of faith quenches all his fiery darts through our faith in God's Word. But we must lift up our faith like a shield as a sign of our faith in God.

Soldiers' shields usually display the emblem of the kingdom they represent. Jesus is who we represent by faith, which makes us Christians. We must believe what the Lord has given us to do and what is required of us by obedience. The obedient of God use their faith to walk daily as children of God. I believe we should have *shield-like faith* as believers in God's army.

A shield held by a Roman soldier was 2 foot by 4 foot. Soldiers would gather behind a wall of shields, side-by-side, forming an outer wall of protection. A soldier would never go to war without his shield! Hebrew 11:1 says: *"Now faith is the substance of things hoped for, the evidence of things not seen."* Faith is the substance of our shield. Together joined as a faith force shield of protection with others of like faith, we can throw up a wall of faith against the devil.

We must guard and protect our faith. It's not just faith that protects, for faith must be in the right hand like an object such as a shield. God is our Shield who protects us knowing that we have faith in Him. He will shield us like a roof over a house. Faith keeps a believer from being defeated in this unseen warfare against the enemy. The devil will shoot arrows of temptation, pride, perversion, greed, money, power, worry, guilt, fear, lust, suffering, etc. at us and only faith in the Lord will get us through trying times of temptation and testing of our faith.

There will be times when the arrows or darts may penetrate our shield of faith, but it will not be until death. On the other hand, there are times when God will penetrate through hardened areas of our hearts that may feel like satan's darts or arrows, but it's the Lord's purifying, refining, and perfecting us through messengers of love. The apostle Paul refers to them as a thorn in the flesh (2 Corinthians 12:7; 1 Corinthians 10:13; Romans 8:28).

As believers in this invisible war we keep our shields up as the fire refines us. Only when our faith is tested, fractured, or wavers will the fire hurt us. The shield of faith must be upheld because our faith will guide our actions. Our decisions each day determine our destiny and outcome in every situation.

Bad decisions are developed out of bad habits and disciplines. Our faith in our decisions must be anchored in God's truth and applied for us to see victory. People must see our faith demonstrated as followers of Him. It's not only in word, but in deeds as well.

Faith in Action Speaks Louder Than Words

James 2:14 says it like this: *"What good is it, my brothers and sisters, if someone claims to have faith but has no deeds? Can such faith save them?"* James 2:18-19 goes on to say, *"But someone will say, "You have faith; I have deeds." Show me your faith without deeds, and I will show you my faith by my deeds. You believe that there is one God. Good! Even the demons believe that—and shudder."*

Faith is more than words only—it must be an action word. Even demons believe there is one God which is true, but their aim is for you to disobey the One true and living God. The opposite of faith is fear. When fear comes, use faith to disarm it. Faith is not just belief, faith is believing and having a plan of action that is followed through in obedience to what God instructs. Making decisions and building habits and disciplines that are based on faith moves you to defeat the enemy of your mind, and you will make wise decisions every time.

While writing this spiritual warfare book, *Unseen Warfare*, you have no idea the amount of ongoing warfare I encountered every day such as distractions, hindrances, delays, mental and physical fatigue, mishaps, financial attacks, and so much more. The unseen warfare I faced daily writing this manual was against everything I stood for and that was the truth and my faith in God to equip you with the rules of engagement to discern, disarm, and defeat the works of the enemy.

My faith has been tested and tried, but I had to persevere because it isn't about me—it's about linking shoulders with other soldiers of faith in God to establish a wall of faith to shield each other so we can win this invisible battle. I couldn't give up writing even when the warfare was unbearable at times. It was you, the reader, I thought of and know that you will muster up enough supernatural strength to break through whatever battle you are facing.

Winning the battle against the invisible is more than just wearing the armor of God—it is knowing how strong and deep your faith is. Our faith is based on the actions in God's Word, believing in the truth of God's Word, and ultimately in the Lord Jesus Christ. Our faith is an important part of our relationship with the Lord as believers. The Bible says, *"without faith it's impossible to please God"* (Hebrews 11:6). The enemy is going to fight you daily to keep you from growing in faith with your heavenly Father.

In other words, faith is how you and I start our walk with God, by believing in His Son Jesus. Faith is connected to our spiritual walk and growth. Faith is what assists you in your stance as a soldier in God's army to fight until the end, as *"Jesus, the founder and perfecter of our faith"* (Hebrew 12:2 ESV). Taking up our faith like a shield is signifying and declaring boldly our total reliance and trust in God in every circumstance that we cannot control, knowing He will lead and guide us.

It is also putting our faith in the Lord's power, His purpose, will and plan for our lives and that by His power to bring it about in our lives and the changing world we live in. Through faith we know that it is God and God alone who forgives us from sin, saves us, loves us, and finishes the work that He started in us. The unseen attacks by the enemy are only to shake our faith, confidence, and trust in the Lord. But we are overcomers!

How to Apply the Shield of Faith

- Ask the Lord to increase your faith if you feel it's being tested (Mark 9:24).
- Set your faith on God's Word, will, character, and promises, not on yours.
- Read, meditate, and speak out loud in prayer Bible verses that build your faith and counteract the enemy attacks against your trust in God.
- Find Scripture verses that feed your faith and fill your atmosphere with decrees and declarations spoken out loud in faith.
- Partner with other like-minded people to build a prayer partnership to hold each other accountable; surround yourself with people who teach and a church that preaches the truth.

5. HELMET OF SALVATION

"and take the helmet of salvation..." (Ephesians 6:17)

The helmet on a Roman soldier in Paul's day referred to the galea, of which many varieties have been discovered. In an artistic and decorative way, helmets were often included a large red plume on top, like a mohawk hairstyle. This type of helmet would not be worn in battle, only during ceremonial occasions.

In antiquity, soldiers on the battlefield could expect all types of things shot or thrown at them including arrows, foul and pungent animal feces, and hails of rocks. So, of course, the helmet protecting their heads was an important part of their armor. Likewise, we must cover our heads from what the enemy will try to whisper in our ears. The helmet of salvation is vital to guard our minds from polluted, perverted, distorted, convoluted, and deception thrown at us before we ever assemble to prepare for war.

The enemy is after your salvation. The devil is a savage enemy! But Jesus is our salvage King! Salvation came to us when we first made the remarkable decision to put our total trust in Jesus' death, burial, and resurrection as the payment for our sin. However, salvation is also worked out through a process of sanctification over time in our Christian walk as believers. It's not an overnight process. The helmet of salvation is just as important as any piece of the armor of God as it covers and protects the soldier's head.

One of the most dangerous battles is the one that takes place in a believer's mind. The war in their natural faculties. The enemy is after our minds. Our head houses our brain that causes us to think and process ideas, thoughts, and memory. We thank God for the skull bone that protects our brains. Wearing a helmet when operating a motorcycle, bicycle, skateboard or working in construction, playing sports or any activity that could cause head damage is necessary. The helmet is needed for a soldier, warrior.

PROTECT YOUR SALVATION

Even in our modern-day military equipment a helmet is important and must be worn. Paul speaks about the helmet of salvation (like the breastplate of righteousness) that must be worn and it rests on the work of Jesus Christ to save us, but also involves believers to maintain it as we go through our walk with Him to work that salvation into every facet of our thoughts. The real spiritual battle that I believe we face is on the battlefield of our mind, which is the centralized spiritual place the conflict or warfare is raged.

It is God who has to break through into our perspectives, paradigms, thought processes, logics and reasoning to free us with truth while the enemy fights to establish strongholds to bind us (John 10:10). Roman soldiers wore helmets to protect their head from injury from the enemy's attacks. Like my favorite football team, the Philadelphia Eagles, has an eagle on its helmet as its team logo, Roman soldiers had a specific emblem on their helmets.

The helmet of salvation sets a believer apart from unbelievers. It's all about conduct, outward expression, and demonstration through our lifestyle and walk that determines whose side or team we belong to, just like a football player. I know the difference between the Philadelphia Eagles and the Baltimore Ravens. Even though both team logos are birds, the birds are distinctly different as are the colors of the players' uniform.

The helmet of salvation displays that we are saved by our faith in Jesus Christ. As the helmet of salvation for believers provides reliable protection against the enemies' attacks, we must also keep in mind that most of the attacks we endure daily are spiritually inflicted and manifest mentally and physically. That is why in this ongoing spiritual battle you must take comfort in your salvation and that you don't forfeit it. Be certain and confident in your salvation in Christ and what He has finished at the cross for you. And you are justified by faith in Him and are considered the righteousness of Christ. Know without a shadow of a doubt who you belong to, that you were purchased for a price, and you will not be forsaken, ever. Salvation means to be rescued, salvaged, and saved.

If you were held hostage as a prisoner of war by the enemy, you were rescued from the hands of the oppressor. Your rescuer would be considered your salvation. Jesus is our Salvation! Jesus, our Superhero! The One who set us free from sin—and when we have faith in Him, we are delivered and set free from sin and death and bondage. We were captives of sin, sentenced to death in need of the Savior through salvation.

Biblically, when we talk about salvation it basically means to be saved from the punishment of eternal life. Romans 6:23 says it like this: *"For the wages of sin is death, but the gift of God is eternal life in Christ Jesus our Lord."* This biblical truth and reality that the helmet of salvation is part of the armor of God points to the Lord who is the only One who can save, rescue, salvage, and deliver His people. I love how First Thessalonians 5:8 describes this particular piece of God's full armor as *"the hope of salvation as a helmet."* We know that Jesus is the hope of glory.

Hope of Glory Helmet

Isaiah 59:17 says, *"He put on righteousness as his breastplate, and the helmet of salvation on his head; he put on the garments of vengeance and wrapped himself in zeal as in a cloak."*

From this passage of Scripture in Isaiah we see that the Lord put on the helmet of salvation. He is the God of war, and the One who can save, deliver, and rescue us from the ongoing invisible war. In addition, we know that the Lord Himself brings salvation to the world because He sent Jesus. Jesus' name means "the Lord Saves." The helmet of salvation guards and protects our mind and brings hope in hopeless situations. The message of the Gospel, the Good News, isn't just about Jesus living, dying on the cross, and being buried—the message is that He rose on the third day with all power in His hand.

In addition, salvation is not about going to Heaven when we depart this earthly life, it's about advancing the King and His Kingdom here and now on earth. We are Christ's extensions on earth; He is making all things new through us for when Jesus returns (Revelation 21:5). When a soldier in Christ puts on the helmet of salvation, we are putting our hope fully in God and the finished work done by Christ. We are to have the mind of Christ (Philippians 2:1-11).

Our mind is very important in controlling our decisions. Consequently, the devil attacks it in a vigorous and deadly way in his war games and strategy. If you cannot focus, concentrate, and think soberly, then he can bring confusion to destabilize you. He wants to create spiritual, mental, and physical unrest to every area of your life. The enemy does not want you to have peace in your in life. Therefore, it's imperative to guard your mind—your goals, concepts, ideas, decisions, will, core values, belief system, perspectives, logic, comprehension, intellect, motives, priorities, etc. (See Romans 12:1-2; James 1:8; 2 Timothy 2:25-26.)

In this invisible battle we encounter daily, it's not just war with these six pieces of the armor of God that we must wear fully but what we are engaging, contending, and waring against in our jobs, careers, ungodly people, places, the world systems, etc. The enemy wants to make our decisions and prevent us from thinking for ourselves. He will attack our minds like he did in the beginning to Eve (Genesis 3:1-7; 2 Corinthians 11:3). He uses the weapon of deception and will do the same to us through the demonic artillery of pride, selfishness, self-ambition, greed, power, and self-centeredness. He actually influences the world through these diabolical methods.

On the other hand, we can discern and disarm his plans by having the mind of God and putting on the helmet of salvation, because only through salvation can we have the mind of Christ and thus do the will of the Lord in our generation. The Bible declares that as a person thinks, that is how they are (Proverbs 23:7 KJV). That being said, to have the mind of Christ as the Body of Christ is to be Christ-like, which starts in our mind—so it must be protected so we can outwit the enemy during spiritual warfare.

It is the devil's plan to tempt God's people so as to minimize the importance of salvation. He would love for us to believe it as a past only encounter of receiving Jesus. However, I encourage the children of God to consider the meaning of salvation today, even more so than the past. Today there are so many more ways for evil to seep into our lives including worldwide Internet social media.

Therefore, always remember that you are saved by the Lord's grace via faith, and therein we must stay. As children of God we have been granted access by faith into His grace in which we abide, and we must remain in it daily (Romans 5:1-2). If at any time we put our sole reliance on our own merit or in the world around us, that separates us from the Lord Jesus Christ and we fall from grace (Galatians 5:4; 1 John 1:7-9).

When we forget the cleansing of our old nature, the apostle Peter tells us that we are spiritually blind and shortsighted if we don't grow spiritually (2 Peter 1:9; Acts 2:38). The enemy opposes anything that develops us spiritually. He tries to thwart God's purposes for salvation and redemption, as well as the Lord's every promise for accomplishing it. The devil preys also on nonbelievers to prevent salvation happening for them (Luke 8:11-12) and promoting sin (Ephesians 2:1-3).

God Is Working for Your Good

Satan will go so far as to break our covenant relationship with the Father and prey on our humanistic nature or inclination to sin. He deceives God's people into believing lies that can potentially hinder our discipleship or effectiveness in God's Kingdom. That's why we are to stand on His promises found in His Word:

Romans 8:28 (ESV): *"And we know that for those who love God all things work together for good, for those who are called according to his purpose."*

John 10:29 (ESV): *"My Father, who has given them to me, is greater than all, and no one is able to snatch them out of the Father's hand."*

Philippians 1:6 (ESV): *"I am sure of this, that he who began a good work in you will bring it to completion at the day of Jesus Christ."*

I am reminded of the story of King Saul and David where in First Samuel 17:38-39 it says:

> *Then Saul dressed David in his own tunic. He put a coat of armor on him and a bronze helmet on his head. David fastened on his sword over the tunic and tried walking around, because he was not used to them. "I cannot go in these," he said to Saul, "because I am not used to them." So he took them off.*

Saul gave David his own tunic, armor, and bronze helmet but it was too heavy for David. He couldn't walk in another man's armor. The armor didn't fit him.

When God places His armor on you, it's the King's armor. It will only work if you walk in the power and might of God, not in your own armor. David couldn't walk in someone else's shoes, only the spiritual shoes that God equipped him with. He could use what he was accustomed to when he defeated the lion and bears as a shepherd. Later he slayed Goliath with the power, strength, and boldness in God that supernaturally and accurately brought down Philistine champion who was an offense to God and to the Israelites.

When David called Goliath an "uncircumcised Philistine," he wasn't calling him a dirty name (1 Samuel 17:26). To be uncircumcised was to be outside of the Abrahamic covenant and the promised blessings of God. When God instituted the sign of circumcision with Abraham, he was living in the land of Canaan.

David was fit to be Israel's future king because he was a man after God's own heart and trusted in the power of God, not in man. He came against the enemy in the power of God, which was his unseen armor that defeated the giant. Guard your mind because mind stirs your decisions and creates your destination, your future.

Don't believe the enemy when he tells you that you fell permanently from glory because you made a mistake or sinned. Don't believe that you are not forgiven and have lost your salvation all together. That's far from the truth—a total lie. You are a child of God and are forgiven when you repent and confess your sins and move on to advance God's Kingdom to fulfill your purpose in God. As soldiers of God, we must accept this helmet of the Lord because it is our salvation.

How to Apply the Helmet of Salvation

- Safeguard yourself by reading, meditating, and studying the Word of God daily and praying to God to reassure you in His truth and your salvation.
- Wash your mind with the Word of God through renewing it daily in God's Word. As Romans 12:2

says, "Do not conform to the pattern of this world but be transformed by the renewing of your mind. Then you will be able to test and approve what God's will is—his good, pleasing, and perfect will."

- Ask God to reveal to you His perfect will for your life and to help you fulfill it.

- Reflect on the Lord's character and faithfulness found throughout the Word of God. Ask the Lord to cultivate the fruit of the Spirit and teach all nine of them to you so you can perfect your Christian walk.

- Guard your mind from carnal, fleshly, earthly, and lustful thoughts. Cast down vain imaginations and toxic thoughts that don't line up with the Word of God (2 Corinthians 10:5). As Colossians 3:2 declares, *"Set your minds on things above, not on earthly things."*

6. Sword of the Spirit

"...and the sword of the Spirit, which is the word of God" (Ephesians 6:17).

The last piece of the supernatural armor of God is the sword of the Spirit. Like the shield, this piece is not worn but wielded to defend or attack. The sword of the Spirit is exactly what is says it is—a spiritual sword that is to be used spiritually. This sword represents the Word of God which the Scripture clearly states. This sword is the most and only lethal weapon a soldier in God's army possesses. It is interesting the only piece of God's armor that is both defensive and offensive. It serves a double-edge purpose as believers are to wield properly the Word of God, the sword of the Spirit.

The Word of God explains and describes what God's Word is like: *"For the word of God is quick, and powerful, and sharper than any twoedged sword, piercing even to the dividing asunder of soul and spirit, and of the joints and marrow, and is a discerner of the thoughts and intents of the heart"* (Hebrews 4:12 KJV).

Even Jesus Christ our Lord used the Word as a sword three times when being tempted and tested by the devil in Matthew 4:1-11:

> *Then Jesus was led by the Spirit into the wilderness to be tempted by the devil. After fasting forty days and forty nights, he was hungry. The tempter came to him and said, "If you are the Son of God, tell these stones to become bread."* **Jesus answered, "It is written:** *'Man shall not live on bread alone, but on every word that comes from the mouth of God.'"* *Then the devil took him to the holy city and had him stand on the highest point of the temple. "If you are the Son of God," he said, "throw yourself down. For it is written: 'He will command his angels concerning you, and they will lift you up in their hands, so that you will not strike your foot against a stone.'"* **Jesus answered him, "It is also written:** *'Do not put the Lord your God to the test.'"* *Again, the devil took him to a very high mountain and showed him all the kingdoms of the world and their splendor. "All this I will give you," he said, "if you will bow down and worship me."* **Jesus said to him, "Away from me, Satan! For it is written:** *'Worship the Lord your God, and serve him only.'"* *Then the devil left him, and angels came and attended him.*

Jesus uses God's Word as a weapon against temptation, bribery, and pride. He didn't have a physical sword in His hand because He is the Sword, the Word. His words were weapons of warfare against every temptation by the enemy. We can presume that the enemy waited for an opportune time to test and tempt Jesus (read

Luke 4:13). Jesus wasn't exempt from this test, and neither are you and I. Satan tested Jesus when He was weak, vulnerable, and accessible. The devil is cunning and will use times of vulnerability and opportunity to get you to succumb to his war game offers and propositions.

Nevertheless, Jesus discerned the plots of the enemy and counteracted each with the Word, which is truth against direct or indirect schemes of the devil. The enemy made three attempts to persuade Jesus to break His fast, commit suicide, and fall down and worship him. Jesus had the same reply, *"It is written!"* Never try to fight the enemy, and those he uses to bait you, with anything that is contrary to God's will and Word. We must wield the Word of God in response to any test and temptation sent by the devil.

We don't wrestle against each other, even though people may act devilish. As believers of Christ we should stand on God's Word and use it to defeat the temptation or test. Even in your weakness, like Jesus you too can overcome the enemy's attempts and temptations every time with the Word of God—the sword of the Spirit. The most interesting outcome between the devil and Jesus is that when He rebuked satan, he left and angels came to minister to Jesus. We have the power to rebuke any demonic temptation that wars against our mind, will, and emotions—our soul.

Wielding Power

We can rebuke too by resisting the enemy in the power in the name of Jesus, not in our own power. The Bible says in James 4:7 (ESV), *"Submit yourselves therefore to God. Resist the devil, and he will flee from you."* Jesus is the Word—the SWORD! As believers we have the sword of the Spirit. The Holy Spirit gives us the supernatural power to wield the Word of God with accuracy to discern, disarm, and defeat the power of wickedness. We live by the Word of God—just as Jesus told satan that *"man shall not live by bread alone, but by every word that comes from the mouth of God."*

The rules of engagement against the invisible enemy are not limited to believers in Christ, because we fight with the truth of God's Word against the enemy who also knows the truth of God's Word. Don't be deceived into believing that the devil doesn't know the Word of God. He does. He predates human existence.

He knows the Word of God and will test you to see if you know it too and if you can you fully live it. That's why we need the Holy Spirit who teaches us all things. He is God's Spirit and can combat the enemy when we don't know it fully ourselves (read John 14:26; 16:13; Romans 8:26-27; 1 John 2:27).

In addition, we utilize the sword of the Spirit of God's armor to offensively and defensively engage with the Word of God and commit to follow all that Jesus Christ has commanded. We must understand that in this unseen warfare battle against the powers of darkness knowing the Word of God is vital for these three simple reasons:

1. It provides truth, light, comfort, revelation knowledge, wisdom, and healing.
2. It is sanctifying and purifying—personally, mentally, and spiritually.
3. It is a weapon of war to be used to advance the Kingdom of God, ward off temptation, and cast down everything that exalts itself against the knowledge of God.

As the apostle Paul concludes the list of the supernatural armor of God with the sword of the Spirit, we must keep in mind that the Word of God is the absolute truth and brings breakthrough freedom to those who receive it. This weapon forged by God through

His Word can discern and destroy the cunning and crafty works of darkness.

Oftentimes when I am preparing to study or minister the Word of God, all kinds of warfare from the enemy comes at me before, during, and after a sermon. The enemy wants to keep us unprepared and distracted so we can't fight effectively. In addition, he comes to pervert the truth of God's Word.

It's imperative to study the Word of God and allow the Holy Spirit to teach you truth. Also it's beneficial to find seasoned teachers, leaders, and Bible readers who can sharpen your sword edge. The enemy wants your sword to be dull, unable to cut through lies, deception, and falsehoods. The apostle Paul wrote to his spiritual son, Timothy, of the necessity to study the Word of truth as a church apostolic leader against false teachers in their day. Paul urges Timothy in Secondv Timothy 2:15 to *"Study and be eager and do your utmost to present yourself to God approved (tested by trial), a workman who has no cause to be ashamed, correctly analyzing and accurately dividing [rightly handling and skillfully teaching] the Word of Truth"* (Amplified Bible, Classic Edition).

The Cutting Edge

Paul, Timothy's spiritual father, urged him to view himself as a worker seeking to please God. Any worker or servant should desire to satisfy the expectations of his or her boss. Timothy was to view his work as unto the Lord and a resident apostle and pastor in the same way. The words "rightly dividing" in Second Timothy 2:15 are translated from the Greek word *orthotomounta*, the present participle form of *orthotomeō*, a compound word made up of two Greek words: *orthos*, meaning right or straight; and *temnō*, meaning to cut.

"Rightly dividing" means to cut straight, to make straight or smooth (Strong's G3178). As soldiers of God we are to accurately know how to use our sword, which is the Word of God. The Word of God gives every soldier the cutting edge and advantage over the enemy's deceptive weapons.

The sword of the Spirit is no play toy, movie prop, or metal ornament for display. It's a real sword used for real spiritual warfare engagement. Paul understood the power of the sword of the Spirit and its lasting blow against the enemy of lies. Jesus defeated the enemy every time with the Word of truth, which is the sword in His mouth. The enemy will eventually give up and go away when he knows the person is armed with the Word of Truth and can quote the Word of God—and lives it as well. You have to absorb the Word of God into you thorough the Holy Spirit so the devil will think twice about messing with you.

How to Apply the Sword of the Spirit

- Apply the truth of God's Word when faced with challenges to compromise. Ask the Lord to show you by revelation what is His original concept and meaning of the Scripture you may be reading and studying.
- Ask the Lord to highlight any erroneous doctrines, teachings, demon spirits or heretical, gnostic, and false Gospel teaching to keep you from being exposed to lies.
- Pray in the Spirit with your heavenly language as you worship, study, read, and during your devotional time with God. If you don't have the gift of speaking in other tongues, ask God to give you the gift, and by faith speak with other tongues in Jesus' name!

SUPERNATURAL WARFARE TONGUES

Lastly, in Ephesians 6:18-20 (NLT), the apostle Paul requests something powerfully and humbly from the Ephesians:

Pray in the Spirit at all times and on every occasion. Stay alert and be persistent in your prayers for all believers everywhere. And pray for me, too. Ask God to give me the right words so I can boldly explain God's mysterious plan that the Good News is for Jews and Gentiles alike. I am in chains now, still preaching this message as God's ambassador. So pray that I will keep on speaking boldly for him, as I should.

Paul says that we are to pray in the Spirit implying that it relates to spiritual warfare, the fully suited spiritual armor of God. We are to pray in the Spirit at all times. Not one or two times, but at all times.

When I was encountering spiritual resistance and demonic visitations when I was in college, the Lord taught me how to pray—basically how to war in prayer! I couldn't speak in my native tongue to fight those spiritual battles. I had to fight in the Spirit with my spirit in the spirit through the sword of the Spirit that came out of my mouth in prayer. Your tongue is a physical weapon against an invisible enemy! The Bible says life and death is in the power of our tongue (Proverbs 18:21 NKJV).

The enemy wants to mute, muzzle, and censor you from praying! Paul gives us a simple but profound key to getting a breakthrough and winning the invisible battle. I saw tremendous breakthroughs in my life in many areas when I shifted my prayer life from praying casual, convenient, lethargic, aimless, and "itemized list" type of prayers to powerful, targeted, intentional, faith-filled warfare-like prayers prayed in the Spirit. Meaning, praying in the Holy Spirit's language (God's language), or praying in other tongues, until I got my breakthrough. There is power in praying in other tongues or in the Spirit language! You can access that power today through the truth of God's Word.

Paul understood prayer and spiritual warfare. The rules of spiritual engagement (ROSE) are activated when you are fully armored in God's supernatural power, and your mouth holds the enemy's defeat. The following are a few Scriptures about the power of speaking in tongues. It's imperative to be immersed in the Holy Spirit and wield God's Word to defeat the works of darkness. Read and study for yourself these Scripture passages that support and emphasize the importance of the New Testament biblical relevance of speaking in tongues:

- First Corinthians 14:1-4 (ESV): "Pursue love, and earnestly desire the spiritual gifts, especially that you may prophesy. For one who speaks in a tongue speaks not to men but to God; for no one understands him, but he utters mysteries in the Spirit. On the other hand, the one who prophesies speaks to people for their upbuilding and encouragement and consolation. The one who speaks in a tongue builds up himself, but the one who prophesies builds up the church."
- Acts 2:1-5: "When the day of Pentecost came, they were all together in one place. Suddenly a sound like the blowing of a violent wind came from heaven and filled the whole house where they were sitting. They saw what seemed to be tongues of fire that separated and came to rest on each of them. All of them were filled with the Holy Spirit and began to speak in other tongues as the Spirit enabled them. Now there were staying in Jerusalem God-fearing Jews from every nation under heaven."
- Romans 8:26 (ESV): "Likewise the Spirit helps us in our weakness. For we do not know what to pray for

as we ought, but the Spirit himself intercedes for us with groanings too deep for words."

- Ephesians 6:18 (ESV): "Praying at all times in the Spirit, with all prayer and supplication. To that end keep alert with all perseverance, making supplication for all the saints."

We can see the benefits of praying in the Spirit at all times, and we can use it in any and all types of prayers and supplications. In other words, every time you pray, you can pray in the Holy Spirit. For example, when I bless my food when I am alone, I first pray silently in the Spirit and then I pray in my native tongue or language. The enemy doesn't know what we are praying when we pray in tongues because we speak mysteries to God (see 1 Corinthians 14:2).

Some may wonder that because the enemy is a spirit being, he could decode the language of God. However, nowhere in Scripture supports that belief to be true. Logically it would make sense, but this is a supernatural language that only the Holy Spirit knows, articulates, and communicates by spiritual transmission to the Father. Even though we don't know what we are speaking when we pray in the Spirit, our prayer is being accepted.

That's why I pray always and as often as I can in the Spirit so that my prayers are not hindered as much as in the second dimension (Heaven) or intercepted by fallen angels (demon principalities).

GOD'S SPIRIT LANGUAGE

When we pray in the Spirit, we ascend to the throne room of God where our prayers requests, petitions, supplications, etc., are rendered and verdicts, edicts, and prophetic revelations of answers are released. God doesn't speak foreign languages as we do, even though He has given us all of them; He speaks only spiritual language.

God's language is spiritual because He is Spirit! Praying is connected to spiritual warfare! That is why the main rules of engagement to conquer the demonic devices and inditements of the enemy is to war in the Spirit with your Spirit language through the Holy Spirit.

Paul didn't make mention that praying in the Spirit is one of God's armor pieces. He gave us a truth that praying in the Spirit after having been fully armored in God's equipment allows you to fight against a spiritually evil supernatural being called the devil and his demons. The apostle Paul basically was telling the Ephesian believers to stay alert and always persevere in supplication for all the saints (Ephesians 6:18).

Paul also asked them to pray for him as well so he could speak boldly God's message. As they pray for him, he will speak the mysteries of the Gospel as an ambassador in chains. He understood that prayer is needed for him to speak boldly as God's bondservant to see breakthrough in that region. We will talk about prayer in spiritual warfare briefly in a later chapter.

The armor and the weapons of our warfare are spiritual. Use them and win the unseen battle with God's power, in Jesus' name! Praying always. Having instructed the Ephesians to put on their armor, Paul now enjoins them to fight by prayer. This is the true method of victorious living. To call upon God is the chief exercise of faith and hope; and it is in this way that we obtain from God every blessing.

Prayer and supplication are not greatly different from each other, except that supplication is only one branch of prayer. As believers in a daily spiritual battle, we are exhorted by Paul to persevere in prayer, praying for each other and those called to preach, teach, and steward the mysteries of the Gospel. As Christians believers, the Bible calls us God's ambassadors in that we have been *"approved by*

God to be entrusted with the gospel" (1 Thessalonians 2:4 ESV), just like Paul the apostle.

As we go through this world, we represent God's Kingdom (John 18:36), and it is our responsibility to reflect the "official position" of Heaven. When you are faced with an uphill battle against the enemy in your spiritual walk with Jesus, know that the Kingdom of Heaven is ready to unleash an army of warrior angels or angelic knights to help you win the invisible war. The weapons of your warfare are already available to you—just discern what they are and use them to disarm and defeat the enemy in God's power and grace!

Chapter 6

WEAPONS OF
OUR WARFARE

I have created the blacksmith who fans the coals beneath the forge and makes the weapons of destruction. And I have created the armies that destroy (Isaiah 54:16 NLT).

The spiritual weapons believers fight with are not weapons of this world. They are spiritual weapons provided by the Lord Himself. God has given us weapons that are not forged by natural hands but by God who has the divine power to demolish strongholds. What are the strongholds in your life and mind that are prohibiting you from receiving your breakthrough? The Bible doesn't go into detail about what the weapons we fight with actually are, but it does tell us what they do—demolish strongholds!

Our biblical paradigm of spiritual warfare is imperative to know so that we know what we are up against. It's not a physical warfare but spiritual. Even though the enemy can influence people against us in the flesh but it's still a spiritual war. In addition, we have to clearly and accurately as soldiers of God in His army to identify the strongholds on the battlefield of our minds and in our lives before we able to know what weapons are used to defend and defeat the works of the devil.

SPIRITUAL WARFARE IS NOT A SPECIAL EVENT

Many believers today tend to view spiritual battles or conflicts in the context of a specific event and may misunderstand the invisible war that wages in their daily lives. Please know that spiritual warfare is an ongoing battle in the spiritual world to weaken believers at best, or cause them to fall at worst. It is the enemy's agenda to drive God's people far away from Him and His divine purposes for their lives.

The enemy wants to unleash weapons of oppression, stress, anxiety, depression, confusion, and a feeling of despair; these are the "results" or "outcomes" of warfare and the aftereffects of the attacks of a very real archenemy of God. Keep in mind that these demonic tactics of the enemy are just part of the attacks sent, but not the battle. The battle is on a much larger scale!

A one-on-one fight is nothing like a war with multiple enemies using weapons against you at the same time. That's why we must look at war and warfare spiritually speaking and take it seriously when engaging.

Oftentimes, believers view spiritual battles as a single event; something that occurs in our lives once in a while, a few times in a lifetime, or a seasonal occurrence of trouble. Whether the fight from the enemy is obvious or not, we must realize that he is continually targeting God's people.

I have known believers who blame everything on the enemy for what goes wrong in their lives. Although the devil is our enemy, I believe every attack isn't from him—rather many are from our unwise decisions, which allows him to attack. Some believer's view spiritual warfare encounters from a self-centered, "me"-only perspective. They often say that they are being attacked, which may be truth. Or that the devil "must be coming against them" at a point in time when they are facing some difficulties in life. And often people say, "I am so anointed that the enemy is coming for me today!" But spiritual warfare is bigger than you and I.

Spiritual warfare is not an event, series of episodes in our lives, or a snapshot in time. It is not something the devil sends our way out of the blue, once in a while, or attacks those who are called to ministry. It is an ongoing battle that involves all believers day in and day out. Truthfully, it is the way of life for God's people. That is why we must discern the invisible works of the enemy.

It is my heartfelt prayer every day that the Lord will equip me and the Body of Christ to victoriously wage war against the works of the enemy to bring tremendous breakthrough and to impact others for the Kingdom of God.

Warfare Unaware

Unconsciously and unaware, we may be ignoring the real battle. There were several times in my life when I was depressed and anxious. The Lord had to reveal to me that I was permitting anxiety to control every aspect of my life. Anxiety and depression were plaguing my mind and body.

Truthfully, I was giving depression and anxiety legal control over my mind, will, and emotions; I was ignoring the battle that I was facing and the war too! I was viewing and evaluating every incident occurring in my life as an isolated event or circumstance. I was looking at every depression that I was facing or anxiety attack by the enemy as a single struggle—but in actuality I was in a whole, unseen battle. A battle in my mind.

The weapons the enemy was using against me were depression and anxiety. The Lord gave me a revelation that I was not just in a battle but in the midst of warfare itself. Therefore, blindly I was preventing God from directing me by His Holy Spirit into truth, I was permitting my anxiety to keep me oppressed, depressed, and stressed, unable to focus. I was focused on the *weapons* of the devil's attacks, not the attacker.

Depression and anxiety had the victory and control over my mind, which crippled my ability to live the life God destined for me. The attack stripped away my joy, peace, and righteousness in the Holy Spirit. In addition, it kept me a prisoner bound by fear and shame. Nobody wants to live in the shadows of evil, powerless, unable to be free and whole.

We too often believe that spiritual battles are massive, glaring attacks on our careers, family, health, our marriage, our business, finances, and ministries. But no, not always or all the time! The devil doesn't always address things by attacking us obviously or noticeably. He starts fights with little subtleties. Discernment through the Holy Spirit must be used to notice the unnoticeable. We need the Holy Spirit's discerning of spirits to identify the devil's weapons. We must keep in mind that the enemy can change his weapons of warfare to whatever will disable his target.

As believers we have to stand guard and alert, knowing that at any time the devil is up to no good and something new. The weapons of our warfare are powerful in the hands of those who can discern the enemy's tactics and then use the necessary weapons to overcome. The Lord was saying to me, "I can't give you the victory in ministry and over depression and anxiety if you can't recognize the enemy's weapons attacking your mind!" Victory only comes when we are honest with ourselves that we need help and can discern what needs to be cleaned, purged, and removed from our lives.

We have to clean house spiritually speaking and evict the unlawful occupants. Or we must address what's dividing our sphere of occupancy! We as warriors of God must eradicate anything that is bringing division, confusion, anxiety, depression, oppression, and stress to our house. The Bible is clear when Jesus says in Mark 3:26-27 (NLT), *"And if Satan is divided and fights against himself, how can he stand? He would never survive. Let me illustrate this further. Who is powerful enough to enter the house of a strong man and plunder his goods? Only someone even stronger—someone who could tie him up and then plunder his house."*

PLUNDER THE PLUNDERER!

We have to plunder the plunderer! In other words, we must arrest, bind, and issue a search warrant against the enemy and have him removed from the premises. Jesus is saying that only a strong man can defeat someone who is weaker. Jesus is stronger than the strong man. He has the authority and power to arrest and evict him. Jesus not only has the power and authority to bind the strong man in his house, He also has the power to take the house as well.

We have the power through the Holy Spirit-delegated authority to bind the strongholds in our lives by evicting the strong man we have given permission to occupy that place and space in our lives. The power that allows the enemy to take up residence is the same power through Jesus' name and authority that will regain control of our spiritual place.

In other words, we must bind the strongholds by arresting the strong man and taking back what he has stolen from us. Don't allow the enemy's weapons of warfare to break your will. The reason why I can speak about this is because I myself was looking at spiritual warfare as an event and not a daily occurrence or a day-to-day part a believer's lifestyle. I had to come to grips with the reality that spiritual attacks, warfare, and spiritual warfare training will be with me for the rest of my human existence.

However, the enemy doesn't have to control, manipulate, or hold me hostage as a prisoner in my mind and life. I came to the realization in my ministry and Christian journey that I can live victoriously in Christ when I allow Him to control all of me.

EVERYTHING ISN'T WARFARE

Warfare doesn't just happen when there are difficulties in our marriage, ministry, business, families, careers, when we lose our employment, or even when we get sick. Those things will happen when you live long enough and because they are part of our natural lives. Everything we go through is not sent by the enemy and we shouldn't automatically assume hardship as being spiritual warfare. We don't want to blame certain things on the devil when we face hardship or delay when in fact it could be God. We must definitely take the time to seriously discern what's happening in the natural and the spiritual realms.

The Bible declares in James 4:7: *"Submit yourselves, then, to God. Resist the devil, and he will flee from you."* The word "submit" in this case, in the blue letter Bible and Strong's Greek Concordance is "a military term that is defined as to "arrange (troop divisions) in a military fashion under the command of a leader." We are in an ongoing spiritual war and Lord is our Commander and Leader. As warriors of God in His army, we are obligated to submit to His commands!

We need to give attention to, submit, and do what the Lord commands, instead of listening to and yielding to our fleshly desires. It's imperative to pursue God in His Word daily. However, we must do more than just read the Word of God. As stated before, the enemy also knows the Word. In fact, atheists, Muslims, and people of other religions read and know the Bible more than some

Christians. But just because they know and read it doesn't mean they live by the truth revealed in it.

Reading the Word of God is also about applying the principles of the truth in God's Word that is powerful in claiming victory in unseen warfare. Reading, studying, and applying God's Word is a lethal weapon of warfare against the enemy! Spiritual warfare involves being in the ranks of God's army and following His commands that allows you to escape and survive the invisible war. When an army totally surrenders and submits itself to the command of its king, commander, or leader, it can move forward victoriously in battle to resist their enemies, causing them to flee before them.

Armies are never assembled or engage in battle without a leader. Likewise, as soldiers of God we are not to employ the rules of engagement in battle without the Lord, our Commander, King, and Leader! We cannot defeat the enemy in our own power—only God can through us!

WARFARE STRONGHOLDS

*For though we live in the world, we do not wage war as the world does. The **weapons we fight with** are not the weapons of the world. On the contrary, they **have divine power to demolish strongholds.** We demolish arguments and every pretension that sets itself up against the knowledge of God, and we take captive every thought to make it obedient to Christ* (2 Corinthians 10:3-5).

We can see clearly in Second Corinthians 10 that evil strongholds do exist. What's good to know is that they can be demolished and destroyed by divine powers. The word "strongholds" in this passage is the Greek word "*ochuróma*" and it means "a fortified, military stronghold; a strong-walled fortress." Also, "a stronghold or fortress" (Strong's G3794) is the Greek root word akin to *ochu-roo*, meaning "fortify and to make firm." Stronghold is used metaphorically in Second Corinthians 10:4, referring to where human confidence is imposed. Simply put, strongholds are fortresses or strong defenses. I will go so far as to say that when the enemy establishes demonic strongholds and thought patterns that imprison people mentally, they are unable to breakthrough mentally if there are demonic fortresses—unless they stand on the Word of God to guard our minds and that place where God occupies according to Psalm 18:2: *"The Lord is my rock, my fortress and my deliverer; my God is my rock, in whom I take refuge, my shield and the horn of my salvation, my stronghold."*

The Lord is our Salvation, fortified Fortress, and Stronghold. The weapons of the enemy are strongholds of lies; he uses them to fortify a place in our lives and mind-sets through oppression, depression, stress, confusion, anxiety, fear, doubt, unbelief, division, and disorders. Note in the Second Corinthians 10:5 it says, *"We demolish arguments and every pretension that sets itself up against the knowledge of God, and we take captive every thought to make it obedient to Christ."*

Oppression, stress, fear, confusion, etc. is referred to as *"arguments and every pretension"* that are set up as strongholds against the knowledge of God in a believer's life. They come to rob us of what the Lord has prophetically spoken over us. In addition, these strongholds come to dismiss the truth of God's Word and contend with or contradict the knowledge of God.

These lies of the evil one are set up to make us believe what the enemy wants us to believe about ourselves and devalue God's worth in our lives. Rather believe his lies, we must rely on the sword of the Spirit, the Word of God. We are commanded to take captive every thought and make it obey the Spirit of truth through

Christ. We will talk about the battlefield of the mind briefly in a later chapter.

The devil's weapons of spiritual warfare include a collection of lies the enemy makes us believe about ourselves and our power in the name of Jesus! It's a façade that the enemy puts up before us. It's our thoughts that the enemy wants to control. If he can deceive and confuse you and turn you farther away from the truth, then he has already won the battle against you. You must guard your mind and use the divine power of God that demolishes every unrighteous thought.

Personally, I never knew this present truth until my mind was under attack, when my life, salvation, and truth in God's Word were challenged. God gives us revelation knowledge and reveals hidden mysteries of the rules of the engagement of the enemy's weaponry against His people. This book reveals the truth by exposing the father of lies and his works.

What has taken us captive? What has become an offense or stronghold? What has taken up residence in our minds that are not of God? What has hindered you from seeing clearly the truth? What has come to blackmail you, keeping you from living victorious? Today is the day for your breakthrough. Truth will make you free from whatever has become toxic and unhealthy to your spiritual atmosphere. Gain or regain control over your mind by the power of the Holy Spirit through the sword of the Spirit.

It's time to take captive of every single thought including abandonment, insecurities, doubt, mistrust, fear, depression, of death, failure, defeat, oppression, etc., which lead you to further away from God and closer to evil, bondage, and sin. Make every thought obedient to Christ and His Word! When a crazy or ungodly thought comes to my mind, I have learned to instantly discard, disregard, and denounce it Jesus' name!

DEMOLISH THE DEMOLISHER

The more harmful thoughts come, the more I use the divine power of God's Word to demolish them or uproot the thought that is trying to sign a lease agreement in my life to reside there, spiritually speaking. As believers we have the power and authority to rebuke those thoughts and evict them. We are to give no place for the enemy in our lives, including our thought mind.

Ephesians 4:27 says, *"In your anger do not sin. Do not let the sun go down while you are still angry, and do not give the devil a foothold."*

We must not open any door or give the enemy any legal access in our lives through sin or through our thoughts. We are not sinning when thoughts come into our minds—but we are sinning when we act out our thoughts. Clearly, we are not to give the enemy any chance or opportunity to infiltrate our thoughts and minds. The devil is an opportunist and he will take full advantage of every opportunity you allow to percolate for any length of time.

Our weapons of warfare are useless if we try to defeat the enemy in our own strength and power. I love what Isaiah 54:17 declares about the enemy's ploys: *"'No weapon forged against you will prevail, and you will refute every tongue that accuses you. This is the heritage of the servants of the Lord, and this is their vindication from me,' declares the Lord."*

This verse doesn't say that weapons will never be formed against us. The absolute truth is that they may form, but will not defeat us. In other words, the weapons will be charged against us, but will not harm us. There are weapons used by the enemy; however, we can put on our supernatural armor of God!

NO WEAPON WILL PROSPER

Isaiah 54 cites the Hebrew word for "weapon," which is *keliy* that means "utensil, implement, apparatus, vessel" and it comes from the word *kalah* that means "something prepared" (Strong's H3627). Unfortunately, it is a weapon of war that has been prepared specifically against and for your demise, as the Scripture reads exactly in the verse that *"No weapon forged against you."* The enemy fashions and forges weapons specifically for each believer!

You are a threat to him so he makes special weapons to render you irrelevant. The weapons aren't to defeat the Lord, but to thwart His children's destinies. Cowardly, the devil would rather pick on Jesus' little baby brother and sister (you and me), because he knows he can't defeat our older Brother.

Yes, we know that the devil's war is ultimately against God, but the enemy is targeting or aiming at His people. Satan knows that he is no match against Jesus who defeated him at the cross. So he will continue to try and defeat anything linked or connected to God. But he's powerless against our all-powerful God made in the flesh of Jesus.

The enemy is powerless as well when he faces God's people because we have the power of the Holy Spirit dwelling inside of us. The devil only bullies those who appear to be weak and nice Christians. He doesn't bother anyone who stands their ground and will go toe to toe with the enemy and doesn't get knocked around in the playground by the enemy. Stand your ground and position in God and remind the enemy of your Big Brother Jesus Christ who defeated him long ago.

When the enemy comes after you when you are vulnerable and weak, just cry out the name of Jesus and he will leave you alone. But there will come a time when you have to stand and face the devil head-on with the power and authority that Jesus has given you. The devil will recognize that he can't mess with you because you have the power of Christ residing inside you. The enemy comes to deceive you, to make you believe that you can't defeat him. But you can! You must believe and trust in what God says about you.

WARFARE BEGINS IN THE MIND

Spiritual warfare often starts in our minds and then like an infection suddenly invades and spreads throughout every aspect of our lives. It is a personal and physical battle where the enemy sneaks in undetected, and then all of a sudden he pillages and destroys the good that was created in our lives. That is why we must recognize and overcome every stronghold of the enemy by the divine power forged by the Lord through truth in His Word.

The devil knows the power of God will defeat him so he will take any chance he gets to catch us off guard to disable and defeat us. Life is no dress rehearsal. This is real life spiritual warfare waged against the elect and chosen of God. This is an ongoing war, not an event in our lives. Standing up to and against the enemy is spiritual warfare. Fighting back with the full armor of God and His divine power through the Holy Spirit is critical.

The enemy isn't a fictional horror movie character Freddie Kruger or a boogey man hiding behind every corner. And he's not someone to blame for every sniffle. But the devil is definitely worth watching for and in prayer staying vigilant, diligent, and standing in the authority and power of the Holy Spirit daily, not occasionally!

Through our relationship with Jesus, God through His Word has given us every weapon we need to resist and defeat the enemy. When the enemy plagues our minds with thoughts contrary to God's will and plan for our lives, we can put on the helmet of salvation to ward off evil. Or when the enemy wants God's people to shipwreck our destiny and purposes, we can stand firm with power from on high that resides in us. The Father will protect what's His and give us the grace to survive and endure this race through life to our heavenly ever after. As soldiers in God's family army, we must at all times maintain a sure foundation in His Word, the Bible, where He lays out specific instructions.

BE UNSHAKEABLE

The only human the enemy is afraid of is someone who stands up against him with the Word of God. He knows he will lose because God's truth is stronger than his lies. He wants to trick you into believing that he can move you. God simply says don't move, stand strong! I love what the following few Scriptures say about being firm and unshaken:

- Psalm 55:22: *"Cast your cares on the Lord and he will sustain you; he will never let the righteous be shaken."*
- Psalm 112:6: *"Surely the righteous will never be shaken; they will be remembered forever."*
- Proverbs 10:30: *"The righteous will never be uprooted, but the wicked will not remain in the land."*
- Proverbs 12:3: *"No one can be established through wickedness, but the righteous cannot be uprooted."*
- Hebrews 12:28: *"Therefore, since we are receiving a kingdom that cannot be shaken, let us be thankful, and so worship God acceptably with reverence and awe."*

When we discern what's going on around us pertaining to spiritual warfare, then we are not easily moved even when we see the enemy as a roaring lion prowling around in search of easy prey to devour. Although we are not to focus on the devil, we are not to be ignorant of his existence. As First Peter 5:8 (ESV) tells us, *"Be sober-minded; be watchful. Your adversary the devil prowls around like a roaring lion, seeking someone to devour."*

The word "prowls" describes the hunting actions of the devil. That word in Greek is *peripatēo,* which basically means "to make one's way, progress, to make do use of opportunities." In addition, prowling is to walk around in a full circle. The devil will prowl around like a lion for an opportunity to pounce on its prey. Spiritual warfare strategy is all about knowing your enemy and how he thinks.

The enemy is waiting for God's people to let their guard down so he can invade their minds, thoughts, and use their very own words against them. He wants you make emotional decisions and be moved by your emotions rather than what the Word of God declares as truth.

THE ROARING LION

The devil is a smart fighter who knows how to defeat his opponents by playing on their minds so they will make a wrong move. He's waiting to pounce on you at any given moment. He is looking for any opportunity. When I played offense as a wide receiver, my opponent, the defensive back, would trash talk me when we were facing each other on the line. Why? Because he wanted me to be distracted; he wanted to get in my head. He wanted me to take what he said personally and get emotional. His game plan was to do something that would cause me to make a bad decision and cost my team the game. But I knew I had to tune out the negative verbal assaults and stand in position, stay focused on the play call to hear, watch, and execute by doing my job as a wide receiver to catch the ball when thrown to me and run for the touchdown.

The devil will trash talk weak-minded people like a roaring lion looking for vulnerability and opportunities to strike. Think about spiritual warfare in this way. There is a reason why the Bible specifically identifies the devil like a roaring lion as a predator in spiritual warfare. Lions mainly hunt their prey under the cover of darkness, like the enemy who hides in the shadows of darkness stalking God's people waiting for a time to attack them. Lions in a gloomy African night use that setting to easily observe and stalk their victims without the threat of detection. It's common for lions to sit by and observe their prey during daylight hours, usually just before sunset, before making a move.

Similarly, if the landscape is illuminated by bright moonlight, they may wait until it's obscured before attempting any sort of hunt. Lions may not be the fastest or strongest predator, however they are the bravest, most intimidating, and deliberate hunters in the animal kingdom. A lion, like the devil, hunts and prowls, seeking the perfect opportunity to attack when it spots the weakest, slowest, and smallest in the herd.

Lions look for any opening to pursue its prey sometimes relying on their keen sense of hearing to detect the cry or distress of an animal. Our enemy, like a lion, uses times of distress, stress, vulnerability, weakness, etc. to target us for an attack. He is waiting for the slightest opening to steal, kill, and destroy us.

When believers look at spiritual warfare just as an event, we are not thinking soberly; rather, we are giving the enemy opportunities to infiltrate our minds and soul. We must keep the supernatural armor of God fully on and ready, knowing an attack is imminent.

Oftentimes we fall prey like an unaware gazelle to the enemy's deceptive strategies, plots, tactics, lies, and mindboggling attacks when we go through day-to-day life thinking or assuming that warfare is something that happens to someone else or when we only pay attention to it when it is a big devastating event.

THE ENEMY IS A WAR STRATEGIST

The spiritual combat you will face daily is not always obvious. The enemy is a master strategist and will not attack you upfront. He uses subtle and cunning tactics to bait you into a trap. Therefore, we must remain sober-minded, empowered by the Holy Spirit to watch and pray. Having done all you can by standing your ground in the battlefield, you will win every battle.

As soldiers of God we must utilize arm ourselves with God's mighty weapons of mass destruction against the enemy. The enemy has always been an invisible terrorist against God's people. He is focused on taking out as many soldiers of God as possible and claiming them as his war causalities. I want to give you forty-four simple weapons of our warfare that we can use to offensively and defensively defeat the enemy. These divine weapons are what I use to overcome the enemy daily. You may even have more than these, that is great because each one is important.

FORTY-FOUR WEAPONS OF WARFARE

1. Weapon of praise: 2 Chronicles 20:19, 21-22
2. Weapon of prophecy: 1 Timothy 1:18
3. Weapon of prayer: James 5:16
4. Weapon of worship: 1 Chronicles 16:23-31; Psalm 86:9-10
5. Weapon of fasting: Joel 2:12; Isaiah 58:6
6. Weapon of thanksgiving: 2 Corinthians 9:11
7. Weapon of love: Matthew 22:36-40
8. Weapon of joy: Nehemiah 8:10
9. Weapon of peace: Philippians 4:7
10. Weapon of forgiveness: Mark 11:25

11. Weapon of the Word of God: Hebrews 4:12

12. Weapon of tongues: (Spirit's language) Jude 1:20

13. Weapon of unity: 1 Corinthians 1:10; Hebrews 12:14

14. Weapon of consecration: 1 Peter 1:15-16; 2 Corinthians 6:17

15. Weapon of intercession: Job 42:8; Acts 8:24

16. Weapon of binding and loosing: Matthew 16:19

17. Weapon of warfare: 2 Corinthians 10:4

18. Weapon of faith: Romans 10:17; Matthew 21:21-22; Hebrews 11:1-2

19. Weapon of 9 gifts of the Holy Spirit: 1 Corinthians 12:7-11

20. Weapon of 9 fruit of the Holy Spirit: Galatians 5:22-23

21. Weapon of accountability to local churches and others: Ephesians 5:21

22. Weapon of confession: James 5:16

23. Weapon of testimony: James 5:16; Acts 4:33; Galatians 2:20; Revelation 12:11

24. Weapon of wisdom: Proverbs 9:10; James 1:5, 3:17; Isaiah 40:28

25. Weapon of identity in Christ: Colossians 3:1-11

26. Weapon of humility: James 4:10; Luke 14:11

27. Weapon of righteousness: 1 John 3:7; Romans 5:1-5; 2 Corinthians 6:4,7

28. Weapon of obedience: Isaiah 1:19; 1 Samuel 15:22

29. Weapon of salvation: Acts 2:38; Matthew 7:21; John 3:3,16

30. Weapon of repentance: (daily) Acts 3:19; Luke 5:32; Matthew 4:17

31. Weapon of favor: Genesis 6:8; Psalm 5:12, 9:17; Ephesians 1:11

32. Weapon of sowing/tithing: Genesis 6:12; 28:20-22; 2 Chronicles 31:4-5

33. Weapon of deliverance: (children's bread) Matthew 15:22-29

34. Weapon of healing: Matthew 15:22-29; Malachi 4:2

35. Weapon of truth: John 14:6; 17:17

36. Weapon of the fivefold ministry body gifts: (offices) Ephesians 4:11-13

37. Weapon of angelic assistance: Psalm 91

38. Weapon of anointed instruments, minstrels and singer: 1 Samuel 16:16

39. Weapon of divine order: Psalm 37:23; 1 Corinthians 14:40

40. Weapon of rest and relaxation: Matthew 11:28-30

41. Weapon of hearing the voice of God: Isaiah 30:21; John 10:27

42. Weapon of discernment: Hebrews 5:14; 1 John 4:1

43. Weapon of attentiveness/alertness: 1 Peter 5:8

44. Weapon of power of decision: Proverbs 3:5-6

Characteristics of spiritual weapons include:

1. They are not worldly, carnal, earthly, or natural.
2. They are mighty, powerful, divine, supernaturally forged, and effective.
3. Their operation/administration is through God only.

WHO IS GOD'S SECRET WEAPON?

The weapons we possess are only mighty through God, not our might. When God is not the Source of our lives, a mighty weapon can become ineffective, remember the sons of Sceva (Acts 19:10-16; 2 Samuel 1:19-27). When the anointing and power of God departed from King Saul because of his disobedience, he was left powerless, ineffective, not anointed by God's Spirit and therefore his weapons of war were insufficient to win in battle.

We must be in right relationship with God and prepared spiritually through our covenant relationship with Jesus while living righteously before Him, detesting the sinful nature so we can operate effectively the weapons of warfare. We not only can handle the weapons of warfare effectively, but we are actually God's weapons of war in His hands. What do I mean we are God's weapons of war?

In the Word of God, the Lord has declared that we are His battle-ax and weapons of war. I love what God declares in Jeremiah 51:20-21: *"You are my war club, my weapon for battle—with you I shatter nations; with you I destroy kingdoms, with you I shatter horse and rider, with you I shatter chariot and driver."* This is powerful truth found in the Old Testament and revelation of how we must see ourselves in the eyes and hands of God. We are His hammer, battle-ax, war club, and weapon of war.

We are not to take this truth lightly! God wants to use you in this unseen warfare. You become one of God's weapons of war on earth when, through the Holy Spirit's empowerment, you destroy demonic strongholds. Therefore, we ourselves are arrayed in the holiness and righteousness of God as His weapons in the spiritual war between good and evil.

Chapter 7

God's Embassy—The Church—Department of Defense

And I tell you that you are Peter, and on this rock I will build My church, and the gates of Hades will not overcome it. I will give you the keys of the kingdom of heaven; whatever you bind on earth will be bound in heaven, and whatever you loose on earth will be loosed in heaven (Matthew 16:18-19).

And God placed all things under his feet and appointed him to be head over everything for the church (Ephesians 1:22).

The Lord God placed Jesus as the Head of the church and everything concerning it. In addition, God put everything under His feet—He has supreme and sovereign rule. We as believers are considered the Body of Christ. Jesus being the Head. If everything is under Jesus' feet, then His feet are part of the body. His feet become our feet, so to speak. We are not the head of God's church or the Body of Christ. But we are the body that hosts and houses His mind, will, and purposes.

In the natural, the neck and shoulders hold the head in place and position. The neck, shoulders, spinal cord, and skeletal structure keep the whole body in place. Likewise the head or leader of an organization, business, home, tribe, nation, country, or whatever is very important. Jesus is the Head of the church and His body, and we need Him to advance the Kingdom and build His church agenda, will, and prophetic purpose.

Place of His Rule

Interestingly Matthew 8:20 says, *"Jesus replied, 'Foxes have dens and birds have nests, but the Son of Man has no place to lay his head.'"* Jesus was replying to one of the scribes as it relates to following Him. Jesus wasn't saying that He was homeless or didn't have any place to stay. He was speaking in regard to the cost of discipleship and leaving everything to follow Him.

We can also draw from His reply that the body follows where the head directs and orders. Jesus was saying that the Son of Man has no place to lay His head also refers to a body (the church) to live or place Himself over. Jesus, as the church and Body of Christ, wants to establish His agenda, purposes, and will in every region, city, community, and nation. Jesus is looking for a place to lay His head upon the shoulders of a willing, able, and stable body.

Today, spiritually speaking, Jesus is searching the earth for the war-ready, embassy base church where He can enforce, engage, enact, empower, equip, educate, and exert His supernatural power and rule of His Kingdom throughout the earth. He's looking for the warrior Bride who can through the power of the Holy Spirit continue to destroy strongholds and works of the devil worldwide. The Bible says in Isaiah 9:1-7 (NLT):

Nevertheless, that time of darkness and despair will not go on forever. The land of Zebulun and Naphtali will be humbled, but there will be a time in the future when Galilee of the Gentiles, which lies along the road that runs between the Jordan and the sea, will be filled with glory. The people who walk in darkness will see a great light. For those who live in a land of deep darkness, a light will shine. You will enlarge the nation of Israel, and its people will rejoice. They will rejoice before you as people rejoice at the harvest and like warriors dividing the plunder. For you will break the yoke of their slavery and lift the heavy burden from their shoulders. You will break the oppressor's rod, just as you did when you destroyed the army of Midian. The boots of the warrior and the uniforms bloodstained by war will all be burned. They will be fuel for the fire. For a child is born to us, a son is given to us. The government will rest on his shoulders. And he will be called: Wonderful Counselor, Mighty God, Everlasting Father, Prince of Peace. His government and its peace will never end. He will rule with fairness and justice from the throne of his ancestor David for all eternity. The passionate commitment of the Lord of Heaven's Armies will make this happen!

Jesus was not born according to the laws and the processes of natural generations; His birth was governed by the civilization of Heaven and the government of God. The nature of His birth was miraculous. The Child was born to a virgin, Mary, his earthly mother: "*...the virgin shall conceive and bear a Son, and shall call His name Immanuel*" (Isaiah 7:14 NKJV). Interestingly, in the Isaiah 9 passage it says that the *"government will rest on his shoulder"* which speaks of His rule, dominion, empire, and burden as King over the people.

"His government and its peace will never end," speaks of a future King, who is Jesus, who shall sit upon the throne of David in His kingdom to order and establish it with justice and judgment forever and ever. Jesus is the Greater David. Jesus is the Head of the church, which is the *ekklesia,* is also King. The shoulder is part of the Body of Christ.

That means we are warriors of God and must bear the burden of the Lord, the responsibilities, and rule with dominion on earth. As members of the Body of Christ, we have a twofold mandate to bring everything under the rule (feet) of Jesus and carry His burden to rule on earth as king-priests.

KINGDOM MANDATE AND CHARGE

We must preach the Gospel as part of the Great Commission so that His Kingdom advances and there is increase into the Kingdom through salvation and conversion. The church releases the Kingdom of God on earth. The rule and dominion of God is our mandate as well, which goes back to Genesis 1:28 (NKJV) where it says: *"Then God blessed them, and God said to them, 'Be fruitful and multiply; fill the earth and subdue it, and have dominion over the fish of the sea, over the birds of the air, and over every living thing that moves on the earth.'"*

God blessed us from the beginning and gave us a fivefold mandate to:

1. Be fruitful (prosper, blessed, produce, harvest)
2. Multiply (reproduce yourself)
3. Fill the earth (increase)
4. Subdue it (govern, manage, and oversee)
5. Have dominion (rule, reign like kings)

These are our Kingdom responsibilities as king-priests and warriors of God. The rule and power of God's Kingdom is unleashed, established, and enforced through the church. The church and the Kingdom of God are not the same. However, the church becomes the base where the government of God through His Kingdom is enforced and exacted through what I call the embassy of Heaven on earth. The church becomes the hub of Heaven on earth. In addition, the church houses God's ascension fivefold officers:

1. Apostles
2. Prophets
3. Evangelists
4. Pastors
5. Teachers

According to Ephesians 4:11, these offices are occupied by believers of Christ. It is interesting to know that there are fivefold officers or five branches in God's church. The United States military also has five branches of leadership: Army, Navy, Air Force, Marines, Coast Guard (and recently added, Space Force). Each branch has specific responsibilities; however, they all work together seamlessly to defend, protect, and guard our country and its citizens from enemies, foreign and domestic.

FIVEFOLD LEADERSHIP MINISTRY BRANCHES

The five branches of the military are organized in such a way that they can immediately be called into action if necessary. Within the individual branches there are specific operations, ranks, and a chain of command. Likewise, with the fivefold ministry officers within the church.

Ephesians 4:11-16 (NKJV) shares the purpose of the fivefold ministry:

And He Himself gave some to be apostles, some proph-
ets, some evangelists, and some pastors and teachers, for the
equipping of the saints for the work of ministry, for the edi-
fying of the body of Christ, till we all come to the unity of
the faith and of the knowledge of the Son of God, to a perfect
man, to the measure of the stature of the fullness of Christ;
that we should no longer be children, tossed to and fro and
carried about with every wind of doctrine, by the trick-
ery of men, in the cunning craftiness of deceitful plotting,
but, speaking the truth in love, may grow up in all things
into Him who is the head—Christ—from whom the whole
body, joined and knit together by what every joint supplies,
according to the effective working by which every part does
its share, causes growth of the body for the edifying of itself
in love.

God doesn't want us to be carried away by every wind of doctrine, people's trickery, and craftiness of deceitful scheming by the
enemy. These fivefold branches of leadership in the church are to
protect the Body of Christ from false doctrine, demon influences,
works of the devil, division, Gnosticism, paganism, ageism, witchcraft, and so much more.

The fivefold officers in the church protect and defend the interests of God's church, Kingdom, citizens, and the Word of God—
which is Truth. When we look at the United States military's five
branches, we can see a similarity with the church offices regarding
the church's fivefold branches:

1. The Army provides soldiers, frontline fighters on the
   ground.

2. The Air Force patrols the air.

3. The Navy's sailors protect the country from the seas.

4. The Marine Corps maintain specialized tactical fighters.

5. The Coast Guard defenders our country's coastlines.

FIVEFOLD MINISTRY OF THE DEPARTMENT OF DEFENSE

The responsibilities of these five military branches are clearly defined and all have a common objective—the security, support, defense, and overall interests of the United States. They are all part of the department of defense of the United States.

The functions of the fivefold ministry in the department of defense of the church are as follow:

1. Apostles *govern* and bring divine order in the Body of Christ.

2. Prophets *guide* and bring prophetic direction in the Body of Christ.

3. Evangelists *gather* by bringing new believers into the Body of Christ.

4. Pastors *guard* and *groom* those who are brought into the Body of Christ.

5. Teachers *ground* those in the Word of God and truth in the Body of Christ.

I would also add the most important ministry which every believer is called to—the ministry of prayer and intercession. Like the newly added branch to the United States military, the Space Force, the intercessors, and prayer warriors in my opinion have the highest responsibility. We are all called to a life of prayer and intercession. We are called to pray for the Body of Christ and hear God's heart for His church. When this is evident, the church becomes the devil's worst nightmare!

The church is the command center for the Commander and Chief—Jesus Christ. As we examine the five natural military branches of the United States, compared to the fivefold ministry branches of the church, there are similarities. First Corinthians 15:46 says, *"The spiritual did not come first, but the natural, and after that the spiritual."* Each military branch and ministry branch has a chief of staff (head) to whom the military and church members are held accountable, just as Jesus is the Head and Chief of the church, ruling with a staff in His hand.

We Spirit-filled believers can go before God with no need of an intermediary, only the Holy Spirit. Those with a greater measure of authority in the fivefold ministry must report to the Commander in Chief—Jehovah Gibbor, the mighty man of war.

We are not facing an individual battle but a body of believers' battle. The victory we will have is as a collective, cooperative, and cohesive unit in God's church as we follow orders from the Lord, and how we respond effectively to them. How we articulately communicate what we heard from the Holy Spirit from the headquarters of Heaven will affect the results of this unseen battle.

LEGISLATE AND ENFORCE HEAVEN'S AGENDA

The church is Heaven's earthly department of defense, which becomes the official agency on earth as an embassy that exacts the foreign policies of its heavenly government through prayer, intercession, and other divine strategies and methodologies. As such, it functions, so to speak, similar to a legislative body. In other words, the institution of the church—the Body of Christ, the *ekklesia*, the called-out ones—serves to divinely enforce and prohibit in the earthly realm any aggressive advancements of the works of the devil and his demonic laws and legislations.

The enemy wants to change what God has instituted on earth. That's why the church is so needed in this hour. The Bible clearly reveals the enemy's ploy in the Book of Daniel. Daniel, the governmental prophet, received a revelation and vision from the Lord. Daniel reported:

> *He will speak against the Most High and oppress his holy people and try to change the set times and the laws. The holy people will be delivered into his hands for a time, times and half a time. But the court will sit, and his power will be taken away and completely destroyed forever. Then the sovereignty, power and greatness of all the kingdoms under heaven will be handed over to the holy people of the Most High. His kingdom will be an everlasting kingdom, and all rulers will worship and obey him. This is the end of the matter. I, Daniel, was deeply troubled by my thoughts, and my face turned pale, but I kept the matter to myself* (Daniel 7:25-28).

This is powerful passage of Scripture where we can see that the prophet Daniel was alarmed by what he received by revelation. It is clear that the enemy's ploy was to make alterations in times and in law by wearing down the saints of the Most High. The wicked one wants to change times and law to serve his own satanic, diabolical, and demonic purposes through the world-supported system and human influences. However, the text goes on to say that the courts of Heaven will convene and bring judgment against the evil one who spoke out in contempt against the Most High God.

The enemy's authority will be stripped, annihilated, and destroyed forever. And the sovereignty, dominion, rule, and greatness of all the kingdoms under the whole Heaven will be given to the saints—you and me. I believe we have come into this new era and Kingdom age.

You may ask, "What does this have to do with me?" As a believer, it has everything to do with you. The evil one has been at war with the saints since the days of Daniel, and today he still has a grudge against us, you, because Jesus defeated him at the cross and by His ascension to the right hand of the Father. The devil wants to regain control.

This ancient war continues because the devil has it out for those who are of the Kingdom of God. This warfare is unseen; however, it has visible repercussions if not discerned and disarmed immediately by the Holy Spirit. We have to understand that this earthly domain and province has been in the enemy's possession or rule; however, through Jesus it was returned to its rightful, legal, and divine Master, Landowner, and King. In the Old Testament, from the patriarchal prophets Moses to Samuel's days, the Lord was the King of the children of Israel. Likewise, in the New Testament, God will reign over His people, the New Covenant believers.

We cannot talk about the church without referencing the Kingdom of God. As we talked about the two kingdoms in previous chapters, it's good to note that the Kingdom of God is soteriological. In other words, it's all about the King and His Kingdom as Savior who brings salvation and deliverance through saving human beings from sin and its consequences, which separates them from the Lord. The unseen warfare between the kingdom of darkness and Kingdom of Light is the object of the divine rulership which is the redemption of people and their deliverance from the works of the enemy.

Kingdom Takeover

The enemy uses his limited power to keep unbelievers blinded of the truth, in darkness, and separated from God (read 1 Corinthians

15:23-28). Jesus put an end to death by His resurrection. He over-took the hostile kingdom of evil! The unseen enemy, the devil, knows what Jesus is capable of and we, His body, must know what we are capable of today. We can depose the enemy by the power of God and advance His Kingdom here and now for Christ!

Furthermore, it must be understood that God's Kingdom is the reign of God in and through Christ, destroying all that is hostile to the divine reign, rule, and dominion of it. God's Kingdom is administrated, enforced, governed, and ruled through the Body of Christ at large on earth. The church of Jesus Christ is the only supernatural, satanic-destroying institution in the universe! There are two kingdoms colliding against each other, as spoken of in the New Testament—the hostile kingdom system of the enemy relentlessly opposing God's Kingdom.

The system of this world refers to the "kingdom of this world" that opposes the Kingdom of God (Revelation 11:15), which we as the Body of Christ must defeat. As the Lord's governmental or ambassadorial agents in the earth, we represent (re-present) the King and His sovereign Kingdom. Therefore, through warfare prayers, intercession, and divine supernatural strategies through the Holy Spirit's intelligence, we have the advantage over the enemy. When we pray as in unity as the Body of Christ, Heaven will invade the earth on our behalf and God's will is accomplished.

Our prayers put angelic forces in the invisible on high alert to work, war, and warn on our behalf as well (read Genesis 18:1;19:29). Prayer keeps us, as soldiers of God, connected to His headquarters in Heaven. Interestingly, the Word of God called us ambassadors. That's why I stated that the church becomes the official embassy of God's government here on earth. In other words, the church is an embassy of the Kingdom of Heaven.

God's Embassy—the Church

The church building is the domain of the fivefold officers, ambassadors, and leadership branch who work and minister to citizens of the Kingdom within the church as well as those who win sinners (unbelievers) to the Lord Jesus Christ. The church is not a hospital, hospice, or shelter—it is a training and deployment center of equipped soldiers, warriors, leaders, and ambassadors! Not to say that the church doesn't provide shelter, medical (healing), and life to those who are lost and spiritually dead (separate from God). However, sticking with what the Bible calls the church, we are governing, judicial, legislative, administrative, military, training, equipping, and ambassadorial center for the people of God.

However, like an embassy, the church does provide a place of refuge, spiritual asylum, and sanctuary. In times of war, the embassy becomes a place where people can run to for protection. The church is where God's people can run to when they are battle weary and worn down by the enemy. In the Old Testament, the altar in the temple is where people ran to when they feared for their lives; and at the altar they grabbed hold of the horns of the altar. They knew what to do in times of distress, fear, confusion, and crisis.

God's presence is at the altar and where wounded and battered soldiers can find peace, joy, and solidarity. No one can touch those who take hold of *the horns of the altar* because we are protected there (read 1 Kings 1:49-51). During the 2020 COVID-19 outbreak, I found refuge in God's presence and peace for my soul. I quarantined and was still and knew that He is God. While writing this book on spiritual warfare, I faced so many battles from the enemy that I wanted to give up and wave the white flag of surrender.

However, I couldn't because I am a war veteran, spiritually speaking. I know what is required and how to overcome the tactics of the enemy. In God's presence is where I found safety and provision and was protected. The enemy doesn't want us to fellowship together and because of the pandemic we were prohibited from gathering in the church building. But we know that we are the Body of Christ and the building Jesus refers to is not built with natural stones. We are living stones being established in Christ. First Peter 2:5 says it like this, *"You also, like living stones, are being built into a spiritual house to be a holy priesthood offering spiritual sacrifices acceptable to God through Jesus Christ."*

The term "living stones" is used as a metaphor to illustrate the secure and intimate relationship believers have with Jesus. Like an embassy where citizens find security, the church is the place we are secure in our relationship with our sovereign King under His rule as ambassadors of Christ. The enemy in the pandemic is purposed to unleash fear, confusion, and disunity.

Although some are ordered to wear a face mask for health precautions, which I understand, I also see a strategy of the enemy to "social distance" us (divide us) to create fear! Fear of catching the disease, fear of dying, and fear of being ridiculed if you don't wear a mask over our mouths. The enemy can use masks to mute, silence, and censor the prophetic voice of the Lord through the church. The devil wants to intimidate the body of believers. However, God is changing the narrative for our good and what the devil meant for evil is backfiring on him. God is giving us our voice back and removing the muzzle so that we can intimidate the intimidator!

The pandemic is creating civil unrest, racial division, economic uncertainty, crisis, and fear. It is a pandemic of fear! We must conquer fear with faith, Christ over crisis and power of God over the pandemic. Social distancing is the enemy's ploy to keep the church from fellowshipping together naturally, although there have been virtual meetings to supplement being in person.

However, there is nothing like God's people coming together in one central meeting place to fellowship in one accord, to learn of our new mission, mandates, assignments and commands, to be briefed on the next prophetic move of the Lord, and to discuss governmental, administrative, and legislative matters concerning the church at large for the advancement of the Kingdom of God.

God's Kingdom Base on Earth

There is a common Scripture quote that we often hear and that comes to my mind: *"For where two or three are gather in my name, there am I with them"* (Matthew 18:20). The enemy is threatened when the church—the *ekklesia*—Body of Christ—the official embassy of the Kingdom of God on earth comes together in worship, prayer, and praise. Hell's agenda is actually exposed, and eradicated in that particular territory!

I am reminded of the apostle Paul who emphasizes the importance of the believers gathering together in Hebrews 10:25 (NKJV) states: *"Not forsaking the assembling of ourselves together, as is the manner of some, but exhorting one another, and so much the more as you see the Day approaching."*

It's imperative now more than ever for us to meet together to support each other by praying and standing strong in the midst of the spiritual battle that rages against us. As ambassadors who are housed in an embassy must serve the purpose of a nation's government, likewise as believers we are called ambassadors of Christ and must represent the domain of Heaven, which is the Kingdom of God's interests here and now on earth through the church, our headquarters!

The United States serves the interests of the country by establishing embassies in different countries around the world. God's Kingdom serves the same purpose and responsibilities, spiritually speaking, that an embassy does for its ambassadors. While the

Lord calls His people soldiers, we can see the function of a soldier biblically speaking in the following passages of Scriptures:

- Psalm 144:1 (NKJV): *"Blessed be the LORD my Rock, who trains my hands for war, and my fingers for battle."*
- 2 Timothy 2:4 (NKJV): *"No one engaged in warfare entangles himself with the affairs of this life; that he may please him who enlisted him as a soldier."*
- 2 Timothy 2:3 (NKJV): *"You therefore must endure hardship as a good soldier of Jesus Christ."*
- Romans 13:4 (NKJV): *"For he is God's minister to you for good. But if you do evil, be afraid; for he does not bear the sword in vain; for he is God's minister, an avenger to execute wrath on him who practices evil."*

God's Kingdom Ambassadors

It is very important to know that we are more than children of God in the Kingdom as citizens; we are also called soldiers and ambassadors! The Lord knows each and every one of us and our spiritual capabilities. The enemy also knows our weakness and how to tempt us, causing us to fall into his baited trap. However, God will make a way of escape for His soldiers who are caught in a snag of temptation by the enemy.

First Corinthians 10:13 declares: *"No temptation has overtaken you except what is common to mankind. And God is faithful; he will not let you be tempted beyond what you can bear. But when you are tempted, he will also provide a way out so that you can endure it."*

As soldiers and ambassadors of Christ you can endure temptation in every battle from the enemy. He is going to attack your old sin nature appetites by enticing and entertaining you by planting seeds in your mind. Keep in mind that our Commander and Chief is gracious, forgiving, merciful and compassionate toward His people. God is not like a drill sergeant barking orders in the face of a new cadet in boot camp training. The Lord will bear you up and strengthen you in times of weakness and vulnerability.

Jesus declares in Matthew 11:28-30: *"Come to me, all you who are weary and burdened, and I will give you rest. Take my yoke upon you and learn from me, for I am gentle and humble in heart, and you will find rest for your souls. For my yoke is easy and my burden is light."*

One of the Scripture passages I stood on in seasons of testing, trials, and tribulations, especially during the COVID-19 pandemic when hope was lost and I was slipping away in fear as a prophetic leader and voice was Second Corinthians 12:9-10 where Paul wrote:

> *But he said to me, "My grace is sufficient for you, for my power is made perfect in weakness." Therefore, I will boast all the more gladly about my weaknesses, so that Christ's power may rest on me. That is why, for Christ's sake, I delight in weaknesses, in insults, in hardships, in persecutions, in difficulties. For when I am weak, then I am strong."*

Even warriors of Christ like Paul, you, and me can go through tremendous hardships, persecutions, difficulties, and times of crisis. Who do we turn to? We turn to the Lord and find safety in His presence and sanctuary at the altar praying, worshiping, and being still before Him. That is why we must connect to a local church and be plugged into that assembly. We should always be accountable to others in the Body of Christ and to a local place of worship. The church is Heaven's earthly department of defense and embassy of the government of God.

The Church Base—The Ambassador's Hub

Before we move on to the next chapter talking about the works of the enemy, we should first define an embassy and ambassador. In the United States, ambassadors are appointed by the President and confirmed by the Senate. Ambassadors are appointed by the highest level of the home government. An embassy becomes the permanent base and home for an ambassador. They are responsible for representing the home country, for handling, addressing, and working out major diplomatic issues, such as negotiations, and for preserving the rights of its citizens abroad. Usually, if a country recognizes another as being sovereign, an embassy is set up to maintain foreign relations with hosting countries, allies, and speak on the behalf of the sending government.

In addition, an ambassador is housed in an embassy located in major cities in foreign nations and provides safety, asylum, sanctuary, and protection for its citizens regarding the home government. An embassy also aids traveling citizens. As the church is Heaven's earthly department of defense, its primary responsibility is to implement military policy and foreign diplomatic policy, as an embassy represents the government of God on earth.

The church houses ambassadors, soldiers of God whose mission it is to provide military forces needed to deter war and defend by protecting the security of the people of God, God's Word which is His policies, by-laws, constitution, and will. The following Scripture reference what ambassadors, or believers in Christ:

- Ephesians 6:20: *"For which I am an ambassador in chains; Pray that I may declare it fearlessly, as I should."*
- Proverbs 13:17: *"A wicked messenger falls into trouble, but a trustworthy envoy brings healing."*

- 1 Corinthians 11:1: *"Follow my example, as I follow the example of Christ."*
- 2 Corinthians 5:20-21: *"We are therefore Christ's ambassadors, as though God were making his appeal through us. We implore you on Christ's behalf: Be reconciled to God. God made him who had no sin to be sin for us, so that in him we might become the righteousness of God."*
- Philippians 3:20: *"But our citizenship is in heaven. And we eagerly await a Savior from there, the Lord Jesus Christ."*

What is the power of the church in this spiritual warfare that we face? The source of the power of the church is through the Holy Spirit and Jesus is the Source. Jesus is the Source of life in the Body of Christ. Jesus is her Head as the sovereign King. The authority of the church is both organic and administrative. Jesus grants that authority through Word of God and in terms of Scripture, which is the Bible. Keep in mind that the church of Jesus Christ has no authority or power apart from the Word of God, and certainly no authority above the Word of God.

Binding and Loosing Power

That being said, the church's power and authority is spiritual, even though believers who are the Body of Christ are physical, natural. The church herself doesn't wield physical, earthly, natural weapons like a sword or rod, rather spiritual, supernatural, divine weapons which are: the Word of God, prayer, worship, intercession, fasting, and much more. Oftentimes we make the church something that God never created or built her to be in the first place. The church is not a secular organization, political machine, entertainment business, hospital institution, or daycare center.

The church possesses a threefold power and authority—prophetic, kingly, and priestly. The church hears and speaks the Word of the Lord prophetically to the body of believers at large in every territory. The church rules, governs, and executes judicial authority as spiritual kings for the best interests of the Kingdom and worship the sovereign King in obedience to Him. Jesus gave His apostles the keys of the Kingdom of Heaven, binding and loosing power, and the rights to open and shut His Kingdom.

We have to understand the power that we possess as the church, which is the greatest entity and force in the universe. In this unseen battle against the enemy, using your spiritual authority is paramount. The church becomes the gatekeeper possessing the keys of the Kingdom. Keys are given to those with access authority. Keys are used to lock or unlock gates, doors, and pathways. When Jesus references keys, He was speaking specifically about access to the Kingdom of Heaven. The church has the spiritual power and authority to open and close the heavens.

Biblically speaking, Jesus lays this foundation of His church in Ephesians 2:20. Jesus' disciples and later apostles were going to be the apostolic leadership of this new institution called the church, and He will grant them delegated authority and power to open the doors to Heaven and invite the world—Gentile nations—to enter in.

In John 3:3, Jesus clearly states that unless someone is born again or regenerated by the Spirit, they will not see the Kingdom of Heaven. Only through the work of the Holy Spirit is someone born again, which through the Word of God brings about a transformed life in a spiritually dead sinner. Faithfully, preaching the Gospel as soldiers of God is the key to the Kingdom of God. We can only see the Kingdom of Heaven, which is eternal, spiritual, and not of this world, with only spiritual eyes.

Matthew 16:19 declares, *"I will give you the keys of the kingdom of heaven; whatever you bind on earth will be bound in heaven, and whatever you loose on earth will be loosed in heaven."* Peter represents the new era apostolic leadership through the church authority and power that can "open doors," speaking to three different groups of people so they can enter the Lord's Kingdom through preaching the Gospel, which is key to the Jews, Samaritans, and Gentiles receiving and entering in:

1. Read in Acts chapter 2, where Peter preached the Gospel on the Day of Pentecost in Jerusalem; where roughly 3,000 Jewish people were saved that day as a result of Peter's message. His preaching basically unlocked the door of Heaven for the Jewish people to enter in and be saved.

2. Read in Acts chapter 8, where the Samaritans received the Holy Spirit after believing the preaching of the Word of God—the Gospel—which was an opportunity key to touch and unlock their hearts. Peter and John were there to witness this powerful event orchestrated by the Lord. Peter's message had unlocked the door for the Samaritans, just like it did for the Jews.

3. Read in Acts chapter 10, where Peter takes the Gospel message to a Roman centurion's household, and they, too, received the Holy Spirit supernaturally that day. There's nothing like home church. Time and time again we see that Peter used the key that unlocked the door for the Gentiles. The "keys" that Jesus had given him worked in each case.

POSSESSORS OF HEAVEN AND EARTH

You also are a key holder able to open and shut the Kingdom of Heaven with the Gospel message as gatekeepers on earth as the church. Again, it's through the local church and collective body of ambassadors, soldiers, and king-priests who are possessors of Heaven and earth with the keys. The New Covenant spiritual order of Melchizedek confirms it in Genesis 14:18-20 where it says:

> *Then Melchizedek king of Salem brought out bread and wine. He was priest of God Most High, and he blessed Abram saying, "Blessed be Abram by God Most High, Creator of heaven and earth. And praise be to God Most High, who has delivered your enemies into your hand." Then Abram gave him a tenth of everything.*

Jesus is the greater Abraham with a better promise and condition, and we are given keys of the Kingdom here and now on earth as king-priest believers. This spiritual warfare that the church is facing is about who possesses the keys—and you are the key holder to the Kingdom through the Gospel. The enemy is fighting you from fulfilling your prophetic destiny and purpose and hindering by blinding unbelievers from hearing the truth that keys does. Of course, we know that keys can be used to lock doors as well as open them.

A major part of the Gospel message when it's preached is that faith is required to receive it and gain access. Without faith in the Lord Jesus Christ as Savior, then the door to Heaven is shut and barred (see John 3:18). Finally, those who responded in faith and repented through the Gospel preached by the apostles were granted access to the Kingdom of Heaven; yet those who continued to harden their hearts and reject the Gospel of God's saving grace were barred from the Kingdom (Acts 8:23).

The "binding and loosing" reference goes on to give us a better understanding of the concept used in Matthew 18:15-20, which also speaks in reference to church discipline, using the same "binding and loosing" language we find in Matthew 16. This authority and power through the church was not to be abused. The apostles were not to usurp Jesus' authority over individual believers and their eternal destiny, they were to exercise authority to discipline erring believers and, if necessary, they could excommunicate disobedient, disorderly, and belligerent church members.

Biblically speaking, Christians today can declare an unrepentant sinner as unsaved ("bound") and a repentant believer in Jesus Christ as saved ("loosed"). The binding and loosing authority and power by the Holy Spirit given to us by Jesus can bind up demonic powers as well and loose bound people who are tormented by demon spirits or works. Knowing what you have access to as children of God is imperative if you want to disarm and destroy the works of the devil.

We cannot destroy the devil *per se* because he's a spirit, meaning there is nowhere in the Word of God that we as humans are able to destroy the devil or demon spirits in our own power, strength, or capabilities. Only through the power of God can we overcome and resist the devil's ploy, schemes, and deceptive plans of destruction. However, as believers in Christ we are instructed to be strong in the Lord, put on the full armor of God so we can stand against the devil's schemes, resist the devil, and become weapons of war in God's hand to shatter demon-influenced nations, kingdoms, and systems of this world with the power of God.

Only God who created the enemy can destroy him. But we do play a major part in this spiritual battle to defeat the enemy. We do have the power to destroy the works of the enemy in our individual lives. Are you ready to disarm and destroy the works of the devil?

The next chapter gives you insight into what those works are. God is establishing churches in every region, territory, city, and nation because there are places where the enemy has influence. There are principalities, power, and spiritual wickedness in high places governing those places.

Ephesians 6:12 (NKJV) says, *"For we do not wrestle against flesh and blood, but against principalities, against powers, against the rulers of the darkness of this age, against spiritual hosts of wickedness in heavenly places."*

Chapter 8

THE WORKS OF
THE ENEMY

Whoever makes a practice of sinning is of the devil, for the devil has been sinning from the beginning. The reason the Son of God appeared was to destroy the works of the devil (1 John 3:8 ESV).

Growing up in church, I heard many messages about God, angels, demons, and Jesus dying for our sins, but not much about *"the works of the devil."* There was no clear answer or specific explanation until I read First John 3:8. Maybe the topic was taboo for the pastors or the churches I grew up in. Maybe they didn't want to engage in that battle or equip believers to fight as soldiers of God. Also, I was not being taught or trained how to operate in my prophetic gift and healing ministry as a young prophetic minister.

Never at the time was I taught how to move in the supernatural, cast out demon spirits, or combat demonic attacks. I had to learn all this through personally studying the Word of God and reading spiritual warfare books and manuals, like the one you are reading. I am writing this for you, to equip and arm you spiritually.

I believe that churches should train and equip believers, not just leaders in deliverance and spiritual warfare. Thank God we have churches that are doing just that. However, I believe this isn't just for the Charismatic or Pentecostal churches to teach and train believers, but every believer should learn how to safeguard themselves in a spiritual attack and in deliverance.

I had a strong interest in learning how to fight against the works of the enemy and of the flesh and live victoriously. I cannot combat the enemy if I don't know biblically what his works are and how he uses them against believers and people. Studying spiritual warfare while growing up as a young prophetic minister and leader, I had four questions in my mind when studying this topic:

1. What did Jesus come to destroy in the first place?
2. What did He destroy?
3. How did He destroy it?
4. How can we as believer's participate personally in His victory in this spiritual warfare?

The first sentence of First John 3:8 opened my eyes to what the works of the devil is—sin. The next sentence reveals the Son of God's purpose for coming to earth in the first place—to destroy the works of sin by the devil. It's clear that those who commit sin are participating in works of the devil. In other words, if a person continues to practice sin, that person is employed by the enemy's department of labor.

Employed by Sin

The primary agenda of the unseen enemy is for people to commit or practice sin. His ploy for those especially called of God is to have them fall into sin by temptation. The works of the devil is to tempt believers and people to sin. When they succumb to the temptation and sin, his work is accomplished. However, Jesus came not to just totally eradicate the guilt of sin (which may enable people to stay like they are and continue the act of sinning right into Heaven) but actually sinning.

In other words, Jesus the Son of Man came to destroy sinning or the practice of sinning continuously. Jesus came to destroy, in my opinion, the viral act of sinning, which has become a deadly pandemic, so to speak, to humanity since the Garden of Eden. It was the devil's quest to find fault in God's creation of human beings. Pride was found in lucifer's heart in Heaven so he was ejected out, along with his rebellious angels now known as demons. Since he fell because of pride in eternity past, this warfare and fight is all about him trying to make sure everyone else falls as well by keeping them from entering the Kingdom of Heaven.

Satan doesn't want people to enter a place where he was rejected and ejected. That's why believers have an intense battle with darkness. Sin is what will keep people from entering Heaven. God had to do something about the plot and ploys of the enemy. He sent His Son Jesus to destroy the works of the devil by becoming the sacrificial Lamb. Jesus' death on the cross and resurrection restored us into right relationship with the Father. Let's look briefly at the Scripture text in First John 3:4-10 from the New Revised Standard Version of the Bible:

> *Everyone who commits sin is guilty of lawlessness; sin is lawlessness. You know that he was revealed to take away sins, and in him there is no sin. No one who abides in him sins; no one who sins has either seen him or known him. Little children, let no one deceive you. **Everyone who does what is right is righteous, just as he is righteous. Everyone who commits sin is a child of the devil;** for the devil has been sinning from the beginning. The Son of God*

was revealed for this purpose, to destroy the works of the devil. Those who have been born of God do not sin, because God's seed abides in them; they cannot sin, because they have been born of God. The children of God and the children of the devil are revealed in this way: all who do not do what is right are not from God, nor are those who do not love their brothers and sisters.

Clearly the Bible states that those who commit sin are guilty. They are already found guilty of lawlessness. Sin is lawlessness! The devil is considered the lawless one. When we practice sin, we become like the lawless one. The antichrist spirit is a spirit of lawlessness—anything opposing the rule, nature, commands, and ways of Christ.

When John referenced everyone who commits sin is guilty of lawlessness, he was speaking about God's law, the expression of the Lord's divine will, purpose, and plan laid out in His Word—the Bible—His constitution and bylaws for believers to know and follow.

The Lawbreakers

When people are lawless, they act without any regard to the law. Laws bring order and are imperative to have in a sinful world (1 Timothy 1:9), and individuals who decide to act lawlessly advance sin in the world. Judges 17:6 and 21:25 speaks of those who did what was right in their own eyes because they had no king over them in Israel. God was their King; however, they wanted to be like other nations to have someone rule over them as king. The word for "lawlessness" in the Word of God is often translated "iniquity."

According to the Scripture, the root of all lawlessness is rebellion. When I think about the word "rebellion," I think about witchcraft that is connected to it. When Samuel the prophet denounces

King Saul for his disobedience to God's commands, the Lord rejects him as king. But Samuel declared:

> *Does the LORD delight in burnt offerings and sacrifices as much as in obeying the Lord? To obey is better than sacrifice, and to heed is better than the fat of rams. For rebellion is like the sin of divination, and arrogance like the evil of idolatry. Because you have rejected the word of the Lord, he has rejected you as king* (1 Samuel 15:22-23).

Samuel states several truths in this passage from First Samuel 15 which caused the Lord to reject Saul as king over His people Israel and choose a man later after His own heart, David. Samuel says that rebellion is like the sin of divination (witchcraft), pride is like the wickedness of idolatry (pagan worship), and obedience is better than sacrifice. In other words, it's better to obey God than to do what you think is right because of your title, position, money, and gifting. God will not be pleased and will look at you as a lawbreaker of His commands, idol worshipper, and witch or warlock, so to speak.

Rebellious people are unruly and do not obey the rules. I love what Proverbs 29:18 (ESV) says, *"Where there is no prophetic vision the people cast off restraint, but blessed is he who keeps the law."* That is why we need prophetic voices, leadership, and prophets today so that we can be governed by God's Word, will, and divine purpose. When there is no prophetic guidance, vision, revelation, direction, and prophecy, the people are unrestraint, left unashamed (naked/exposed), unruly, undisciplined, and lawless in their conduct. However, blessed are those who keep the law. The Lord blesses those who obey His Word.

Not all warfare comes from the devil; at times, we must do a self-examination to make sure we are in right standing with the

Lord and that we are not disobeying Him. It's one thing to have the enemy fighting against you. But it's another for the Lord to be resisting you as well. The devil likes to see the Lord resisting His own people because of unrepented sin in their lives. Warfare could be something we brought on ourselves. If so, we can change that by repenting and obeying God's voice.

THE ANTICHRIST SPIRIT

Lawbreakers carry on the spirit of the antichrist and reject God's ways, laws, and methods; they embrace the works of satan. Lawlessness is basically rejecting the Lord. The works of the enemy are to counter the works of the Lord in the life believers. As a murderer, the devil's responsibility and purpose is to work against God, who is Life, with death ploys through sin and lawlessness for people to commit. As a liar and deceiver, satan works against the Lord, who is absolute Truth, with temptation and deception ploy to rebel.

In the lives of unbelievers, the work of the devil is to keep them from coming to saving faith in Christ. Lawlessness is the agenda of hell. Second Thessalonians 2:8-12 says:

> *And then the lawless one will be revealed, whom the LORD Jesus will overthrow with the breath of his mouth and destroy by the splendor of his coming. The coming of the lawless one will be in accordance with* **how Satan works. He will use all sorts of displays of power through signs and wonders that serve the lie, and all the ways that wickedness deceives** *those who are perishing. They perish because they refused to love the truth and so be saved. For this reason God sends them a powerful delusion so that they will believe the lie and so that all will be condemned who have not believed the truth but have delighted in wickedness.*

It's important to know that Jesus overthrew the lawless one when He came to destroy the works of devil through sin. There are those today who refuse to love the truth and to be saved; those God will turn over to a reprobate mind. However, the righteous, who possess the nature of Jesus Christ and walk in obedience will hate the deeds of lawlessness. We can see how it affected Lot, where the Scripture states he was a godly man living in Sodom who, *"was tormented in his righteous soul by the lawless deeds he saw and heard"* (2 Peter 2:8). And David as king and psalmist stated emphatically, *"I abhor the assembly of evildoers and refuse to sit with the wicked"* (Psalm 26:5).

We as believers and followers of Christ are to be law-abiding citizens of the Kingdom (1 Peter 4:15). It's clear that the works of the devil are not the aftereffects or consequences we endure in a spiritual battle. The question is what, why, and who are we fighting at the same time. We can be fighting sin, the devil, and our appetites. In addition, we have to understand and discern that there are three different frequencies that we have to decipher:

1. The Voice of God—the Holy Spirit's language—prophetic Spirit of God
2. The voice of man (self or others)—the human spirit
3. The voice of satan—the devil—demon spirits

This spiritual battle is not easy and there are multiple levels, layers, and dimensions of invisible warfare. Therefore, you must possess the prophetic insight and discernment of the Holy Spirit who can assist you in discerning any battle. Not all warfare is against the devil, but against his works and strategy to cause you to commit sin. When you sin, you give him legal right to go before God to have you sentenced to death by reason of the sin you acted upon.

JESUS PAID THE PRICE FOR FREEDOM

If the devil can seduce people into addictions—strongholds such as pornography, alcoholism, drugs, entertainment, sex, immorality, homosexuality, perversion, etc.—then he entraps us in bondage to sin that can break our bond and communication with the Father. Fortunately for God's people, Jesus' sacrifice on the cross fulfilled many protections for us. Colossians 2:15 (NLT) says, *"In this way, He [Jesus] disarmed the spiritual rulers and authorities. He shamed them publicly by his victory over them on the cross."*

Jesus paid the ultimate price on the cross by taking up the penalty for our sins—and in turn giving us His righteousness. Therefore, the devil has no power over the eternal destiny of believers in Christ. Keep in mind, even though Christ died and three days later resurrected, which destroyed the works of the devil, doesn't mean he won't tempt believers to commit sin. But because Christ's death on the cross allowed Him to bear all of God's wrath against that sin, the Lord will not hold the sin against His people—you and I (Romans 8:1).

Furthermore, we now have the supernatural gifts of the Holy Spirit who dwells inside believers, which causes them to become like Christ in nature. The Holy Spirit seals every individual whose faith and belief is in Jesus Christ—and satan's demonic works and powers cannot remove them from the promises of the Lord (Ephesians 4:30). The only way believers can destroy the works of demonic powers is overcoming the lust of the flesh, lust of the eyes, and the pride of life that the world offers. We are not to love the world but love the Father. Those who love the world, the Father is not in them.

> *Do not love the world or anything in the world. If anyone loves the world, love for the Father is not in them. For*

everything in the world—the lust of the flesh, the lust of the eyes, and the pride of life—comes not from the Father, but from the world. The world and its desires pass away, and whoever does the will of God lives forever (1 John 2:15-17).

This Scripture from First John 2 cites three major temptations that the enemy uses of world to cause believers to fall:

1. *Lust of the flesh:* the power that is unseen (behind the scenes) that produces sin as its outward display or demonstration.

2. *Lust of the eyes:* the power through visualization that incites sinful motives, desires that produce sinful activities.

3. *Pride of life:* the power of self-gratification for more power, fame, recognition, prestige, and to be worshipped by others.

First, what is lust of the flesh? The lust of the flesh is a physical, or body, temptation, desire, pleasure, passion, and urge to do some sinful activity that gratifies the flesh. Basically, it is an overpowering sinful desire that pleases any physical need. The lust of the flesh is what God forbids. These include:

- Drug use (marijuana, pills, cocaine, alcohol, etc.)
- Gossip
- Sexual sins (pornography, orgies, masturbation, fetishes, etc.)
- Speaking slander, accusation, and lies
- Physical violence
- Overeating
- And so much more

Overcoming the Works of the Flesh

Paul the apostle provides some biblical examples of the "works of the flesh" in Galatians 5:19-21 (NKJV) where it says:

> *Now the works of the flesh are evident, which are: adultery, fornication, uncleanness, lewdness, idolatry, sorcery, hatred, contentions, jealousies, outbursts of wrath, selfish ambitions, dissensions, heresies, envy, murders, drunkenness, revelries, and the like; of the which I tell you beforehand, just as I told you in time past, that those who practice such things will not inherit the kingdom of God.*

Keep in mind that many of these mentioned works are what happen when we succumb to the lust of the flesh. Therefore, Paul gives a fair warning that those who do such things will not inherit the Kingdom of God. The works of the flesh are things humans naturally tend toward that are contrary to God's design for us (Romans 1:28-29).

In other words, individuals who pursue sinful lifestyles characterized by immorality, anger, divisiveness, drunkenness, etc., are giving evidence that they are not saved (see Matthew 7:20). When people are truly saved, they will not indulge themselves or entertain works of the flesh. The greatest spiritual warfare is the war within us!

The Holy Spirit will help you overcome these temptations and bodily urges. Paul goes on to say in Philippians 3:2-3 (NLT) that *"we who worship by the Spirit of God are the ones who are truly circumcised"* and to put no confidence in the flesh. We are the righteousness of Christ through faith. However, we as Spirit-filled believers in this unseen battle with satan are to *"Watch out for those dogs, those workers of evil..."* In this unseen warfare we have to delight ourselves in the Lord and He will give us the desires of our heart (Psalm 37:4).

WHAT IS LUST?

However, they must be God's desires and will for our hearts. Not worldly desires, fame, and power. The enemy will use the lust of the flesh and any bait for us to take. We must understand that lust is sin using our own passion, desires, and wants against us to meet its purposes in our lives. Let's look at two primary characteristics of the word "lust" that distinguishes it from the natural, organic, and pure desires that God gives His people:

1. The Word of God describes lust as an "evil" desire. Just as the Bible uses the words "hunger and thirst" for righteousness in Matthew 5:6 to describe a holy longing and desire for the Lord.

2. Lust possesses an overpowering influence and urge that oftentimes becomes irresistible to fight off or ignore. This overwhelming power by lust can be unparalleled and almost impossible to conquer. You may have experienced this battle within your body when your heart is lusting after something and it seems that lust has control over you. And at times it commands you to do what lust wants you to do.

Strangely, lust will have you believe that if you do not get what you passionately desire, you will cease to exist because of it. Universally, it's sad to say that after you get what you desired and lusted for, you discover that having it fell short of what you expected and it didn't satisfy you as completely as you thought it would.

I am reminded of this Scripture: *"But each person is tempted when they are dragged away by their own evil desire and enticed. Then, after desire has conceived, it gives birth to sin; and sin, when it is full-grown, gives birth to death"* (James 1:14-15 NKJV). Fulfilling lustful desires does not satisfy. Only God can satisfy and fill those empty places within us.

The devil wants to you to love the world and forfeit your connection with God. Giving our lives to Jesus is a sacrifice, just as He gave His life for us for our sins. We defeat the works of the enemy every time when we humble and deny ourselves.

Paul makes it plain in Galatians 2:20 where he states: *"I have been crucified with Christ and I no longer live, but Christ lives in me. The life I now live in the body, I live by faith in the Son of God, who loved me and gave himself for me."* So is it really worth giving in to temptation and succumbing to the works of evil and to the world's sinful offers? Mark 8:36 declares, *"What good is it for someone to gain the whole world, yet forfeit their soul?"* This spiritual warfare is more than just a battle of the fittest—it is a battle for your soul.

Second, what is the lust of the eyes? The lust of the eyes is the temptation to gaze or look upon something that we have no business looking at. In addition, it also means to look upon something with desire, craving, or pleasure, even though the Lord has instructed us not to look upon such sinful things. To covet with envy someone's wife, husband, gifts, life, etc. is lust of the eyes. The sin of coveting is the prime example of succumbing to lustful visuals.

To yearn or strongly crave something that belongs to another is coveting. For example, the lust of the eyes includes watching pornography and lusting after other peoples' material possessions such as houses, cars, income, position, status, family, appearance, careers, etc., which are unlawful and sinful.

I am reminded of this type of example in Second Samuel regarding King David and Bathsheba, the woman with whom David committed adultery:

One evening David got up from his bed and walked around on the roof of the palace. From the roof he saw a woman bathing. The woman was very beautiful, and David sent someone to find out about her. The man said, "She is Bathsheba, the daughter of Eliam and the wife of Uriah the Hittite" (2 Samuel 11:2-3).

As David watched Bathsheba taking a bath, lust caused him to lose focus and fall victim to his urges. He was supposed to be out on the battlefield with his men, but instead he began desiring someone else's wife because of what he saw with his eyes. When he saw her nakedness, it triggered a strong, lustful desire to take her for his own. Later David concocted a plan to have her husband killed in the line of duty. Consequently, God judged David harshly for his sin (read 2 Samuel chapters 11 and 12).

Third, what is the pride of life? The pride of life is that temptation for self-glory, gratification, and for excess greatness, power, and fame. The sin that the Lord hates the most is pride. When this is the sin was discovered in lucifer (beautiful angel), he lost his position and later became satan (the adversary—demon). Let's look at some examples of this sin of pride:

- Strong desire for others to highly esteem you; self-glory (making a name for yourself) and directly or indirectly through orders and accomplishments want others to worship you or look to you as a god or idol.
- Strong desire to feel more important than anyone else around you, to be highly valued by everyone surrounding you; the center of attention, topic, or agenda.
- Strong desire to get all the credit, glory, attention, and accolades for things others or the Lord has done.

- Strong desire to sit in seats of power and to have influence over others in a way that boasts one's own ego for the sake of bragging rights. Pursue positions of authority and accomplishing things for your benefit rather than to benefit others. To use others as steppingstones or pedestals to elevate yourself to appear flawless or perfect. Desire to be served and be great—yet Jesus states that, *"The greatest among you will be your servant. For those who exalt themselves will be humbled, and those who humble themselves will be exalted"* (Matthew 23:11-12).

Two Ongoing Battles

We can clearly see that this topic is very important to understand when it comes to discerning, disarming, and defeating the works of the enemy concerning the three major temptations that the devil uses as bait. I can list a bunch of demon names and go into the whole kingdom of satan, but my objective in writing this book is to get to reveal the premise and strategy of the enemy for victorious Christian living. There is so much to cover; however, this book is specifically aimed to assist you winning the invisible battle with your spiritual weapons and identifying who you are up against. The two battles we face daily are:

1. The War Within
2. The Battlefield of the Mind

That is why I have this chapter and the next one, Invisible Battlefield of the Mind, back to back as the works of the enemy works through the temptations of this world—the works of the flesh (lust of the flesh, eyes, and pride of life)—and the war in the battlefield of our minds that the devil uses as a rule of engagement against God's people. Victory is all about how we respond to the attacks of the enemy through lustful, sinful offers of the old sin nature.

The devil will feed our egos so much that the more prideful we become, the harder we will fall. Humility is the only way up in God's Kingdom. I have learned a powerful revelation throughout my life as a believer that the greatest attack on your life by devil will precede one of the greatest Holy Spirit-personal awakenings and outpourings that you have ever encountered.

Don't allow the devil to blow hot air in your balloon, because eventually that balloon will pop or deflate. Pride of life is the ways of the world, not of the Kingdom of God. I have experienced competition, jealousy, envy, character assassination, gossip, division, pride, and haughtiness from my fellow believers' in Christ. We must unify and love one another. We are not to be workers of the flesh which are the ways of this world and age. The devil knows that God opposes pride. The following is a powerful passage of Scripture in James 4:1-6:

> *What causes quarrels and what causes fights among you? Is it not this, that your passions[a] are at war within you? You desire and do not have, so you murder. You covet and cannot obtain, so you fight and quarrel. You do not have, because you do not ask. You ask and do not receive, because you ask wrongly, to spend it on your passions. You adulterous people! Do you not know that friendship with the world is enmity with God? Therefore whoever wishes to be a friend of the world makes himself an enemy of God. Or do you suppose it is to no purpose that the Scripture says, "He yearns jealously over the spirit that he has made to dwell in us"? But he gives more grace. Therefore it says, "God opposes the proud but gives grace to the humble."*

This Scripture warns against the spirit of pride; but later in James 4:7-10 it states that we are to submit ourselves to God. Then we can resist the devil and he will flee from us. The Lord is looking for those who can draw near Him and He toward them. God isn't looking for those who are indecisive or doubleminded.

God is looking for those with clean hands and pure hearts whom He can use. This invisible battle is not on the natural battlefront, it is on the battlefield in our minds. Overcoming the three main temptations is key to overcoming and winning the war in our flesh, our physical body.

First Corinthians 10:13 says, *"No temptation has overtaken you except what is common to mankind. And God is faithful; he will not let you be tempted beyond what you can bear. But when you are tempted, he will also provide a way out so that you can endure it."*

THE POWER OF CHOICE

How should you respond to temptations? My answer—ask yourself what would Jesus do and what did He do according to the Word of God. When tempted by satan, Jesus wielded the Word of God and rebuked him. We can do the very same thing Jesus did by using the Word of God to stand and fight and resist the devil. We don't need to rebuke satan because when we use the Word of God against his erroneous and deceptive plans, he is already rebuked by Jesus who is the living Word.

There is always an escape route when we face temptations by the enemy like Jesus faced—because we have the power of choice. We can choose to not give in to or yield to the temptations of the enemy. The greatest weapon against the works of the devil is our power of choice. With our gift of free will from God, we can choose to fall, or stand tall on God's Word. It's between obedience or disobedience. It's about the work of the flesh or the work and fruit of the Spirit.

TUG-OF-WAR: SPIRIT AND FLESH

God is calling His people to walk by His truth in Ezekiel 36:16-38 and Romans 8:9-11. The spiritual battle is with yourself. That is why we must be honest with ourselves before God with a pure, earnest, and sincere heart to repent and confess our sin or faults to Him. Freedom is ours in the Spirit; however, the flesh is weak—but the spirit is willing according to Matthew 26:41. There is a battle going on between the flesh and the Spirit of God within believers. Always watching and praying is a great antidote to overcome temptations of the enemy.

Galatians 5:16-18 clearly explains this internal battle: *"So I say, walk by the Spirit, and you will not gratify the desires of the flesh. For the flesh craves what is contrary to the Spirit, and the Spirit what is contrary to the flesh. They are in conflict with each other, so that you are not to do whatever you want. But if you are led by the Spirit, you are not under the law."*

Those who are led by God's Spirit are the children of God. We only defeat sin by the Spirit of God. We defeat the works of the flesh by willingly walking by the Spirit. Spirit-led believers obey Abba God who is Spirit. Workers of the flesh disobey God and are workers of iniquity and are led by the devil, their father (John 8:44).

We are children of God when we are led by the power of His Spirit who brings us into the spirit of adoption, which makes us children of God and coheirs with Christ (Romans 8:17). Let look at more specifically here in Romans 8:13-17:

> *For if you live according to the flesh, you will die; but if by the Spirit you put to death the misdeeds of the body, you*

will live. For those who are led by the Spirit of God are the children of God. The Spirit you received does not make you slaves, so that you live in fear again; rather, the Spirit you received brought about your adoption to sonship. And by him we cry, "Abba, Father." The Spirit himself testifies with our spirit that we are God's children. Now if we are children, then we are heirs—heirs of God and co-heirs with Christ, if indeed we share in his sufferings in order that we may also share in his glory.

Our natural body came with a sin nature when Adam and Eve disobeyed God and was judged by God for disobedience. We are born into sin naturally. Psalm 51:5 says, *"Surely I was sinful at birth, sinful from the time my mother conceived me."* And Ecclesiastes 7:20 declares, *"Indeed, there is no one on earth who is righteous, no one who does what is right and ever sins."*

BECOME A LIVING SACRIFICE

We can be in the world but not of it; that is what Jesus says in John 17:14. There has to be a distinction between those who are of God and those who are of the devil. God is not raising up hypocrites, those who say one thing but do the total opposite. We must be like Christ not only in word but also deed. People know we belong to the Lord through our fruit (actions, deeds, and lifestyle). In this spiritual battle we die daily to our own wants and desires and give them to the Lord. It's a daily crucifixion, so to speak.

In addition, Romans 12:1-3 says:

Therefore I urge you, brothers and sisters, in view of God's mercy, to offer your bodies as a living sacrifice, holy and pleasing to God—this is your true and proper worship. Do not conform to the pattern of this world, but be transformed by the renewing of your mind. Then you will be able to test and approve what God's will is—his good, pleasing and perfect will. For by the grace given me I say to every one of you: Do not think of yourself more highly than you ought, but rather think of yourself with sober judgment, in accordance with the faith God has distributed to each of you.

It must be understood that a good thing may not be a God-led thing. Humans in the flesh make unwise decisions that come with serious consequences. Any deed not empowered by the Holy Spirit—is a "work of the flesh" (Romans 8:8; 14:23). Our decisions and work must be done in love for God and in holy faith.

There is a tug-of-war going on between the flesh and the Spirit of God in believers. The devil knows this. When we gave our lives to Jesus at salvation, the Spirit of God started to move upon our minds and causes us to have a repentant heart, making it possible for us to make decisions that are solely of the Holy Spirit, rather than the flesh (read Galatians 5:16; Ezekiel 36:27; Romans 8:4; Colossians 3:5-8).

EVIL IS ALWAYS PRESENT

Jesus destroyed the work of the devil on the cross; and likewise, spiritually speaking, when we die to self and are crucified with Christ, the devil's works are also destroyed and our old sin nature dies (Romans 6:2,11). However, I must say that the flesh doesn't die so easily, because the flesh is going to do what the flesh does and is. The tug-of-war, or the war within, doesn't discriminate and will challenge even the most dedicated follower of Jesus Christ.

As mentioned before, Paul wrote so eloquently of this war within in Romans 7:21-23: *"So I find this law at work: Although I want to do good, evil is right there with me. For in my inner being I delight in God's law; but I see another law at work in me, waging war against the law of my mind and making me a prisoner of the law of sin at work within me."*

The Lord wants us to walk in freedom and to be free in the Holy Spirit. The devil wants us to be free too, but his freedom is lawlessness but bound by sin. God's freedom is not a license to do whatever we want or this hyper-grace teaching "once saved, always saved" without repenting of sin because we are saved by grace. But we must not take the Lord's freedom for granted; if we do, it opens opportunity for the flesh to tempt us.

Galatians 5:13-15 says, *"You, my brothers and sisters, were called to be free. But do not use your freedom to indulge the flesh; rather, serve one another humbly in love. For the entire law is fulfilled in keeping this one command: 'Love your neighbor as yourself.' If you bite and devour each other, watch out or you will be destroyed by each other."*

Acts of the Flesh

It's important not to give the devil an opportunity to tempt us because of our spiritual freedom. We are called to freedom, but don't use it and abuse it for an opportunity or excuse to sin in the flesh. We as believers are set free by the Holy Spirit and we are to walk in the Spirit, not fulfill the works of the flesh. In addition, we are to love each other when the devil comes to bring division, hatred, and deception which are works of the flesh.

The Bible reveals a list of acts of the flesh:

- Sexual immorality—the evil ascribed to sexual acts that violate social conventions
- Impurity—the quality or condition of being impure
- Debauchery—excessive indulgence in sensual pleasures
- Idolatry—worship of idols or extreme love, reverence for something or someone

- Sorcery—the practice or use of magic, especially black magic, also witchcraft
- Hatred—intense dislike or ill will toward something or someone
- Discord—disagreement between someone or lack of harmony
- Jealousy—the state or feeling of being jealous
- Rage—violent, uncontrollable anger, vehement desire, and aggressive behavior
- Rivalries—competition for the same objective or for superiority in the same field
- Divisions—disagreement between two or more groups, typically producing tension or hostility
- Factions—a small, organized dissenting group within a larger one, especially in politics, or state of conflict within an organization
- Envy—a feeling of discontent or resentful longing aroused by someone else's possessions, qualities, or luck
- Drunkenness—the state of being intoxicated or intoxication
- Orgies—a wild party, especially involving excessive drinking and unrestrained sexual activities or an excessive indulgence in a specified activity
- Lies—not telling the truth, an intentionally false statement, present false impression to be deceptive or deceitful

These acts of the flesh are what the devil uses against believers of Christ and people in general to keep them in a lifestyle of sinful lawlessness. Apostle Paul gives a strong warning to the Galatian believers not to practice such things because workers of the flesh will not inherit the Kingdom of God. Let me be clear, though, acts of the flesh are not always as obvious as the ones listed.

Anyone can fall prey to these works of the flesh and can even be found within mega ministry leaders, public Christian figures, believers, and even I have faced these daily challenges of the flesh—but I overcame by choosing not to yield to them with the help of the Holy Spirit.

Unfortunately, there are some so-called Christian ministry leaders, ministers, and public figures who are workers of the flesh. They basically pursue their own personal calling to gain popularity and have selfish ambitions under the guise of serving Christ and advancing the Kingdom, but inwardly they are not serving God. There are false prophets, teachers, and apostles who transform themselves into apostles of Christ.

The Bible says of them, *"For such men are false apostles, deceitful workers, masquerading as apostles of Christ. And no wonder, for Satan himself masquerades as an angel of light"* according to (2 Corinthians 11:13-14). There are some who appear to be followers of Christ but they are deceivers, transformers, and masqueraders. It's all about people's motives found in their hearts. Satan can transform himself or mutate into an angel of light, but he's full of darkness. The true light of God comes through a pure vessel. A bad tree cannot produce good fruit and a good tree cannot produce bad fruit (Matthew 7:15-20).

FRUIT OF THE SPIRIT

In ministry, I have faced much division, competition, character assassination, jealousy, malice, and toxic behaviors from those confessing to be believers of Christ. This should not be among believers. This is why Diotrephes was rebuked in 3 John 1:9. Trying to please the Lord from selfish motivation potentially leads to unhealthy competition, bitterness, division, slander, unforgiveness, and overtime, burnout (Galatians 1:10).

Since the acts of the flesh were listed, we should list the godly characteristics of the fruit of the Spirit revealed in Galatians 5:22-23:

1. Love
2. Joy
3. Peace
4. Patience
5. Kindness
6. Goodness
7. Faithfulness
8. Gentleness
9. Self-control

It is imperative to understand and seek to produce the fruit of the Spirit to overcome the acts of the flesh. The "fruit" of the Spirit outlined in Galatians 5:22 could be defined as "deeds, actions, or results." The result or the work of the Spirit in a believer's life will produce love, joy, peace, forbearance, kindness, goodness, gentleness, and self-control. Let's look at each one briefly as biblically speaking we may not know the meaning of the fruit of the Spirit.

I believe if we are going to win the invisible war within, we must know the opposite of the acts of the flesh. Our biggest fight is the flesh and the soul and is why we need the Holy Spirit. We need to cultivate the fruit of the Spirit working in our lives—and it's not an overnight process. For some it can take a lifetime to fully develop all nine fruit of the Spirit. Thank God for His grace and mercy! We must arm ourselves with the knowledge of the Spirit of

God for our benefit. This book is not meant to be exhaustive on every subject; however, we must uncover and tackle the mysteries of God that assists us to discern, disarm, and defeat the works of the enemy through the flesh.

Love—Greek word *agape*, which means affection, good will, benevolence, charity, and love feasts (Strong's G26).

Joy—Greek word *chara*, which is often translated joy or delight. It means "calm delight" (Strong's G5479). In the Bible, joy can be also viewed as gladness, the realization of the Lord's favor and grace working in a person's life. Possessing biblical joy is expressed happiness that is not dependent on ones' own circumstances. James 1:2-3: *"Consider it pure joy, my brothers and sisters, whenever you face trials of many kinds because you know that the testing of your faith produces perseverance."*

Peace—Greek word *eirēnē* and the exemption of the havoc of war, as well as wholeness, concord and harmony with the Lord and others. In addition, it means "one's peace, quietness, rest and set at one again" (Strong's G1515). Living a life of peace is being safe and secure both mentally and physically. The divine security that the Holy Spirit provides. Romans 8:6: *"The mind governed by the flesh is death, but the mind governed by the Spirit is life and peace."*

Patience—Greek word (*makrothumia*), which means "patience, endurance, constancy, steadfastness, perseverance, longsuffering, and slowness in avenging wrongs" (Strong's G3115). Patience is possessing forbearance. The Holy Spirit empowers believers to withstand challenging situations in life with endurance and perseverance in times of crisis, warfare, and troubles.

Kindness—Greek word (*chréstotés*), which means "moral goodness, integrity, usefulness, and benignity" (Strong's G5544). In the King James Version of the Bible, this word is translated "gentleness," which links it to the meaning of a gentleman or gentlewoman, someone who behaves properly, with moral integrity and kindness. Ephesians 4:32 (NKJV): *"Be kind to one another, tenderhearted, forgiving one another, even as God in Christ forgave you."* Proverbs 11:17: *"Those who are kind benefit themselves, but the cruel bring ruin on themselves."* First Corinthians 13:4: *"Love is patient, love is kind...."*

Goodness—Greek word (*agathōsynē*) means uprightness of heart and life, goodness, and kindness" (Strong's G19). Goodness is an action word and displayed through one's character. Second Thessalonians 1:11 (NLT): *"We keep on praying for you, asking our God to enable you to live a life worthy of his call. May he give you the power to accomplish all the good things your faith prompts you to do."* Psalm 23:6 (NKJV): *"Surely goodness and mercy shall follow me all the days of my life; and I will dwell in the house of the LORD forever."* James 3:13 (NLT): *"If you are wise and understand God's ways, prove it by living an honorable life, doing good works with the humility that comes from wisdom."*

Faithfulness—Greek word (*pistis*) means faith and faithfulness. Faithfulness in use is faith, belief, trust, confidence; fidelity, faithfulness. Faith is the Holy Spirit's working evidence in the life of believers. Faithfulness combines dependability and trust based on our confidence in God and His eternal faithfulness. Faith is a supernatural gift from the Lord and cannot be given by humans. Proverbs 28:20 (NLT): *"The trustworthy person will get a rich reward, but a person who wants quick riches will get into trouble."* Second Corinthians 5:7 (NKJV): *"For we walk by faith, not by sight."* Proverbs 20:6 (NKJV): *"Most men will proclaim each his own goodness, but who can find a faithful man?"*

Gentleness—Greek word (*prautes*) in the King James Version was translated "meekness," but because being meek seemed weak, modern translations of the Bible use "gentleness" to mean mildness of disposition (Strong's G4240). Philippians 4:5: *"Let your gentleness* *be evident to all. The Lord is near."* Titus 3:2: *"...to be peaceable and considerate, and always to be gentle toward everyone."* Proverbs 15:1: *"A gentle answer turns away wrath, but a harsh word stirs up anger."*

Self-Control—Greek word (*egkrateia*), which means "self-mastery, self-restraint, self-control, continence" (Strong's G1466). In other words, the ability to control your flesh (body) and its sensual desires and appetites both mentally and physically through the help and supernatural power of the Holy Spirit. Proverbs 25:28: *"Like a city whose walls are broken through is a person who lacks self-control."* Proverbs 16:32: *"Better a patient person than a warrior, one with self-control than one who takes a city."* 1 Peter 4:7 (ESV): *"The end of all things is at hand; therefore be self-controlled and sober-minded for the sake of your prayers."*

THE HOLY SPIRIT HELPS OVERCOME THE WORKS OF THE FLESH

The nine fruit of the Spirit are in total contrast with the works of the flesh, detailed in Galatians 5:19-21. We destroy the works of the flesh, which is laced with the works of the devil, when we please God in our lives. It is not by a "work," so to speak, but by the "fruit" that the Spirit alone can produce. Committed to prayer, the Word of God, worship devotion, and staying in God's presence is a preventative to avoid the acts of the flesh. When we are constantly submitted to the Holy Spirit and permit Him to give us day-to-day divine directives in every aspect of our lives, we will overcome every temptation (Ephesians 5:18; Galatians 5:25).

In this unseen warfare, the devil will not prevail if you deploy the Holy Spirit to work inside you to conquer the works of the flesh. You are new creature and your mind can be daily renewed. The Word of God says, *"Therefore, if anyone is in Christ, the new creation has come. The old is gone, the new is here!"* (2 Corinthians 5:17).

You are not what people or the world call you unless your actions, fruit, deeds, or works say otherwise. As we move on to the next chapter, think about what nature you carry. What works daily are you fulfilling—the works of the flesh or the fruit (deeds, acts, works) of the Holy Spirit? People will see you only by what you produce. They only know you by the fruit that you bear.

SATAN AND HIS DEMONS' NATURE

When I think about the works of the devil I often think of his nature and character. His name speaks of the type of spirit and enemy we are facing in this unseen warfare. Satan's biblically known names in alphabetical order and not capitalized:

- abaddon—Revelation 9:11
- accuser—Revelation 12:10
- adversary—1 Peter 5:8
- angel of light—2 Corinthians 11:14
- angel of the bottomless pit—Revelation 9:11
- anointed covering cherub—Ezekiel 28:14
- antichrist—1 John 4:3
- apollyon—Revelation 9:11
- beast—Revelation 14:9-10
- beelzebub—Matthew 12:24
- belial—2 Corinthians 6:15
- deceiver—Revelation 12:9
- devil—1 John 3:8
- dragon—Revelation 12:9
- enemy—Matthew 13:39
- evil one—John 17:15
- father of lies—John 8:44
- god of this age—2 Corinthians 4:4

- king of Babylon—Isaiah 14:4
- king of the bottomless pit—Revelation 9:11
- king of Tyre—Ezekiel 28:12
- lawless one—2 Thessalonians 2:8-10
- leviathan—Isaiah 27:1
- liar—John 8:44
- little horn—Daniel 8:9-11
- lucifer—Isaiah 14:12-14
- man of sin—2 Thessalonians 2:3-4
- murderer—John 8:44
- power of darkness—Colossians 1:13-14
- prince of the power of the air—Ephesians 2:1-2
- roaring lion—1 Peter 5:8
- rulers of the darkness—Ephesians 6:12
- ruler of demons—Luke 11:15
- ruler of this world—John 12:31-32
- satan—Mark 1:13
- serpent of old—Revelation 12:9
- son of perdition—2 Thessalonians 2:3-4
- star fallen—Revelation 9:1
- tempter—Matthew 4:3
- thief—John 10:10
- wicked one—Ephesians 6:16

The works of the devil is his job description, as we see throughout the Bible. This ancient archenemy of God and His people has one purpose, to win the battle for our mind. The Holy Spirit is our Helper and assists you when you partner with Him in spiritual warfare—that gives the victory!

You have the power to fight and resist what you cannot see. We must also understand the nature of satan and demonic spirits. People often mistakenly believe that the devil is a caricatured spirit being that has red horns, a pitchfork, and sits somewhere with fire surrounding him. His power and influence are broader and more dangerous than that. His nature is rebellious, as are his demons.

The nature of satan and demonic spirits include:

- Evil in nature (Judges 9:23)
- Possess extraordinary supernatural strength (Mark 5:1-18)
- Fear the Lord (James 2:19)
- Move around, travel (Mark 5:7-12)
- Work supernatural miracles (Revelation 16:13-14)
- Possess and express feelings (Matthew 8:29)
- Able to recognize individuals with spiritual power over them (Acts 19:13-15)
- They "preach" doctrines (teaching of devils) (1 Timothy 4:1)
- Impersonate or mimic individuals (1 Samuel 28:3-9)
- Possess their own will (Matthew 12:43-45)
- Primarily responsible for every wickedness known to humanity (Ephesians 6:11)
- Possess their own desires (Matthew 8:28-31)
- Possess unique, strange, human-like personalities (Acts 19:15-16)
- Able to communicate and speak (Mark 5:6-7)
- They understand their fate (Matthew 8:29)
- Powerful unseen beings (Mark 5:1-18)
- They understand and possess knowledge (Acts 19:15)
- Cleverly intelligent and wise (1 Kings 22:22-24)

- Not natural beings or human (Ephesians 6:12)
- Able to fellowship, gather, and congregate (1 Corinthians 10:20-21)

As we look at these demonic and satanic nature of these spirits, God gives us the ability to recognize by discerning not just the names but what they are capable of doing. Let's look at a list of the scope of demonic or satanic activities, operations, and evidence of their presence. If we are not able to recognize their operation, administration, and activities at work against us, then how can we win this spiritual battle or conflict effectively? We as warriors of God must discern and detect them by their unseen presence by their natural manifestation.

The generalized scope of satanic/demonic operations in both a broader and diverse sense:

- Fear and intimidation: (2 Timothy 1:7)
- Wrestling, fighting, quarreling: (Ephesians 6:10-18)
- Bondage: (Romans 8:15)
- Jealousy: (1 Samuel 19:1-11)
- Confusion, disorder, strife: (James 3:15-16)
- Evil, wickedness: (Luke 11:26)
- Vexation: (Matthew 15:22)
- Grief: (1 Samuel 1:7-8)
- Torments: (Matthew 15:22)
- Oppression: (Acts 10:38)
- Sickness, disease: (Matthew 4:23-24)
- Idolatry: (1 Kings 22:53)
- False prophecy: (1 Samuel 18:8-10)
- Strange fire (illegal/illicit worship): (Leviticus 10:1)
- False doctrine, error, heresy: (1 Timothy 4:1-2)

- Violence: (Mark 9:22)
- Deafness, dumbness: (Matthew 9:32-33)
- Blindness: (Matthew 12:22)
- Deception: (1 John 4:1-6)
- Manipulation: (Leviticus 25:17; 2 Corinthians 11:14
- Lying: (1 Kings 22:21-24; Proverbs 12:22;
  1 Timothy 4:2)
- Persecution: (Revelation 2:10)
- Transformation, disguise: (2 Corinthians 11:14)
- Stealing, thief: (John 10:10)
- Betrayal: (John 13:2)
- Convulsions: (Mark 9:20)
- Murder: (Psalm 106:36-38)
- Worldliness: (Luke 11:26)
- Lust (John 8:44)
- False accusation, slander, witness:
  (Revelation 12:9-11; 1 Peter 3:16; Exodus 23:1;
  Leviticus 19:16; Deuteronomy 19:18-19)
- Temptations: (James 1:13-18; Luke 4:13, 22:40
- Curses, hexes, incantations, spells: (Deuteronomy
  18:10-12)
- Lawlessness: (2 Thessalonians 2:1-12)
- Immorality, perversion: (1 Corinthians 7:2)
- Rebellion: (1 Samuel 15:23; 2 Thessalonians 2:1-12)
- False worship: (Deuteronomy 32:17)
- Discord, disharmony: (Proverbs 6:16-19)
- Provocation: (1 Chronicles 21:1)
- Witchcraft, magic, sorcery: (Exodus 22:18;
  2 Chronicles 33:6; Acts 19:19)

- Mediums, necromancers: (Leviticus 20:6; Isaiah 19:3)
- False prophets, teachers, apostles (Matthew 7:15; 2 Peter 2:1; 2 Corinthians 11:13)
- Workings of demonic influences in humans: (2 Timothy 3:1-5)
- Works of the flesh: (attributing to demonic influences: (Galatians 5:19-21)
- Seducing: (1 Timothy 4:1)

We can clearly see from this list of the nature and activities of the demonic spirits that none should be operating in the life of a born-again, Spirit-filled believer. These are not the characteristics of a child of God or the Spirit of God—rather, they are the nature of the antichrist. If any of these characteristics are working within you or someone you know, it's time for healing, deliverance, and breakthrough. The power of darkness and the influences of these demonic activities should hold no place in the life of the believer. Get free and receive God's love and embrace by partnering with the Holy Spirit.

Chapter 9

INVISIBLE BATTLEFIELD OF THE MIND

Do not be conformed to this world, but be transformed by the renewal of your mind, that by testing you may discern what is the will of God, what is good and acceptable and perfect (Romans 12:2 ESV).

Let this mind be in you, which was also in Christ Jesus (Philippians 2:5 NKJV).

Spiritual warfare starts in the battlefield of our minds. That is the place where the enemy creates strongholds that can be hard to contend against. He plants thoughts of unbelief, fear, confusion, lies, condemnation, perversion, and doubt that become strongholds. In other words, we must look at strongholds as thoughts or ways of thinking that the devil may inject into people's minds. If people believe the lie(s) of the devil, next they will act out those lies. For example, there are those who believe that homosexuality is not a sin, so that is considered a spiritual stronghold based on a lie from the enemy (1 Timothy 1:10; Romans 5:12,18).

DEMONIC STRONGHOLDS OF THE MIND

The devil attacks our minds causing us to fight against spiritual strongholds, which is fighting against the thought(s) that holds people, marriages, families, communities, and even nations in spiritual bondage. You can look at a stronghold as a pattern of thought established in the mind of a person. The lies can come many different ways such as hearing unbiblical teachings, doctrines of devils, teachings of false prophets—anything contrary to God's will and law.

When a thought becomes a stronghold that is later acted upon, it becomes a culture or way of life for a set of people. Through this war strategy of the enemy, many cultures are established. It started with a thought that became a way of doing things, way of life. As you think in your heart and mind, so you are (Proverbs 23:7 KJV). You do and become what you believe in your heart. Thoughts can be from the mind of God, our own thoughts, or they can be planted in our minds by the enemy.

Our mind is the most powerful part of ourselves. The power to defeat the enemy is the power of decision. Our thinking controls our actions; action dictates the direction our life is heading.

Unfortunately, this is why some people don't give their lives totally over to Jesus as Lord. If they decide not to fully follow Christ, they will continue to live defeated lives, feel condemned, guilty, unworthy, inferior, and be susceptible to any other mental attack the devil sees fit to employ.

God doesn't want His people living in spiritual bondage when they are actually spiritually free. Freedom and breakthrough happen in our minds as we penetrate and claim victory over demonic strongholds. On the invisible battlefield, we have the power of

God through the Holy Spirit to destroy the spiritual strongholds of the devil.

The children of God will no longer lived defeated lives but victorious lives, and this truth begins in the mind. The devil tries to hold people captive by their thoughts, which hinders them from living victoriously day-to-day.

Knowing your identity, calling, and purpose for living gives you an advantage over the enemy. It's imperative to know who you are in Christ so you are not vulnerable to the deceitful lies the enemy tries to place in our minds. When people don't know their identity or have no clue of their sense of purpose on earth, the enemy can use that void to plant seeds of doubt and insecurities.

HOLY SPIRIT'S POWER TO BREAK YOLKS

We need the power of the Holy Spirit to destroy demonic yokes that are strangling us and weighing us down. Through growing in the Word of God and maturing in the things of the Spirit, we become supernatural agents able to break through every challenging circumstances in our lives.

God told His people that He will break the yoke of bondage that was placed upon them by the Assyrians. Jesus reassures His disciples in Matthew 11:28-30 saying, *"Come to me, all you who are weary and burdened, and I will give you rest. Take my yoke upon you and learn from me, for I am gentle and humble in heart, and you will find rest for your souls. For my yoke is easy and my burden is light."*

Only the power of the Holy Spirit and God's Word can guarantee a win in Jesus' name! The Word of God is power packed with truths that when we study, read, understand, and abide by what it says, we will live a victorious life in the Holy Spirit and in God's Kingdom.

The Word of God has transformative power to change, alter, and reset our thoughts and lives. We should allow the Word of God to flood our minds with truth that defeats the lies of the enemy every time. Knowing the truth will always keep you free from deceptive plans and works of the devil on the battlefield.

I know what it's like to fight for life. For me it started when I gave my life to the Lord at the age of seven. I had to fight for my peace, joy, love, and to be in right relationship with the Lord. There were times in prayer when ungodly thoughts would come, even while in God's presence. I would feel badly and thought I sinned. However, it was just the enemy trying to trick me and cause me to feel unworthy and make me doubt that God heard my prayers. Evil was trying to control my thoughts.

It's so easy for our minds to become the devil's playground. We must guard our eyes, ears, and mouths when it comes to what we see and hear and say. Believing ungodly thoughts can plague our minds and give the enemy legal access to cause chaos within us.

DON'T FALL PREY, PRAY!

One thing I had to overcome as a young believer was forgetting the sins of my past. The enemy wanted me to continue to feel guilty and condemned and prevent me from the truth that I was forgiven by the Lord. Satan wants us to believe we are not saved and free and forgiven. He wants us to act on lies and continue to sin. That's trick of the enemy!

The devil brought up my past and planted thoughts that I had not been forgiven. He wanted to make my past, my future so I would never fulfill my God-given purpose and destiny. I lived in torment, guilt, self-condemnation, and rebellion. I had to fight for my mind (sanity) and denounce those lies in my mind. I had to believe God's Word and totally accept His promise of forgiveness.

God continues to forgive me every time I repent and confess to Him. Jesus died for me and you!

NO MORE CONDEMNATION

If you are like me and even now battling the pressuring weight of condemnation, guilt, shame, and have taken it to heart, here is a verse to memorize and believe: Romans 8:1 says, *"There is now no condemnation for those who are in Christ Jesus."* This means that when your screams thoughts of condemnation at you, it's a lie. Feelings of condemnation betray your full devotion and trust before God.

Again, guard your thoughts and don't allow the devil to fill your heart and mind with guilt and condemnation. Keep in mind that your past isn't your present and the past is the past. No one has the right, power, or authority to dig up old bones like a dog of what the Father has already buried and forgotten. The following Scriptures will bless your heart and mind when you truly believe:

- First John 1:9 (ESV): *"If we confess our sins, he is faithful and just to forgive us our sins and to cleanse us from all unrighteousness."*

- Isaiah 43:25 (ESV): *"I, I am he who blots out your transgressions for my own sake, and I will not remember your sins."*

- Second Corinthians 5:19 (NLT): *"For God was in Christ, reconciling the world to himself, no longer counting people's sins against them. And he gave us this wonderful message of reconciliation."*

- Hebrews 10:17 (NLT): *"Then he says, 'I will never again remember their sins and lawless deeds.'"*

- Psalm 103:11-12 (ESV): *"For as high as the heavens are above the earth, so great is his steadfast love toward those who fear him; as far as the east is from the west, so far does he remove our transgressions from us."*

Therefore, as children of God we must live lives of obedience. Living lives of repentance and forgiveness. Forgiving others and ourselves. The enemy already has enough ammunition, don't arm him with anymore. Rid yourself of old thinking patterns and lies of the enemy. Know that you are Christlike!

Don't Die on the Battlefield

Don't die on the battlefield of the mind on the frontline believing the lies of the enemy in this unseen warfare. The enemy wanted me dead when I first gave my life the Lord. He played with my young mind; and because of that, I was thrown into a realm of spiritual combat.

When I gave my life to the Lord, life as I knew it was amazing. There was a hunger for God's presence and supernatural encounters. My pursuit of happiness was in my prayer and worship time with the Lord. Also, reading my Bible and faithfully going to church was my only outlet to escape the reality of pain, rejection, and misunderstanding when I returned home. At church I found peace, joy, and purity in an environment full of love, unity, and inspiration in my home church—the Union Baptist Church located in Wilmington, Delaware.

However, after giving my life to Jesus and having all this zeal as a seven-year-old new believer, later, in my adolescent stages of life I was faced with many unspoken challenges that a child shouldn't have had to experience. Meanwhile, attending this popular Baptist church and listening to weekly life-changing messages was not a cure-all antidote to some of my life's day-to-day struggles at home. Oftentimes, I would go home from out the presence of God in church to a contradicting and convoluted atmosphere.

During that time, my mother wasn't a Christian and my father was a practicing Muslim.

Not growing up in a Christian home was one of the battles I had to endure. In addition, we were living in one of the roughest neighborhoods in Wilmington, Delaware. At the time, it was, in my opinion, a complete war zone. My life was a spiritual battlefield as a young black male who was a follower of Jesus. I became numb to all I witnessed including violence, drug activity, crime, prostitution, and poverty.

However, my mother made sure that within the four walls of our home, it was a different world than the reality outside. I recall a time when I was five years old looking out my bedroom window from the top of my bunkbed seeing an unresponsive man lying on the ground with bloody puncture wounds all over him. Later I found out that our next door neighbor stabbed her boyfriend to death in self-defense as she was a victim of domestic violence. I heard gunshots every other night from drug and gang activities. This is just a fraction of what I encountered as a young believer.

My mother told me to stand up for myself whenever faced with neighborhood bullies. Every day was a fight to survive and be normal. This wasn't the life that my mother wanted for her children. Every day was a battle and fight to be seen and heard. My mother did her best by providing a stable indoor environment for my siblings and me.

However, life to me at that time living in the projects was very unpredictable. It was a daily battle of the fittest. I firmly believe, though, that God was preparing me for future spiritual warfare engagement so I could become the man of God He called me to be.

As a five-year-old, the traumatic imagery of that deceased man outside my bedroom window was the enemy playing tricks on my mind even then. I came to realize that it wasn't a trick, but life's reality handed to me. Later, those heartbreaking images played over and over in my head and left me bewildered at times in my walk with Christ while growing up. Giving my life to the Lord was something I thought would free me from life's problems, cares, and pain. I assumed that being born again would also change the trajectory of my life and that suddenly I would live in a perfect world.

Oh how soon I realized that I was in a spiritual battle. Giving my life to Jesus caused me to be a target on the devil's hit list. As a child I found myself in a real war mentally, physically, and spiritually. The enemy wasn't happy with my decision to surrender my life and will to the Lord and become a child of God.

In spite of what was going on in my surroundings, I realized that Jesus was my only hope, peace, joy, and comfort in a hostile environment. However, when life continued to hit hard, I eventually succumbed to what was given me. Furthermore, being in God's presence made me feel invincible and invisible to reality. I had to come to grips with as a kid and teenager growing up for Christ.

Suicidal Thoughts

Being raised by a single mother and no father figure, life wasn't easy. Honestly, there was one point in my life when I wanted to commit suicide by jumping out of that same bedroom window because my mind and emotions got the best of me. I couldn't see the point of living and would rather be with Jesus. Perhaps at the time I wasn't aware of the invisible war going on within.

Who would have thought that a zealous kid who was worshipping God, fasting, praying, and loving going to church wanted to take his own life when he was at home? I didn't comprehend that the archenemy of God was using the method of mental torment to attack my mind at a very young age.

Those whispers from the devil put suicide in my mind and caused deception, making me think that my life was a total wreck. Truthfully, at the age of 12, I hadn't lived long enough to take on the responsibilities of adulthood and wanted to end my life. That was the invisible war going on in my mind—and it all started as a thought. Where did that thought come from? Why was that thought ever conceived? What triggered that type of plan of action? Satan.

It's no secret that satan targets the minds of the believers. It is his plan to establish mental strongholds—no matter the age of the believer. Our mind has strongholds that can be positive or negative. Negative strongholds must be penetrated by the Word of God and the Spirit of truth for breakthrough to ultimately take place and root. If the devil can change our mind about ourselves then he has the advantage. We must contend for the liberty of our sanity and peace in the Holy Spirit.

I am reminded of the many drug addicts and abusers that I see day-to-day and my heart cries out for them because they are like zombies walking around, literally out of their minds. What addicts see, say, and do is unbelievable. Drug abuse leads to hallucinations, mental disorders, and many times opens the door to demonic possession or embodiment. I always wonder what happened to cause these people to get to this point in their lives? Growing up I heard the phrase, "The mind is a terrible thing to waste." So very true that is.

YOU CONTROL YOUR MIND

The mind controls the body. Therefore our mental faculties must be sober, stable, and equipped to withstand any stealth attack of the enemy. The Bible calls the adversary a roaring lion: First Peter 5:8-9 (NLT) declares: *"Stay alert! Watch out for your great enemy, the devil. He prowls around like a roaring lion, looking for someone to devour. Stand firm against him, and be strong in your faith. Remember that your family of believers all over the world is going through the same kind of suffering you are."*

Keep in mind that the devil never had authority or power over believers. Only when believers give him the keys can evil enter their lives. The good news is that although satan is described as a "roaring lion," in reality he has no actual authority and power over God's people unless we yield it to him. That can happen when we turn our backs on God and the lion seizes that opportunity to invade our mind with destructive thoughts.

A supernatural boldness comes to those who stand up against the wicked one. The enemy knows the power of a person's mind. If he can consume you with overwhelming thoughts of negativity, you become a fallen casualty in the battlefield of your mind—and he wins.

He wants to establish strongholds in your mind to get the best of you. But the Bible says we have the mind of Christ, which I believe is impenetrable! The Bible says in James 1:8 that a double-minded person is unstable in all ways. People who have doubts are thinking about two different things at the same time and can't make up their minds about anything. This is one of the enemy's plans to bring confusion to God's people.

As I was studying the word or term "double-minded," I learned that it comes from the Greek word *dipsychos,* meaning "a person with two minds, double souls or two spirited." Also, it means "wavering, uncertain and doubting and divided in interest" (Strong's G1374). Interestingly, this particular word only appears in James 1:8 and 4:8. James 1:6-8 states doublemindedness: *"But when you ask, you must believe and not doubt, because the one who doubts is like a wave of the sea, blown and tossed by the wind. That person should not expect to receive anything from the Lord. Such a person is double-minded and unstable in all they do."*

Guard Your Thoughts

God doesn't care for anyone who is double-minded, two-faced, or those who are neutral. The devil loves when people, especially believers, can't make up their minds and are unstable. I look at a hypocrite as a person who is double-minded, have split personalities depending on the circumstances, and are two-faced.

A hypocrite puts on a false appearance of virtue or religion or contradicts their stated beliefs or feelings. We are not to be double-minded people but sober minded in the things of God. A doubter, cheater is considered double-minded. Even Jesus Christ speaks and describes them as people who serves two masters (Matthew 6:24).

Mental Illness and Disorders

When I talk about the power of the mind, I oftentimes think about people whether young or old who suffer from mental disorders or illnesses. Here is a list the twelve of the most common mental illness and disorders:

1. Schizophrenia
2. Bipolar Disorder
3. Phobias
4. Borderline Personality Disorder
5. Manic Depression
6. Anxiety Disorder
7 Obsessive Compulsive Disorder
8. Panic Attacks

9. Eating Disorders

10. Antisocial Personality Disorder

11. Paranoia

12. Post-Traumatic Stress Disorder (PTSD)

Mental Health America (MHA) states:

> Most people believe that mental health conditions are rare and "happen to someone else." In fact, mental health conditions are common and widespread. An estimated 44 million Americans suffer from some form of mental disorder in a given year. Most families are not prepared to cope with learning their loved one has a mental illness. It can be physically and emotionally trying, and can make us feel vulnerable to the opinions and judgments of others.

MHA goes on to define what mental illnesses as:

> Brain-based conditions that affect thinking, emotions, and behaviors. Since we all have brains—having some kind of mental health problem during your life is really common. For people who have mental illnesses, their brains have changed in a way in which they are unable to think, feel, or act in ways they want to. For some, this means experiencing extreme and unexpected changes in mood—like feeling more sad or worried than normal. For others, it means not being able to think clearly, not being able to communicate with someone who is talking to them, or having bizarre thoughts to help explain weird feelings they are having (https://www.mhanational.org/recognizing-warning-signs).

MENTAL WARS

As we can see, mental illness and disorders can open doors to torment people and hold them captive. If not addressed and carefully evaluated by those equipped, anointed, educated, and trained in the areas of healing, deliverance, and mental health, the devil will win the battle of the mind. Mental illnesses and disorders can be heredity and/or demonic strongholds that must be dealt with, with the power of God and His truth.

The enemy wanted me to commit suicide or go into deep depression because of my childhood trauma. There are many reasons that people open themselves unknowingly to attacks by the enemy that comes after their minds. Doors can open through trauma that can potentially affect a person mentally, spiritually, and physically.

According to the American Psychological Association (APA), trauma is "an emotional response to a terrible event like an accident, rape, or natural disaster." However, an individual can experience trauma just out of their response or in relation to any or an event that they find emotionally, mentally, or physically threatening or harmful. Keep in mind that a person who may be going through some spiritual warfare and life challenges could experience one or many levels of trauma, privately or publicly, whether they are Christian believers or not. They may feel:

- Hopeless
- Angry
- Confused
- Unable to concentrate
- Anxiety
- Depressed
- Fear

- Sad
- Numb
- Shame
- Denial
- Irritable
- Guilt
- Unworthy
- Unloved
- Abandoned
- Victimized

These emotions can happen to anyone. Trauma can plague the way we function day-to-day and can be acute, chronic, or complex. A *Medical News Today* article describes three attributes of trauma (https://www.medicalnewstoday.com/articles/trauma), including:

1. Acute trauma: Results from a single stressful or dangerous event

2. Chronic trauma: Results from repeated and prolonged exposure to highly stressful events. Examples include cases of child abuse, bullying, or domestic violence

3. Complex trauma: Results from exposure to multiple traumatic events

OUR DECISIONS DETERMINE OUR DESTINY

God wants us to win the invisible war and gain full control over our thoughts and mind. He wanted to break the mental torment that I faced even as a child. The Bible clearly addresses where mental illness comes from in Deuteronomy 28:15 (NKJV): *"But it shall come to pass, if you do not obey the voice of the LORD your God, to observe carefully all His commandments and His statutes which I command you today, that all these curses shall come upon you and overtake you."* And Deuteronomy 28:28 (NKJV) tells us, *"The LORD will strike you with madness and blindness and confusion of heart."*

We can see from these passages in Deuteronomy 28 that believing anything outside of God's will and His Spirit, which is love and truth and power, becomes probable cause for the enemy to mentally torment people's thoughts.

DISOBEDIENCE OPENS THE MIND TO THE DEMONIC

A prime example of disobedience opening the door to the demonic is when Saul disobeyed God (1 Samuel 15:10-34). As a result of his disobedience, the Lord removed the kingdom from his rulership and the Holy Spirit departed from him as well, which gave place or room for an evil spirit, a tormenting spirit (1 Samuel 16:14). Saul was troubled and faced depression; some scholars say he was double-minded and dealt with schizophrenia. Whether Saul's diagnosis was that he was suffering from manic depression, chronic bipolarism, schizophrenia, paranoia, or mood swings, the biblical facts remain that he was facing tormenting spirits.

Tormenting spirits are not of God; they are demon spirits plaguing Saul's emotional, mental, and physical state. In short, King Saul suffered greatly at the latter part of his reign trying to cope with his mental health issues. There was time when he succumbed to paranoia, demonstrating extreme mood swings (at the end of First Samuel 11).

The plan of the enemy is to drive you crazy so you give up on the promises of the Lord and are unable to fulfill God's purpose. I believe that in this spiritual warfare, believers and especially leaders must seek help from spiritual leaders as well as seek professional help such as therapy. There is nothing wrong, in my opinion, with seeking professional help from those who are well-equipped to get you back in a better state of mind.

The Word of God and the indwelling work of the Holy Spirit can stabilize our minds and keep us in perfect mental health. I must say that many leaders suffer from mental illness and disorders but hide their torment silently. Just because you are going through depression, stress, or oppression doesn't mean you are not a believer, or the Spirit of God has left you. There are times of weakness mentally, physically, etc., when we must seek help from others so we don't have to fight alone.

Suicide by megachurch and ministry leaders has been too common in recent years. It is heartbreaking to know that pastors with all that influence are fighting in silence behind the scenes with unseen evil spirits. Discerning of spirits and the power of discernment is absolutely vital today! We have no clue what people are facing day-to-day or what they are wrestling with. A person may appear well externally but fighting for their life internally and mentally. This invisible battlefront is where the war in the mind is facing the forces of hell.

REMEDY FOR BREAKTHROUGH

We don't just need a diagnosis of the problem and the noticeable symptoms, we need a prognosis by the power and wisdom of God to drive out demonic spirits and evil thoughts. It's more than just reading and studying your Bible daily, it's having the Spirit of God help you overcome the warfare within your mind. Saul needed David to play for him because of his manic depression; and when David played, Saul received temporary relief from the tormenting spirits and they would suddenly leave (1 Samuel 18:10).

If the anointing and power of God through playing the harp by David can bring instant healing and deliverance, how much more would happen when people carry the indwelling power and force of the Holy Spirit each and every day. Worship, praise, prayer, fasting, studying the Word of God, and having other likeminded people stand with you can help you win the battle when it comes.

The following are some symptoms of mental illness that you or someone you know may be facing. Catching it early and getting help is the best decision one can make. The devil wants to play with and in your mind, but the Lord wants to free you or anyone you know, love, and care about! Anything outside of Jesus is a lie! Read through these symptoms and take appropriate action to free yourself through God's mercy and healing:

Mental illness symptoms in adults, teens, and adolescents:

- Irate feelings
- Substance use or abuse
- Erratic or unpredictable behavior
- Various unexplained physical ailments
- Dramatic mood swings
- Increased inability to cope with day-to-day activities and responsibilities
- Social distancing and withdrawing
- Irregular sleeping and eating patterns
- Perplexed or confused thinking
- Hallucinations (seeing and hearing what's not there)
- Excessive anxieties, fears, paranoia, and worrying
- Delusional thought patterns
- Extended periods of depression, irritability, or sadness
- Suicidal thoughts

Mental illness symptoms in older children and preadolescents:

- Regular outbursts of anger
- Intense anxiety and fear
- Rebellious and/or disobedience to authority, truancy, theft, and/or vandalism
- Increased inability to cope with day-to-day activities and responsibilities
- Irregular sleeping and eating patterns
- Short attention span
- Substance use
- Incompetent when managing personal responsibilities at home and/or at school
- Frequently complaining of physical ailments

Mental illness symptoms in children:

- Consistent temper tantrums
- Grades decline despite great efforts
- Constant nightmares
- Irregular sleeping and eating patterns
- Sudden changes in academic performance
- Excessive anxiety, depression, and worrying; i.e., refusing to go to bed or school
- Hyperactivity
- Signs of rebellion, disobedience, and aggressive behavior

KNOWING THE LORD'S MIND-SET

God has been speaking to me a great deal about understanding strategies of spiritual warfare. I titled this book *Unseen Warfare* on purpose, because we are not always aware of the enemy's devices, schemes, and tactics against believers. Therefore, my heart and compassion for the Lord's people is for them to be equipped spiritually, to be able to discern, disarm, and defeat the works of the enemy in their personal lives.

As a child, I had no clue what was going on with me. One minute I was in church worshipping and loving God, and when I went home from church I was hit with unusual warfare including crazy thoughts, erratic behavior patterns contrary to God's Word, and abnormal feelings and emotions.

We must keep in mind that the enemy doesn't play by the rules, and he's not fair. It is his primary strategy and plan of attack to send a barrage of thoughts of defeat, doubt, fear, and confusion. I initially heard the term "battlefield of the mind" when I read the book by popular Bible teacher Joyce Meyers in her best-selling book, *Battlefield of the Mind: Winning the Battle in Your Mind.*

The enemy is after the soul of believers because it houses our mind, will, and emotions. The devil would love for you to worry, doubt, become confused, depressed, angry, and harbor feelings of condemnation, unforgiveness, and fear, which are all attacks on the mind. The enemy wants the upper hand and advantage by downplaying God's loving and merciful thoughts toward you.

One of my favorite Scriptures about the thoughts of God toward His people is Jeremiah 29:11: *"For I know the plans I have for you,' declares the LORD, 'plans to prosper you and not to harm you, plans to give you hope and a future.'"*

The Lord's mind-set concerning those He loves is that of a prophetic future filled with a plan of success, prosperity, fruitfulness, good health, and well-being—not suffering. At the very young age of seven, there was a strategic plan by the adversary to derail and cause me to forfeit my prophetic destiny by having me take my own life. However, God supernaturally intervened and broke the power of low self-esteem, rejection, anxiety, abandonment, confusion, identity crisis, and fear.

Keep in mind that the devil doesn't know God's prophetic purpose, plan, and destiny over our lives until it is prophetically released, uttered, and spoken. Even Jesus Himself faced demonic assassination decrees by Herod when there was a prophetic announcement of a King and Governor who would soon come to rule God's people. An invisible war is equally as real as natural wars. God wants to open our spiritual eyes to understand the biblical perspective about the spiritual realm.

THE ENEMY'S DEVICES

Paul wrote in Second Corinthians 2:11, *"In order that Satan might not outwit us. For we are not unaware of his schemes."*

The Lord will not allow the enemy to take advantage, outwit, outsmart, or have the upper hand on His people. God will unleash new rules of engagement from Heaven through His Holy Spirit to shed light on what is hidden and expose and cast off the darkness as warriors of the cross.

This invisible war is not for the faint of heart or chocolate soldiers ready to melt under the heat of pressure. It is for prepared warriors of Christ who are armed and dangerous against the kingdom of darkness. If there is a natural war being fought, there is always a spiritual one as well.

The unseen realm, spiritual realm, or invisible realm, is a world in itself. It's the supernatural natural world of the spirit. There is a real civilization and activities happening in the invisible or unseen realm around us. What's happening in the natural realm is equally happening in the spiritual realm. There is the kingdom of darkness and the Kingdom of Light. Darkness and light are at war—but light always dispels darkness. We have to know what kind of enemy we are facing.

Be Spiritually Disciplined

God never tempts His children and never sets up a suicide mission for His warriors to be destroyed by the enemy. However, the Lord will at times lead us into places of testing. The devil uses those schools of testing as a ploy to tempt us into sinning against God. However, Jesus is the greatest example and champion on how to overcome the temptations of the devil and the acts of the flesh. He is the model we can follow to win the battle against the flesh.

I love what the apostle Paul wrote in First Corinthians 9:27 (NLT), *"I discipline my body like an athlete, training it to do what it should. Otherwise, I fear that after preaching to others I myself might be disqualified."* Paul learned how to command his flesh to do what he wanted it to do. He compared it to athletes working out or conditioning themselves for a game. Paul mastered the flesh to win, and not be disqualified in his race of faith to preach the Gospel.

You can win this spiritual battle in your flesh, mind, and finish your course in what God has called you to do in your generation. You have the power to conquer your fears and anything that comes to take your mind. You have the power to think for yourself and do the unthinkable in the power and might of God. Jesus defeated the works of the flesh and the devil by His obedience to the Father, and He had you in mind when He did it. He won the war that you too can win your own spiritual battles.

We defeat the enemy every time with having a winning mindset. You are a champion of Christ! That basically means that when Jesus defeated the enemy, He won with a flawless victory and the scoreboard was 31-0. We must think like champions to win like champions and do what champions do—win. Champions know how to beat all odds and endure every obstacle on their way to victory. They can see the finish line and, like Paul, win.

To have the mind of Christ is taking our thoughts captive in obedience as children of God. Paul goes on to confirm this by saying that in this invisible battle for our mind, is to "take captive every thought to make it obedient to Christ." To win this battlefield of the mind is to regain control if the enemy has duped you into sin. Furthermore, to control your mind is to control your actions, whether good or bad. On the winning side of this warfare are those who know how to control themselves. Growing up in a hostile neighborhood, I felt like all my life I had to fight; but most of my fights could have been avoided if I just walked away.

Sometimes it's not the person who gets the last word or the most blows in a fight who wins. It's the person who is the wisest and most calm. I had to learn how to control my emotions and how to respond. The devil uses our weakness and our possibilities to lure us into traps and unnecessary warfare. It's important to note here that our thoughts have the power and potential to paralyze or motivate us, to catapult us into a series of despair, or spiral things out of control, or thrust us to the heights of greatness and launch us into realms of unstoppable breakthroughs.

Spiritually Minded

Our thoughts have the power to mislead us or lead us, lead down a path of deception or guide to the center of truth anchored in God's Word. The Bible reveals to us that human wisdom is faulty at best, leading humankind to call good evil and evil good. That's why the apostles didn't teach human wisdom; they taught the wisdom of God and the things of the Spirit, which is God's mind. Paul says in First Corinthians 2:13 (NLT), *"When we tell you these things, we do not use words that come from human wisdom. Instead, we speak words given to us by the Spirit, using the Spirit's words to explain spiritual truths ."*

We are fighting an internal battle on every front in any given moment that has the potential and power to either draw us a step closer to Christ who is the Truth, or pull us farther away from the Truth who is Christ. We can feed our self-centered, self-absorbed, self-destructive, deceived thinking until we become engulfed and enslaved by the ungodly, sinful thought processes—or we can refocus and realign our perspective, paradigm, and mind-set of the truth of God's Word, believing and receiving it as His revealed Word setting us free.

Again, it's no surprise why the enemy always targets the mind— it is the primary battlefield. The frontline defense against it is self-control and standing firmly on the truth of God's Word. The devil bombards every believer's mind with explicit sexual images, past painful memories, and seducing thoughts. He employs this tactic through myriads of demon forces throughout the world system that he controls and rules. That's why we should always mind our own business, which should be the things of the Spirit of God. Satan understands that if he can control our mind, he can control our body.

Christian believers are to set our minds on the Spirit. To mind the Spirit is to spiritually think of, relish, and love what is godly, eternal, invisible—not earthly or carnal. Minding the things of the Spirit is that revealed, which God the Father through the Holy Spirit works in us, moves us toward, and promises to give us. Living life according to the flesh inevitably produces a mind given over to the things of the flesh, because it reveals the presence of death (deadness to God and to spiritual things). However, living the life according to the Spirit inevitably produces a mind given over to the thing of God who is Spirit, because His Spirit is life and fullness.

How to Guard Your Mind
on the Battlefield

The simplest two ways to guard your mind in this invisible battle is to 1) discern and test your thoughts; and 2) reject ungodly thoughts. Let's dig deeper into both ways.

One: We must always discern with the help of the Holy Spirit what thoughts and ideas are ungodly, placed by the devil or self that must be rooted out of our minds. Psalm 19:7 reveals: *"The law of the LORD is perfect, reviving the soul. The statutes of the LORD are trustworthy, making wise the simple."*

This verse uses the word "simple," which is a Hebrew word basically meaning open-minded. I hear people say that they are open-minded, which is not biblically the way to think, it's carnal thinking. In ancient times the Jews would describe an individual who was simple or open-minded as someone whose mind was like a revolving door. Basically illustrating that anything and everything came in and went out. They were like an open door, so to speak. In their view, an individual who was considered simple was a gullible person who believed anything and everything they heard, even without credence.

We are to trust in the ways of the Lord and not be worldly or carnal in our thinking. We are to be stable-minded and not simple-minded in the way we think when it comes to thoughts and images that should be rejected. The psalmist David was simply stating in Psalm 19:7 that we are to be filling our minds with God's Word, which is perfect and able to revive our mind, will, and emotions, because we become wise in discerning what is not of the Lord (Hebrews 5:14).

Throughout Scripture, wisdom primarily speaks of God's knowledge or the knowledge of God in total cooperation and in obedience to Him (Proverbs 9:10). That is one reason the Bible describes those who say there is no God as "fools" (Psalm 14:1).

Unfortunately, an individual who does not study or know God's Word will have a difficult time discerning and testing what is not good and therefore have difficulty protecting themselves from the trickery plans of the enemy.

That person's mind will constantly be consumed and bombarded by perverted visuals, sexual images, seducing ideas, comments, conversations, ungodly thoughts and lusts strategically purposed by the enemy to deceive, control, expose, and destroy them. Moreover, people who are not knowledgeable of the Word of God will become simple (open-minded), lacking the power, fortitude and discernment to shut any doors opened through sexual thoughts, talks, and imagery. Many times these people will not only accept, but also cultivate the evil.

Clearly, we must safeguard ourselves against ungodly thoughts. For example, when watching a television show in a hotel room after returning from a powerful glory, prophetic, or healing service, we have to be careful what we choose to watch because the devil will want to erase the godly experience and replace it with evil. Also, we have to choose the types of music we listen to—staying away from anything that is sexually provocative or incites violence.

In addition, we must be careful when in the workplace and marketplace. Do not be pulled into risqué or trash-talk conversations that could stir up lustful desires or hurtful gossip. Remember that being "open-minded" means accepting what pollutes our soul— while the wise person recognizes what dishonors God's temple, your body (1 Corinthians 6:19).

So, the first way to guard our minds is by discerning what is ungodly by testing it against God's Word. The second way is to reject ungodly thoughts by using the Word of God.

Two: We must test what comes in our minds by the Word God—and if ungodly we must reject it. In the natural, for an example, if a bottle of water looks clear and fresh, I can drink it. But if it looks murky and brown, I will smell it, and then I will reject it by pouring it out or discarding it.

If I drink it even though it smells and looks toxic, the consequences are on me because I didn't use the common sense God gave me.

Are you guarding your mind? Are you taking every thought captive and making it obedient to Christ? Are you filling your mind with God's Word? Are you resisting the devil's attacks so that he flees from you? If so, the Holy Spirit will continue to equip you to win the battle every time. If not, God wants to give you the gift of discerning spirits to discern, disarm, and defeat the works of the enemy today!

PART THREE

DESTROYING THE WORKS OF THE ENEMY

Chapter 10

SUPERNATURAL POWER OF DISCERNING OF SPIRITS

Whoever is wise, let him understand these things; whoever is discerning, let him know them; for the ways of the Lord are right, and the upright walk in them, but transgressors stumble in them (Hosea 14:9 ESV).

One powerful supernatural weapon against the devil is having the supernatural ability to discern spiritual things such as demons, angels, truth, error, seasons and times, divine, demonic, the presence of God, and the presence of evil. God wants to equip every Spirit-filled believer with the power of discerning of spirits. Many things are occurring in and around us that we can see with our natural eyes. But it takes spiritual magnifying lenses to see beyond the natural.

You don't have to be a prophet, seer, or intercessor to see into the unseen realm. What does it mean to discern things in the invisible or spiritual dimension? To gaze into the spiritual realm may not always mean having the ability to see beyond the natural realm. Perhaps for you it means you can think and perceive from a spiritual place and mind-set—able to detect spiritual matter and things concerning that dimension.

Looking Beyond the Obvious

To be victorious in this unseen warfare, we must have the supernatural power of the Holy Spirit to understand, engage, and examine what is happening beyond the realm of natural sight. What does the Bible say about the word "discern"? Researching this word from a biblical perspective I found that it means "properly, to scrutinize, investigate, interrogate, determine." It also means "to ask, question, discern, examine, judge, search" (Strong's G350).

Basically, to discern is the ability to properly examine, hold investigation, to discriminate or make determinations. To discern is closely related to wisdom that a believer must have in times of crisis, warfare, and in your spirituality. Hebrews 4:12 says this about a discerner: *"For the word of God is alive and active. Sharper than any double-edged sword, it penetrates even to dividing soul and spirit, joints and marrow; it judges* [the "discerner" of] *the thoughts and attitudes of the heart."*

For us to win the spiritual battle against the works of the devil, we have to discern by judging, examining, investigating, searching out, and inquiring of the Holy Spirit and the Word of God, which is the sword of the Spirit. Furthermore, as soldiers of God in this battle, knowing the Word of God is imperative to fight against falsehood. Discerning is not assuming; it is properly assessing and examining the facts. If a person doesn't study and know the Word of God (the Bible), they will fall victim to walking in error and susceptible to becoming double-minded or unstable.

The Word of God has the power and edge to cut through the toughest situation to get to the root. Like a surgical scalpel is sharp enough to pierce and cut through all the flesh to get to the bone, joint, and marrow as the Scripture describes what the Word of God can do. Discerning of spirits is a powerful gift from God used to detect falsehood and anything contrary to the ways, will, and presence of God. It interests me that the Word of God can cut thorough the soul and spirit. That's how spiritually sharp the double-edged sword is.

We need this type of weapon when we are fighting against an intelligent, cunning, and manipulative enemy—the devil. Possessing the power of a discerning heart and mind displays the divine insight, intelligence, and wisdom of God that transcends beyond what is seen and heard in the natural. The Word of God can only be "spiritually discerned." Without the Spirit of God, our natural minds would consider things of the Spirit as foolish because humans are unable to discern them spiritually.

A DISCERNING HEART

First Corinthians 2:14 (ESV) says, *"The natural person does not accept the things of the Spirit of God, for they are folly to him, and he is not able to understand them because they are spiritually discerned."*

The Spirit of God gives believers the power to spiritually discern things of the Spirit, which is spiritual discernment. Keep in mind we must possess the power and gift of the Holy Spirit to be activated into those things that the Spirit of God desires to disclose and declassify for His people.

When the enemy comes with false doctrines, teachings, and lies that are contrary to what God declares in His Word and prophetic words over your life, you can discern the intent, motive, heart, and agenda of the devil behind the lies he speaks or teaches through people. I love what King Solomon asked for in a dream—a discerning heart, supernatural intelligence, wisdom of God, and rightly administrate and govern the kingdom. He was best known for his power of discernment, making many wise decisions and moral judgments as a young king (1 Kings 3:9,11).

Today, in a dark world, believers are to be discerning by God's Spirit. It was the prayer of the apostle Paul for believers in Philippi *"to discern what is best...for the day of Christ"* (Philippians 1:10). In times like these we are to be like King Solomon who was wise enough to ask for a discerning heart to govern what is God's and concerning the things of God such as His people. The righteous should desire to seek the Lord for discernment as their objective in this spiritual battle raged against us. We have to discern spiritually what we are spiritually contending against.

Hosea 14:9 (ESV) confirms this: *"Whoever is wise, let him understand these things; whoever is discerning, let him know them; for the ways of the Lord are right, and the upright walk in them, but transgressors stumble in them."* Having the power of discernment allows us to judge righteously and spiritually filtering through the Word of God as the standard or plumb line that calibrates everything pertaining to God. Believers should have discernment when it comes to the many voices we hear, whether our own voice, the voice of God, or the voice of the enemy or demon spirits.

Truth Combats Error

The Word of God coupled with the Spirit of God assists in what we receive as truth or discard as false. It's important to know that a discerning person will always recognize the truth of God's Word by the Spirit and acknowledge its invaluable worth and power to combat error: *"All the words of my mouth are just; none of them is crooked or perverse. To the discerning all of them are right; they are upright to those who have found knowledge"* (Proverbs 8:8-9). The Word of God admonishes believers to *"hate what is evil; cling to what is good"* (Romans 12:9).

In times like these when the devil is influencing world systems and now infiltrating the church with heresy, antichrist spirits and agendas, some call what is right wrong and wrong right. In other words, justifying the wicked and condemning the just are both abominations to the Lord (Proverbs 15). This is why spiritual discernment is so necessary in this hour.

Believers must be able to discern truth from error! Unless we have true discernment, how can we determine what is evil and what is good? To maintain the purity of the Gospel, the Body of Christ must determine, distinguish, examine, and investigate truth from heresy. Wisdom and nobility were what I believe the Berean Jews possessed when it came to the message they heard Paul preach. They were noble, not novice.

Acts 17:10-12 (ESV) says, *"The brothers immediately sent Paul and Silas away by night to Berea, and when they arrived they went into the Jewish synagogue. Now these Jews were more noble than those in Thessalonica; they received the word with all eagerness, examining the Scriptures daily to see if these things were so. Many of them therefore believed, with not a few Greek women of high standing as well as men."* These Jews possessed the power of discernment by examining, searching out, and inquiring daily to see if what was preached is accurate or true. They had unique wisdom to properly discriminate between what is best, and what is merely good.

Have you ever heard someone make a comment that you knew was not true? Or could you detect someone was lying by examining their body language? We are not to ignore the Holy Spirit indicators that go off in our spirit. To discern is also having the ability to hear the voice of God and respond accordingly in obedience. There are red flags, a gut feeling or burden you may feel when you hear or see something that doesn't sound or look right. It could be the

Spirit of God getting your attention to search out a matter and discern if it's demonically motivated or God inspired.

As king-priest believers, we should search out things in a discerning and just way by God's Spirit. Proverbs 25:2 (King James Version) says, *"It is the glory of God to conceal a thing: but the honour of kings is to search out a matter."* The Holy Spirit imparts the supernatural gift of discernment to enable, empower, and equip believers who ask for it to clearly recognize and distinguish between the influence of the Lord, the devil, angels, demons, the world, and the flesh in a given situation.

THE POWER OF DISCERNMENT

I believe that the Body of Christ—the church—needs the power of discernment to warn the body at large prophetically what the devil is up to in times of danger to keep them from being led astray by false teaching. (See also 1 Corinthians 12:10, Acts 5:3-6; 16:16-18; 1 John 4:1.) It takes the power of discerning of spirits to understand times and seasons (1 Chronicles 12:32).

In times of crisis, turmoil, pandemic, economic depression, and civil unrest, discerning the times is imperative to know what is on Heaven's agenda and God's will for that time. People can sometimes forecast the weather by determining what is happening in the sky and the signs we see. But God is looking for those who can spiritually discern the moves of God's Spirit. The Bible even talks about nations lacking discernment and sense (Deuteronomy 32:28).

God is raising up leaders in the Body of Christ who possess the wisdom of discernment and common sense. The power of discerning spirits is the power and ability to think, perceive, comprehend things of God against what's not of Him and distinguish and judge what they are righteously and accurately.

I am reminded of the story of Paul and Silas in Acts 16:16-18:

Once when we were going to the place of prayer, we were met by a female slave who had a spirit by which she predicted the future. She earned a great deal of money for her owners by fortune-telling. She followed Paul and the rest of us, shouting, "These men are servants of the Most High God, who are telling you the way to be saved." She kept this up for many days. Finally, Paul became so annoyed that he turned around and said to the spirit, "In the name of Jesus Christ I command you to come out of her!" At that moment the spirit left her.

We can see that what the woman spoke was true of who they worshipped, but Paul was annoyed by not just what she said, but by the source that was speaking through her. He discerned the source of her power and influence was ungodly. We must be able to detect and discern by judging prophecy as in First Corinthians 14:29 (ESV), *"Let two or three prophets speak, and let the others weigh what is said."* The prophetic word must be judged by two or three seasoned prophets within a local assembly in order and protocol.

In addition, First John 4:1 (ESV) says, *"Beloved, do not believe every spirit, but test the spirits to see whether they are from God, for many false prophets have gone out into the world."* Today as it was then, we see a rise of false prophets, teachers, and false-christs who have gone out into the world system; the enemy is using them to deceive many and possibly the very elect of God (Matthew 24:24). Just because someone is operating in healing, signs and wonders and accurate prophetic words doesn't mean they are of God.

That is why the supernatural gift of discerning of spirits can detect and deflect false charismatic personalities, movements, and gifts. Jesus says in Matthew 24:24, *"For false messiahs and false prophets will appear and perform great signs and wonders to deceive, if possible, even the elect."* Therefore even Spirit-filled believers can be lacking true discernment. So, we should not be impressed by supernatural workings, as they may be of the devil, used as a weapon of deception. When you have the vital gift of discernment, you will not be deceived.

SUPERNATURAL POWER OF
DISCERNING OF SPIRITS

What is the power of discerning of spirits? It is one of the nine gifts of the Holy Spirit that edifies and blesses the church as a whole. Every believer can ask for this gift (1 Corinthians 14:1). May our prayer be like David when he said, *"I am your servant; give me discernment that I may understand your statutes"* (Psalm 119:125). The power spiritual gift of discernment is also known as the gift of "discernment of spirits" or distinguishing between spirits.

Discerning of spirits will save your life when the enemy is trying lure you into a trap or have you engage in gossip, slander, hatred, and conspiracy against people—especially God's people. Love is the greatest antidote against people bringing division, hatred, and dissention. The love of God becomes kryptonite against the works of the enemy including hate, racism, jealousy, anger, etc. We must discern not only spiritually but intelligently through God's Word.

If your discernment is low, sharpen your sword today so that you can wield it accurately and precisely when offensively and defensively fighting against the works of the devil, acts of the flesh, and navigating in God's Words of wisdom. Jesus discerned and perceived what is in the heart of His disciples and the religious self-righteous murderous leaders. Matthew 9:4 says, *"Knowing their thoughts, Jesus said, 'Why do you harbor evil thoughts in your hearts?'"*

Jesus wasn't a mind reader, he was a discerner and could judge their motives and secret intents. It takes the power of discerning of spirits or discernment to perceive the plots, plans, and evil intent of the enemy, even through people. Believers must conduct themselves like Kingdom "spiritual" citizens. There is a different standard we live by—holiness and righteous living. We are to live in peace and show ourselves friendly—while standing strong against evil.

Oftentimes, we have to discern and use wisdom when in engaging in the world system and living among worldly and ungodly people. God's people are hated by the world so at times we must operate under the radar (read Matthew 10:22; John 7:7; 15:18-25). In sending out His apostolic twelve disciples, Jesus says to them all, *"I am sending you out like sheep among wolves. Therefore be as shrewd as snakes and as innocent as doves"* (Matthew 10:16). In this verse, Jesus was basically cautioning them in His commissioning that they were to be alert, wise, and compassionate. They needed to discern with wisdom to judge their environments and people they would meet along the way. As believers and children of God called to share the Gospel, we are shunned, persecuted, and hated because of Whom we serve.

PERCEIVING THOUGHTS

Like Jesus, you have the same Holy Spirit power and ability to perceive people's thoughts, if you ask for and activate it:

- Matthew 22:18: *"But Jesus, knowing their evil intent, said, 'You hypocrites, why are you trying to trap me?'"*
- Mark 2:8: *"Immediately Jesus knew in his spirit that this was what they were thinking in their hearts, and he said to them, 'Why are you thinking these things?'"*
- Luke 6:8: *"But Jesus knew what they were thinking and said to the man with the shriveled hand, 'Get up and stand in front of everyone.' So he got up and stood there."*

- Luke 11:17: *"Jesus knew their thoughts and said to them: 'Any kingdom divided against itself will be ruined, and a house divided against itself will fall.'"*

Reading people's hearts and discerning their intents so we can respond correctly and with godly wisdom is invaluable. Jesus knew what He was sending His disciples into and what kind of spiritual and natural climate they would encounter. The world then, as it is now, is hostile to those who follow Jesus Christ—not incidentally hostile, but intentionally and purposefully hostile. The world is compared to the nature of wolves—vicious.

So within the seven spheres of society, "How can we advance Christ's Kingdom effectively without becoming predatory ourselves in those environments?" I used to work in corporate America in banking where I had to let my light shine brighter in a dark place. With the Holy Spirit's daily aid, I overcame obstacles and was faithful to Christ.

He instructed us to be Christlike in a godless world. As we fight daily against forces of evil, worldly temptations, and works of the enemy, our response and actions should be a combination of godly wisdom with the gentleness of a dove to win unbelievers to Christ. With the power of discernment, you become an inconspicuous soldier, not attracting attention to yourself, rather doing everything for God's glory to populate Heaven for Christ.

Before we move on to the next chapter, I want share examples of the discerning of spirits at work. Discerning of spirits gives believers the ability to sense:

- God's presence, the Spirit of God
- Angelic or celestial beings
- Truth
- Anointing and breakthrough

- Holy Spirit working and gifts
- Supernatural (good or evil) through power of darkness
- Witchcraft, sorcery, black magic, and curses
- Spiritual senses opened (sight, hearing, tasting, touch/feel and smell)
- Foul odors (sickness, disease, death or spoiled food, rodents)
- Fresh aromas (flowers, frankincense, oils, powders, rain, corn, and bread)
- Spiritual portals, gateways, doors, and ladders
- Demon spirits
- Error
- Confusion
- Deception, manipulation
- Lies
- Division, disorder, dissention
- Honesty, love, transparency
- Climate changes or temperature (naturally/spiritually)
- Weather pattern, signs, times, and seasons
- Divine blessings, favor, glory, and power of God
- Gifting, mantles,, specific callings, charismatic gifts
- Fivefold ministries and leadership
- Character, personalities, flaws, and genetic codes/ DNA
- Past, present, and future prophetic trajectory
- Voice of God
- Human spirit (soul)
- Voices of the enemy or demonic whispers
- Vibes, energy, and projections

- Body language
- Spiritual language

Chapter 11

PRAYER WEAPON IN SPIRITUAL WARFARE

Confess your sins to each other and pray for each other so that you may be healed. The earnest prayer of a righteous person has great power and produces wonderful results (James 5:16 NLT).

Have you ever tried to go into prayer to spend time with God but were hindered, delayed, or distracted by a sudden phone call, text message, unexpected emergency, or request of your time? It could be possible that an unseen enemy is trying to keep you from receiving your breakthrough in prayer. It could also be that the enemy is working through people, places, and things to stop you from entering into the presence of God. Why? Because the devil understands that prayer is the secret weapon of war against his works.

Prayer is simply communicating with our Creator and receiving what is our portion as children of God. The enemy is threatened by those who spend time in the glory of God. He doesn't want us to hear God's voice and/or receive Holy Spirit intelligence and empowerment and war strategies to overcome the works of the enemy against us in spiritual battles.

When we think about this invisible warfare between God and satan, we may wonder, *What does this spiritual conflict have to do with us if it's between them?* Keep in mind that you have been hand-picked by the Lord to have a personal relationship with the Father. This relationship is supernatural and therefore spiritual. We are one with Him, so His fight is our fight.

PRAYER—THE COMMAND CENTER

The Word of God reveals that there are three forces fighting for our attention and audience as well as fighting for ownership of our heart—the world, the flesh, and our enemy the devil. However, God's power is stronger than all three. The place of prayer is the command center for the Holy Spirit to speak to you about any pending unseen dangers, threats posed, and divine intelligence. The power of prayer is needed in times of war, crisis, pandemic, national insurrection, civil unrest, etc.

You should never underestimate the power of your prayers because it draws you closer to God and away from the world, flesh, and the enemy. In the Western world or culture, personal and financial success, accolades, physical appearance, and liberty from responsibility to the wider community are examples of what the world encourages people to make priorities and put them before the Lord. But the Word of God admonishes His people to closely walk with Him. We are to *seek first the Kingdom of God*. Therefore, we should watch and pray and be alert to the influences around us.

The enemy's plan is to stop you from entering into the place of prayer. Prayer shouldn't be viewed as a battlefield but a bunker of protection and roundtable to receive prophetic directives, insight, wisdom, and peace that comes from being in God's presence. The enemy's plan is to send God's people off course in their relationship with Him. To go back to the beginning, the enemy tempted Eve in the Garden of Eden so that God's people would fall and be separated from Him. The influences of the world may be tempting, but you can overcome each one by staying anchored in the Word of God, in the Spirit, and remove anything contrary to His Word.

There will be times before, during, and after prayer when the enemy will try to fight you in your in mind, tempting you to reject what the Scripture declares about the Father and your relationship with Him. Or about your faith to believe His promises, calling, and destiny for your life aren't true. Thinking these thoughts are tactics of the enemy and are nothing but subtle lies. You have the power to reject those thoughts! Do it immediately and the devil will flee.

Different types of prayers have the power to: request angelic assistance in the battle, breakthrough revelation and answers: healing: deliverance and miracles: and wisdom and direction from the Holy Spirit. Just ask and you will receive!

BREAKTHROUGH WARFARE PRAYERS

Moreover, there are times when we have to war in prayer for ourselves, our family, nation, community, churches, and things that God places on our hearts. Prayer is the place where we engage at times in warfare over what's blocking prayers, answers, and breakthrough from strongholds. When I think about warfare prayers, the first thing that comes to mind is breakthrough. I am not going to cover every aspect of prayer but will speak only of prayer that brings breakthrough, which is the theme of the believer and of God, the Lord of the breakthrough.

Breakthrough happens when believers engage in warfare prayers. Sometimes we pray quickly through our grocery list of things and move on; however, if we don't pray through warfare battles thoroughly we won't experience breakthrough. In addition, we have to know what is on the Lord's heart and partner with the Holy Spirit to pray them into the earth. The Bible says to pray that His Kingdom will come and His will be done on earth as it is in Heaven (Matthew 6:10). Then our prayers will align with what the Lord wants to establish in our lives, city, region, territory, government, nation, and world.

Prayer is the only way to bring Heaven to earth through the church—the Body of Christ. There are corporate prayers and fasting, intercession, worship and prayer, and other types of prayers that work when we decide to engage the King for answers. I always say that *prayer only works when we work our faith in prayer!* As soldiers of Christ in His army and Kingdom, we must pray for breakthroughs. Breakthrough is a military term and the agenda in prayer is to see an opening or breach as a result of it.

We are not to stop or cease from praying until something drastically happens, changes, and manifests! (See 1 Thessalonians 5:17.)

We have various ways to pray—prayers for peace, joy, healing, financial liberty, deliverance, salvation for love ones, etc.—and the main objective in all prayer, in my opinion, is for "sudden breakthrough." Are you looking for a breakthrough in your life? Do you feel like your prayers have hit a glass ceiling or closed heaven? Are you tired of praying and not seeing any results or answer to them? It's possible that you are on the brink of a breakthrough and the enemy wants to discourage you and have you to believe that your prayers will never get through. Keep praying!

DON'T STOP PRAYING

I encourage you to know that God wants you to receive your breakthrough just as desperately as you do. There are things we have to contend for in this walk as children of God. There are prayer requests, petitions, and supplications before the Lord that will take time to receive. However, when you pray in faith and believe what you ask for is the Lord's will—know that the Father heard you and will respond. James 5:15-17 says:

*And the prayer offered in faith will make the sick person well; the Lord will raise them up. If they have sinned, they will be forgiven. Therefore confess your sins to each other and pray for each other so that you may be healed. **The prayer of a righteous person is powerful and effective.** Elijah was a human being, even as we are. He prayed earnestly that it would not rain, and it did not rain on the land for three and a half years.*

It's clear from this passage in James 5 that there are prevailing prayers of breakthrough when we are the righteous of God. The prophet Elijah had to power through prayer and God's judgment to close the Heaven that there was a famine in the land for three and a half years. However, it was the same prophet who prayed fervently and persistently until he broke through and rain fell on the land. Most often our greatest breakthroughs come when we pray without ceasing.

Oftentimes, God causes a supernatural delay for our own protection. Not that He wants us to beg or plead in prayer, but to cooperate with His time and realize that some requests are not for now. Therefore, we must pray according to His will, plan, and purpose on earth. Most of our prayers are not God's will for us. As soldiers in God's army, we are engaged to see breakthrough and victory in the battles.

Elijah didn't pray once and the heavens gave rain. The prophet continued to pray until he heard something in the spiritual realm that gave him confidence and assurance that God heard him and the breakthrough was coming. Prayer ended the drought! You have to realize that rain is in your mouth when you pray. Elijah heard the sound of abundant rain when he was praying and his head was between his knees. He heard the rain in the spiritual realm before he saw it in the natural realm.

What have you been contending for to see manifest in your life? God is saying that you will have to see or hear it first in the spiritual before it comes through in the natural. For example, I was contending for a vehicle because my car was about to die. I needed an answer to what my next car should be. I prayed and prayed with no response until one night I dreamt about a beautiful diamond silver Mercedes Benz C300. I awakened from that dream feeling that the Lord was being specific about my next vehicle. Cars in dreams represent ministry, and I believed the dream was twofold for me. God was upgrading me in the spirit and also upgrading my transportation.

Several months later my Chrysler 300 totally broke down and I heard the Lord say to me, "Hakeem, today is the day to go in faith and get that Mercedes Benz C300." I obeyed Him after several attempts to back out; and even with no job, I drove off the lot that day with a brand-new Mercedes Benz C300. My point is, I had to see in the spiritual realm through a dream what I had been praying and preparing for. Prayer can prepare us for what is next if we are open and alert to the Holy Spirit's invitation into God's presence. Breakthrough is our portion as believers. We must contend for the faith and the promises of God. Prayer shouldn't be our last resort—it should be our first priority.

PRAYER AS A WEAPON AGAINST INVISIBLE EVIL FORCES

We are to seek the Kingdom of God first and His righteousness and all these things will be given to us (Matthew 6:33). Sometimes we don't pray for things even though God wants to bless us with them. As His people we are to pray for spiritual things, gifts, and wisdom that allows us to steward what He blesses us with. Warfare praying is not for the faint of heart, it's for those who are ready and willing to fight in prayer as if their lives depend on it. Breakthrough prayer benefits those who are relentless, unwavering in their faith to see God's glory invade the earth. When you pray, you must envision that what you are believing the Lord for is already in your possession.

Prayer is a weapon against doubt, unbelief, fear, witchcraft, double-mindedness, control, manipulation, death, debt, etc. What does breakthrough mean to you and how do you pray for one? I will use the term "spiritual breakthrough" as having personally reached a new level, dimension, and height in your spiritual walk with the Lord. Breakthrough is not limited to just something that happens spiritually, it can be applied to all spheres of activities in society such a medical or scientific breakthrough, for example. There is a science and spiritual aspect when it comes to prayer.

The Word of the Lord spoken in prayer takes shape and form first in the spiritual realm and manifests in the natural world, which brings the breakthrough or outcome of prayer. God breaks into the natural dimension through His people. The Lord needs a physical body to carry His purpose and destiny to be fulfilled on earth. Through the church—His body of believers—we accomplish His will. That is why the enemy hates the prophetic, prophets, and those who are called to pray.

Prayer is more than words we memorize and recite, it is our spirit life through the Holy Spirit who conceives and manifests the unseen to the seen. The devil only fights and resists prayers prayed by the saints in the heavenly (unseen) because it has the power to destroy anything that is not God's will on earth and in the natural sphere. It is the will of the Lord for the civilization of Heaven to invade the earth. Prayer becomes the deliverer or courier of God's Word to be birthed and established in the earthly realm.

That's why God sent His Son who is the Word of God to save the world and redeem humankind, returning them to their rightful place. Breakthrough only comes when believers continue to pray and speak the Word of the Lord until the power of darkness is expelled. We are to push back darkness and share the love of Christ to a lost world. Breakthrough is our portion.

Strategic Prayer Movement of Breakthrough

God is raising up an army able to move troops in corporate prayer and fasting that will breach the enemy's frontline plans. Breakthroughs in a spiritual sense is when individuals give their lives to Jesus, or receive divine revelation or prophetic understanding of a deeper a biblical truth, or receives an answer to prayer, or has victory over the power of sin or the works of the flesh. Breakthrough prayer is key for supernatural release. Peter received a breakthrough when he escaped prison on death row after the church came together to pray and he received angelic help.

> *Peter was therefore kept in prison, but constant prayer was offered to God for him by the church. And when Herod was about to bring him out, that night Peter was sleeping, bound with two chains between two soldiers; and the guards before the door were keeping the prison. Now behold, an angel of the Lord stood by him, and a light shone in the prison; and he struck Peter on the side and raised him up, saying, "Arise quickly!" And his chains fell off his hands. Then the angel said to him, "Gird yourself and tie on your*

sandals"; and so he did. And he said to him, "Put on your garment and follow me." So he went out and followed him, and did not know that what was done by the angel was real, but thought he was seeing a vision. When they were past the first and the second guard posts, they came to the iron gate that leads to the city, which opened to them of its own accord; and they went out and went down one street, and immediately the angel departed from him. And when Peter had come to himself, he said, "Now I know for certain that the Lord has sent His angel, and has delivered me from the hand of Herod and from all the expectation of the Jewish people" (Acts 12:5-11 NKJV).

The power of corporate praying caused the angel to release Peter from prison.

Furthermore, Hannah received spiritual breakthrough in prayer when she was barren and wanted a boy child. For years she prayed asking the Lord, and finally she conceived and Samuel was born. His birth was a tangible answer to her ongoing prayers. She didn't give up praying even when she was ridiculed, mocked, and put to shame because she was unable to have children. Her faith and persistence yielded her what she asked for: *"For this child I prayed, and the LORD has granted me my petition which I asked of Him"* (1 Samuel 1:27 NKJV).

Breakthrough prayers through intercession, faith, and patience are prime examples in the lives of Simeon and Anna. Their faithful service and witness allowed them to live to see the promised Messiah—Christ. It took unflinching faith and warfare over doubt, impatience, and uncertainty for them to win the battle until they saw what God had spoken and promised them. Warfare prayer is a prayer of tactics, methods, and techniques used by some charismatic, prophetic, apostolic, pentecostal, and certain denominations, streams, organizations, churches, and circles.

This art of prayer primarily focuses on using prayer as a weapon to contend against the spiritual or supernatural forces of evil, especially regarding daily life, proclivities, obstacles, struggles, and bad habits. Growing up in the Baptist denomination, I was not accustomed to hearing terms like breakthrough and warfare prayers. It was after I received the baptism of tongues and was baptized in the Baptist church that in my private time with God, I found myself intensely praying while listening to worship music and speaking in other tongues. The Holy Spirit would place someone on my heart and mind who was dear to me, and I would prayerfully go to bat for them.

Oftentimes, the people I prayed for and warred in prayer for would tell me later that they received a breakthrough in their life. The Holy Spirit taught me how to pray with warfare methods that bring results. Warfare prayers are prayers prayed for the purpose of breakthrough for or about something specific while waging war against an unseen opposition, entity, force, or spiritual enemy bent on making believers unhappy by thwarting their prophetic purpose, dreams, vision, and desires.

There is no question or second guessing that this invisible battle with evil isn't real. Therefore, when we pray this type of warfare prayer, it's targeted at a real unseen enemy, satan and his demon troops (Ephesians 6:12). Paul concluded his admonishment and commandment for believers in Ephesians 6:18: *"And pray in the Spirit on all occasions with all kinds of prayers and requests. With this in mind, be alert and always keep on praying for all the Lord's people."* We are not to pray occasionally, we are to pray always.

SECRET WEAPONS—FASTING AND PRAYING

When I think about all kinds of prayer that the apostle Paul was referring to, I think about prayer with fasting. Dealing with stronger demonic powers, forces, and strongholds of the mind requires different types of warfare prayer strategies to weaken and conquer the enemy. The Bible says in Mark 9:29 (ESV), *"And he said to them, 'This kind cannot be driven out by anything but prayer.'"* To wrestle different of kinds of demons requires different kinds of prayers. We can see that Mark 9:29 implies that only prayer can drive out demons. The art of prayer is not just praying, but praying and fasting becomes a lifestyle that draws us closer to God and away from the enemy.

We must be led by the Spirit of God when we engage in warfare-type prayers and use the Word of God as our basis and grounds for the rules of spiritual engagement. In other words, the enemy is not going to retreat or back down if our warfare prayers are not laced in faith and the power of the Holy Spirit and the Word of God. There is nothing wrong with praying the Scriptures, decreeing and declaring the Word of God, when it's in fact His Word and not our own. We can run the risk of saying all these warfare prayers, yet they are ineffective when done for self-gain, attention, and not in God's will. There are people I know who pray prayers against other believers and expect God to approve and validate their charismatic or prophetic witchcraft prayers. This is not in accordance with God's Word or will.

We are not called to pray against or wish ill will against another believer. Or speak judgment in the name of the Lord because someone offended us, etc. That's a total violation of Scripture and we will receive judgment and condemnation from the Lord. We are not to use our spiritual gifts as weapons of war against each other in the Body of Christ. Warfare prayers should be used against the evil unseen enemy trying to stop God's will being done on earth. When we pray prayers against each other, we are basically guilty of conspiracy and treason against citizens of the Kingdom of God.

The Lord is obligated to defend His Kingdom children and by His law (Word) to protect them (Ecclesiastes 8:4). Our prayers as soldiers the armed services of the Lord should be targeted on evil. God only answers believers' prayers who have the right heart, motive, and are aligned with His will. That's why some prayers are not answered. James 4:3 says, *"When you ask, you do not receive, because you ask with wrong motives, that you may spend what you get on your pleasures."*

Warfare prayers should not be empty words or vain repetitious prayers that we expect the Father to grant. I am reminded of the Sermon on the Mount where two general guidelines on prayer were given by Jesus: to pray in private, not to be seen by other, and don't repeat empty phrases (Matthew 6:5-8). Then Jesus goes on to instruct His disciples on the protocols of prayer when approaching God by saying that they should pray like this: *"Our Father in heaven, hallowed be your name, your kingdom come, your will be done, on earth as it is in heaven. Give us today our daily bread. And forgive us our debts, as we also have forgiven our debtors. And lead us not into temptation, but deliver us from the evil one"* (Matthew 6:9-13).

POWER OF FORGIVENESS TO WIN UNSEEN BATTLES

An often overlooked key in prayer is forgiveness, saying that those who are forgiving will be forgiven (Matthew 6:14-15). God will not answer people's prayers if past or present offenses, unforgiveness, grudges, anger, and strife is in their heart toward others who have wronged them or even vice versa. Breakthrough in prayer only comes when we acknowledge who we have wronged or have wronged us and forgive. Forgiveness is an action word.

We are to forgive if we are going to win spiritual battles. Prayer as a weapon in spiritual warfare requires a militant and Kingdom mind-set and position. It's standing on God's promises and words to see them come to pass in our life or in the lives of others. We are called to pray together. There are schools of prayer and prayer movements God is raising up that teach what Paul says in Ephesians 6:18 *"all kinds of prayers."* As Christian believers we can learn and be equipped in the art of prayer.

The Art of prayer is not one single method of prayer but there are various ways to pray that will bring supernatural results individually and corporately. It's important to note that when we are praying spiritual warfare types of prayer that Jesus and the agenda of the Kingdom becomes the primary focal point and aim. There is nothing wrong with praying bold, direct, faith-filled prayers to take control over our spiritual atmosphere and climate that seem to be under attack by the enemy. I don't know anyone who prays in battle and is smiling and happy.

Warfare prayers are to be assertive and aggressive only when their energy and focus is the Word of God with clapping, dancing, stomping, and shouting. The Bible says in Deuteronomy 28:7: *"The LORD will grant that the enemies who rise up against you will be defeated before you. They will come at you from one direction but flee from you in seven."* Keep in mind that satan only responds to force, power, and authority; he does not respect conversation, church programs, and lectures; neither does he regard anyone's spiritual title or position.

In addition, satan is not moved by who people think they are, call themselves, or their worldly knowledge, rather he is moved by what God's people are capable of doing to him. He is threatened by those with power, authority, and influence who can disrupt and defeat his satanic agenda. When you have the force of Heaven backing you in prayer, you don't have to fear the enemy and what he can do—you will be the feared one. You don't have to be intimidated—you will intimidate the intimidator. It takes aggressive force in prayer and in your spiritual identity hidden in Christ to tame the enemies of your destiny.

Warfare Prayers Work Only in the Power and Name of Jesus

Don't allow passivity to keep you from assertively praying warfare prayers by the Word of God to get instant results. It's time to rise up in your prayer position and arm yourself with the right decrees, declarations, proclamations, and prophetic utterances by the Holy Spirit in prayer to see Heaven and angelic movement on your behalf. Be an active prayer warrior. *Only spiritually active soldiers are battle ready believers armed and dangerous by the Holy Spirit to overcome the plans of the enemy.* Warfare prayers are weapons against the enemy—our will, wants, and desires should not get in the way. God knows what we need when we ask Him in prayer.

Therefore, there isn't anything wrong with praying boldly and faithfully, as long as we remember that the Lord is our Commander and Chief in this spiritual army. In these types of warfare prayers we can use first person statements such as "I declare," "I decree," "I prophetically pronounce," "I superimpose," "I uproot, overthrow, tear down," "I overrule," "I smash," "I rebuke," etc. Even though we use this terminology, we must know that we do not have ultimate power without the power in the name of Jesus and the One who can defeat the devil.

We pray, prophesy, work miracles, cast out demons and so much more in the power and name of Jesus and the anointing that

God has given us at birth. My point is that we are acting agents and ambassadors sent in His name. Therefore, when we pray like this, if we are not careful, pride can set in and the enemy would have us to believe that it is *our* will being done rather than "The Lord's will be done." Speaking boldly, directly, and passionately in the authority of the Holy Spirit is important when we understand that prayer is not in yelling, screaming, and beating the air—it is in knowing the Word of God in faith and understanding the power it has when released in faith.

If you are facing spiritual warfare on any level trying to steal or occupy your space, know that the Lord will give you warfare strategy to win. Joshua 10:7-8,10 tells the story of Joshua, Moses' assistant and war general. His responsibility after the death of Moses was to lead the children of Israel into their Promised Land. However, there were settlers who were already occupying the land that God promised them. There are prophetic promises and dreams that the Father wants you to seize and occupy. But there will be a fight with the current tenants or occupants. The Promised Land was already occupied by five kings.

Therefore, Joshua had to lead the people to evict them. To get this land meant war. Likewise, it will not be an easy task to drive out the principalities occupying the spiritual realm. However, the Lord will be faithful in assisting you as He was with Joshua in conquering the Promised Land.

The task was daunting for Joshua because the five kings formed an alliance to attack Joshua and God's people. They knew Joshua's reputation as a war general, the power of the Israelites' success, and they had every intention of preventing them to take their land. I love how this war general used prophetic intelligence to thwart their wicked plans:

So Joshua marched up from Gilgal with his entire army, including all the best fighting men. The LORD said to Joshua, "Do not be afraid of them; I have given them into your hand. Not one of them will be able to withstand you." After an all-night march from Gilgal, Joshua took them by surprise. The LORD threw them into confusion before Israel, so Joshua and the Israelites defeated them completely at Gibeon... (Joshua 10:7-10).

CHANGE YOUR FOCUS

Joshua gathered his entire army of his best warriors, marched all night, and after the Lord threw the enemy into confusion, Joshua and his men defeated them utterly. In spiritual warfare the Lord also says to us, don't be afraid of the enemy. He will confuse the enemy on your behalf and you will advance and receive what belongs to you.

I must say that when you are praying in a spiritual tactical mode, do not to channel your energies and focus on satan. Biblically, there is no evidence that believers ever addressed the devil, only Jesus spoke to the evil one directly. We are to direct our prayers to the One who defeated and destroyed the enemy. We don't have the power to rebuke satan or speak to him—but we *do* have the power to cast out his demons and destroy his works. Rebuking the devil, the Bible reveals, is accomplished by God, not us.

Jude 1:9 says: *"Even the archangel Michael...did not himself dare to condemn [satan] for slander but said, 'The Lord rebuke you!'"* The only guideline believers have is to submit to the Lord, and resist the devil and he will flee (James 4:7). The Bible doesn't say rebuke him and demand him to do things in our power and strength. We resist him by the power of the Holy Spirit who gives us all the authority to do so in Jesus' name! Only the name of Jesus rebukes and drives out demons!

When we pray in a warfare posture, we are not commanding the Sovereign God to do anything because we use decrees, declarations, and the Word of God. We pray targeted prayers partnering with God and being led of God's Spirit to become like sharp shooters striking the mark of sin and the works of the flesh or of the devil trying to have a place in our lives and minds. We strike the mark in prayer as prayer assassins to destroy, remove, and disarm anything contrary to God's will and purpose in our lives.

STEALTH PRAYER WARRIOR

As prayer warriors, intercessors, we pray for the sole purpose of victory in this invisible battle for the glory of Christ and His Kingdom. We decree and command through the Word of God so we can experience breakthrough in every area, in the authority and power of God through the Holy Spirit. Praying warfare prayer means praying according to Scripture, trusting in the Lord's power we possess, and submitting our will to His while in the battle.

Prayer connected with the *logos* and *rhema* word of God will deploy and discharge the correct weaponry against the enemy. Targeted prayers will shift nations, cities, and regions that have been highjacked by the enemy. Warfare prayers and prophetic words by the prophets are the proper tactics needed to win the invisible battles. Prayer changes everything when we change our strategies to pray. Effective prayers bring about breakthroughs in your life.

In this unseen battle, prayer is an invisible shield that protects from you from the evil one and keeps him from detecting you. Prayer camouflages God's people so that the enemy will not see your next move. When you are a prayer warrior, you become like a "stealth fighter" going undetected and under the enemy's radar. You strike the mark in prayer when you become a stealth prayer warrior.

Chapter 12

ANGELIC WARRIORS OF GOD

For he will command his angels concerning you to guard you in all your ways (Psalm 91:11).

Angels are unseen beings who are at the command of the Lord. They are spiritual forces of good while demons are spiritual forces of evil. God has created them for a specific purpose, and they serve Him and His purposes. Angels are used in the realm of spiritual warfare to fulfill and protect the interests of God and His Kingdom. If the Lord would open your spiritual eyes to the unseen or invisible realm right now, you would see these incredible beings.

In addition, in the spiritual world you would witness a battle in the heavens between angels and demons. The Kingdom of God has an angelic army. There is a civilization in the unseen realm, and in Heaven there is a real Kingdom, city, citizens, God the King Ruler, and an angelic military governed by the Ministry of defense, God.

ANGELIC ALLIES

The angel army is at the command of the King of kings and Lord of lords. As soldiers in God's army on earth, we have angelic aid helping us fight against the evil forces of hell. They are not at our command, but the Lord's command. Angels only respond to the voice of God's Word and are willing and able to fulfill it. The angels of the Lord hearken only at the voice of the word of God. Nothing else but the word of God that is voice-activated. The Lord's word accomplishes His desires and divine purposes and plans that He sovereignly sees fit.

Isaiah 55:11 (NKJV) says, *"So shall My word be that goes forth from My mouth; it shall not return to Me void, but it shall accomplish what I please, and it shall prosper in the thing for which I sent it."* And Psalm 103:19-21 (NKJV) declares about His angel's stance: *"The LORD has established His throne in heaven, and His kingdom rules over all. Bless the LORD, you His angels who excel in strength, who do His word, heeding the voice of His word. Bless the LORD, all His hosts, you ministers of His, who do His pleasure* [will]*."*

Throughout the Bible, especially in the Old Testament, we see many activities done by these super beings of God called angels. They are used of the Lord to bring judgment to whole cities and enemies of God, and they also fulfill unique roles and responsibilities by: assisting humans in spiritual conflicts; delivering prophetic revelation, messages; strengthening God's people; providing protecting, defense, guidance; answering prayers; releasing judgments, decrees; and more.

We must understand that God has given His people angelic allies that are our unseen partners and servants of the King and His Kingdom, which we have access to if we pray to the Lord to deploy them. Angels are unseen secret service-like beings ready to take out any unseen enemy of the Kingdom of God.

What are angels according to the Bible? Hebrews 1:14 describes them as *"ministering spirits sent to serve those who will inherit salvation."* These angelic warriors and messengers are battle-ready! The word "angel" basically means messenger.

I Saw an Armored Angel in My Room

There was a time in prayer when I was asking the Lord to show me what angels look like. I was going through a rough season and undergoing a lot of spiritual attacks. I was reminded in the Word of God that angels can come to our rescue as they did with Peter who was in jail. As I was in prayer lying on my face in my dark room, suddenly I saw a bright light and when I looked up I saw the silhouette of a man. The more I looked, the shape of the man became more visible and clearer.

To my surprise there was standing in front of me an angel that was fully armored, including a sword. I was so afraid that I closed my eyes in disbelief, awe, and fear. I opened my eyes again and he was still there standing tall. He was massive and muscular and had no wings, as television usually depicts. I knew he was an answer prayer and God was showing me my guardian angel.

Right after that supernatural encounter, I had dreams of this angel all the time; but the crazy part was that the armored angel in my dream looked like me without the helmet. Everything else was identical to what appeared in my room.

I believe that God showed me my guardian angel that is fighting for me in the spiritual realm in my dreams. Angels are on assignment concerning those who will inherit the Kingdom. Your angels are fighting on your behind in the unseen realm. In my dreams they are fighting over my prophetic destiny to see it fulfilled in the natural. We must pay attention to our dreams. Let me be very clear—we are not to worship angels and focus on them. But we do need to know their assignment and role in our lives as believers. Remember, the enemy can transform himself into an angel of light to deceive us with a false Gospel (2 Corinthians 11:13-15).

ANGELS AMONG US

I shared my angelic encounter because God was confirming to me personally as a seer prophet and showing me that He sent His angelic warriors to fight for me in that rough season of warfare I was going through. I know that angels surround us and are among us in the spiritual realm. In a dream, Jacob saw angels ascending and descending on a ladder from earth to Heaven (Genesis 28:12). They were going back and forward, up and down between realms. We have to know that angels exist just as much as demons do. Angels are positioned and ready to engage in the spiritual battle to help you win.

Jesus received the ministry of angels after His victory over satan's temptations in the wilderness for forty days and nights. The Bible says, *"Then the devil left Him, and behold, angels came and ministered to Him"* (Matthew 4:11 NKJV). In addition, Jesus, of course, also understood the power of prayer and the ability to ask His Father to deploy more than twelve legions of angels. In Matthew 26:53 (NLT) He told the devil, *"Don't you realize that I could ask my Father for thousands of angels to protect us, and he would send them instantly?"*

A legion of angels is approximately between 6,000 and 7,000. If you do the math that 12 times 6,000 is 72,000. Jesus had the ability to summon at His command a host of at least 72,000 angelic warriors. There are times throughout the Bible when one angel had the superpower and ability to wipe out a whole city. That's how mighty these beings are. King David on the threshing floor saw an angel destroying Jerusalem.

> But *as the angel was preparing to destroy Jerusalem*, *the Lord relented and said to the death angel, "Stop! That is enough!" At that moment the angel of the Lord was by the threshing floor of Araunah the Jebusite*. **When David saw the angel**, *he said to the Lord, "I am the one who has sinned and done wrong! But these people are as innocent as sheep— what have they done? Let your anger fall against me and my family"* (2 Samuel 24:16-17 NLT).

We can clearly see from the passage in Second Samuel 24, an angel has the ability to do God's bidding and carry out His judgment no matter what. This wasn't just in the unseen realm. David saw this angel on the threshing floor. The sovereign Lord will at times allow us to encounter His angels in many ways at His discretion. Again, we are not to seek them out, just know they are available in the spiritual realm to help us break through.

In the New Testament in the Book of Revelation, angels are directly involved in spiritual engagements and battles: *"Then war broke out in heaven. Michael and his angels fought against the dragon and his angels fought back"* (Revelation 12:7).

Angelic Dispatchment

Clearly, Revelation 12:7 specifically states that a war broke out in the heavenly realm between the archangel Michael along with his angels and satan along with his rebellious angels also known as demons. One of the powerful ways to employ angels from God is through prayer. There is an angelic intervention when prayer is involved. God deploys angels during spiritual warfare prayer.

We should ask ourselves what role do Christian believers play in how angels are released and engaged in our spiritual warfare? I believe we are to engage in warfare prayer that activates angels.

As we decree and declare the Word of the Lord, they will respond when it's prophetically spoken.

When the prophet Daniel prayed and fasted for twenty-one days, there was also a spiritual battle taking place in the heavenly realm, also known as the second heaven. Interesting to note is that his prayers influenced and triggered the battle (see Daniel 10:1-14). Principalities and powers were engaged in battle with Gabriel and Michael as the chief princes (angels of God). Angels then and now are engaged in battle in the unseen realm in the second heaven fighting against demonic principalities and powers—and fighting for the glory of God and His children.

In addition, these powers influence world rulers of darkness and unseen wickedness or evils in high places. That is why the apostle Paul admonished believers of the purpose of putting on God's supernatural armor. He understood that our conflict in this world is a spiritual one; warfare involving cunning, deceitful, trickery, and the works of the devil, as opposed to a human-to-human conflict. Unfortunately, human beings are used by the devil and play significant roles in assisting him in accomplishing evil.

FIGHTING UNSEEN AND SEEN DEMONIC INFLUENCES

We must keep in mind that demonic entities or spirits are the true power behind people who are in direct opposition to the things of the Spirit of God, knowingly or unknowingly. Paul wrote in Ephesians 6:12 (NKJV) says, *"For we do not wrestle against flesh and blood, but against principalities, against powers, against the rulers of the darkness of this age, against spiritual hosts of wickedness in the heavenly places."* He mentions four forces believers fight *against* in the unseen realm.

1. Principalities
2. Powers
3. Rulers of darkness
4. Spiritual hosts of wickedness in high places

The concept of principalities is understood by a Greek word *arche* (pronounced *ar-khay*) (Strong's G746), which means "commencement, chief (in various applications of order, time, place, or rank), first, magistrate, power, principality, principle, and rule." Paul was speaking of these unseen principalities as ruling demon spirits possessing executive authority or governmental rule in the world system. These ruling powers usually are involved in a particular race, people, territory, or nation. In other words, principalities and powers are at work in and around a municipality—a city or town.

These ruling spirits only operate within their jurisdiction; outside of that, they have no authority. But inside the specific region, landscape, or territory, they have authority. Just like a city police officers only have authority within their specific jurisdiction to make an arrest. County or state police jurisdiction may have more scope of authority than a city police officer because of its reach. However, federal agents (FBI and CIA) have greater authority than all, yet they too have to stay within their authority.

My point is that the Lord has angels at His command, and they are assigned delegated authority to guard, protect, and watch over certain regions of the world. A principality basically refers to and covers a specific region, territory, or country geographically. That's why we see in Daniel 10 where Michael is an angelic chief prince and divine (godly) principality assigned to watch over and protect the nation of Israel. Satan has demonic principalities assigned over certain regions and geographical places too. Demon spirits are wickedly ruling world kingdoms that oppose the truth of God's Word.

In Matthew 12:24, the devil is called in Greek "beelzebub" meaning "lord of the house," speaking of satan who is the prince of evil spirits (Strong's G954). These evil spirits are subject to him and operate under his rule, dominion, and power.

It is the primary objective of the devil to deceive nations under his evil influence and prohibit them from coming into the knowledge of God's truth and salvation through Jesus Christ His Son. In Revelation 20, the enemy is described as a deceiver of nations. The Greek word for "deceive" is *planaho*, which basically means to "cause to roam from safety, truth or virtue, go astray, seduce, roam about, wander, lead aside from the right way, and to be out of the way (Strong's G4105). Angels, on the other hand, carry out the truth of God's Word and will for nations of the world.

Second, the apostle Paul mentions the word "powers," which in Greek is the word *exousia,* which means power of choice, liberty of doing as one pleases, the power of authority (influence) and of right (privilege) (Strong's G1849). Even though the word power is unclear to as Paul's meaning, it is closely associated with the meaning he uses in other passage of Scripture. These are all high-ranking, evil supernatural powers, and the power of sin and evil in operation in the world system.

WHEN WICKEDNESS IS IN POWER

Third, Paul mentions "rulers of the darkness of this age." If Paul was living in the 21st century, he would refer to workers of evil who deal out gross poverty, terrorism, heinous crimes against humanity, drugs, gangs, and cults, etc. There are a few Christian writers who would go so far to relate the powers to world rulers who practice black magic and have close associations with demonic pagan gods such as the Ephesians' Artemis, and seems to be in line with the pagan culture of ancient times when temples were dedicated to demonic pagan deities.

I am reminded of Proverbs 29:2 (NLT) *"When the godly are in authority, the people rejoice. But when the wicked are in power, they groan."* We need righteous and godly leadership in all levels of government and the workplace. When evil doers are in authority, people are confused, perplexed, and mourn. That's why prayer, fasting, unity, and godly leaders in the church and in the seven spheres can unseat demonic powers and influences.

In addition, I believe that organizations such as Planned Parenthood that conducts abortions could be likened to pagan acts of children sacrifices and more evil such is found in Second Kings 16:3, *"He followed the ways of the kings of Israel and even sacrificed his son in the fire, engaging in the detestable practices of the nations the LORD had driven out before the Israelites."* These horrible practices and abominations are ruled by wicked powers. This is the reason why we need righteous leaders in government and in power who will veto ungodly laws and pass righteous legislation in nations, territories, and regions worldwide.

Fourth, there are what Paul calls "spiritual wickedness in high or heavenly places." The word "wickedness" is the Greek *ponēria* and means depravity and particularly in the sense of malice and mischief, plots, sins, evil purposes and desires (Strong's G4189).

This type of wickedness or malice is likened to a curse. We will talk more about demonic curses in the next chapter. When I think about spiritual wickedness in heavenly places, the devil comes to mind as the prince of the power of the air. Evil demonic spirits operate in heavenly places. Satan's organization of demon spirits works evil and mischief in our natural atmosphere. The toxicity of these evil spirits pollute our environment as they operate in the very air we breathe, and transcend beyond this natural realm.

People controlled by spiritual wickedness in high places are influenced by the enemy and the kingdoms of this world. They are in no way associated with God's eternal Kingdom. Even though satan is called the prince of the power of the air, Jesus is called the Prince of Peace and of Life (Isaiah 9:6 and Acts 3:15). There is a distinct and clearly defined difference between satan's kingdom and God's Kingdom. Jesus says in John 18:36, *"My kingdom is not of this world. If it were, my servants would fight to prevent my arrest by the Jewish leaders. But now my kingdom is from another place."* Christ's Kingdom is not of this world system plagued by darkness! It is of Heaven where He sits at the right hand of God.

BATTLE-READY ANGELIC WARRIORS

Paul told the Ephesians believers to be fully suited in God's armor to be victorious in a spiritual battle. Angels are stationed and battle-ready to fight invisible forces of supernatural evil that are operating and influencing their visible human agents concerning philosophical, social, religious, political, and cult issues. It is the devil's greatest success to deceive nations, which he can do because people lack true discernment. Believers must arm themselves with discernment and lean on God's angelic help to rescue us and defeat the technologies and methods of the enemy.

Sometimes prayers, petitions, and supplications we send to God are held up by territorial demon spirits. Demonic delay can hinder, interception, and interrupt God's prophetic plan and destiny for your life. On the other hand, sometimes God's delays are for His people's protection, revelation, perseverance, and cooperation with His perfect timing. That's why prophetic intercessors, watchmen, prayer warriors, and corporate prayer and fasting is needed to partner with Heaven to see breakthrough in nations and territories for salvation, healing, deliverance, and the advancement of the Gospel.

Angels are dispatched and deployed into battle for us and solely for God's eternal purpose. We bind and loose in the power and name of Jesus. We don't bind and loose things with vain words or unbiblical rhetoric. It's must be spoken and done in accordance with the Word of God and prophetic unction of the Holy Spirit. We don't command God's angels, nor do we do their job. They work *with* us as we cooperate with the Lord and in His timing.

No More Sneak Attacks

In addition, we don't bind and reinforce things in the second heaven; we ascend in prayer as we are seated with Jesus on the right hand of the Father, where we fight (see Luke 22:69; Romans 8:34; Colossians 3:2). We fight with Jesus on Daddy God's lap, spiritually speaking, and there is where things are placed under the foot of Jesus. We must let the angels of God do their job as we do ours in concert with the Holy Spirit who knows the mind of God. Jesus is making intercession for us, the saints! You are on the winning side of the Kingdom battlefield.

When we stop praying could be the time the enemy decides to strike. Be alert in prayer by watching and staying alert. Why? Because you never know when he will try a sneak attack. Like a car or home alarm, you must be ready to react when a thief is sneaking into your life wanting to steal, kill, and destroy you. With the Holy Spirit living inside you, you are not alone in the spiritual battle. There is a host of angels surrounding you in the spiritual realm. As we call on the name of Jesus, let's expect a release of God's heavenly warriors—angels sent on your behalf! The Scripture declares in Psalm 34:7: *"The angel of the LORD encamps around those who fear him, and he delivers them."*

The messenger angels interpret God's will, protect, provide guidance, bring answers to prayer, announce, warn, instruct, bring judgment, encourage, sustain, deliver, and intercede on behalf of believers in battle. Many Christian believers today have not been taught the function and sphere of angel activity as it relates to spiritual warfare. Consequently, we have not availed ourselves because of ignorance or full understanding of what we have at our disposal.

Angels are "unemployed," so to speak, because we have not asked God to activate them on our behalf. Consequently, they are unemployed and have nothing to do—except of course to worship the King of glory. We don't have to fight this war alone; we can accept the angelic aid available because we are citizens of His Kingdom.

MINISTERING SPIRITS

In other words, we have access to angelic military support! Hebrews 1:7 (NKJV) says, *"And of the angels He says: 'Who makes His angels spirits and His ministers a flame of fire.'"* Angels are ministering spirits assigned to minister to you and me. You can ask the Lord to dispatch His angels to assist you in any battle at any time. One of David prayers was *"...with the angel of the LORD driving them away! ...with the angel of the Lord pursuing them!"* (Psalm 35:5-6 ESV). King David understood the power of angelic warriors standing guard in the invisible to assist him against his enemies.

The following are some biblical accounts of angels participating in warring against the adversary that you can study and read on your own: Second Kings 19:35; Second Chronicles 32:21; Isaiah 37:36; Revelation 12:7.

Colossians 1:16 (NKJV) says, *"For by Him were all things cre-ated that are in heaven and that are on earth, visible and invisible, whether they be thrones or dominions or principalities or powers. All things were created through Him and for Him."* We know that the origin of angels started with God who created them. Psalm 148:2 (NKJV) says, *"Praise Him, all His angels; praise Him, all His hosts. …Let them praise the name of the LORD: for He commanded and they were created."* The Word of God reveals that there are multitudes of angels (Luke 2:13-15) who are apparently classified and categorized according to the duties they fulfilled for the Lord.

The following are the main classifications of angels:

Angelic Messengers

Messenger angels are most likely the largest in number. These are the *"ten thousand times ten thousand"* angels visualized by Daniel (Daniel 7:10), who carry out the will of God in Heaven and earth. This is the group that usually relates to the believer in terms of spir-itual warfare. They interpret God's will, protect, provide guidance, bring answers to prayer, announce, warn, instruct, bring judgment, encourage, sustain, deliver, and intercede on behalf of believers.

Angelic Elects

First Timothy 5:21 says of these angels, *"I charge you, in the sight of God and Christ Jesus and the elect angels, to keep these instructions without partiality, and to do nothing out of favoritism."* Biblically, no further information is provided concerning this particular angelic group.

Cherubim

The Bible first speaks of cherubim in Genesis 3:24: *"After he drove the man out, he placed on the east side of the Garden of Eden cher-ubim and a flaming sword flashing back and forth to guard the way to the tree of life."* Cherubim are armed with torched swords ready to stand guard over the things of God. Furthermore, Ezekiel descriptively reveals cherubim have four appearances: the face of a lion, ox, man, and an eagle (Ezekiel 1:3-28; 10:22). This also speaks of the living creatures surrounding the throne of God covered in eyes by the crystal sea of glass in Revelation 4:6. This particular class of angels is considered the guardians of the Lord, which is in the highest order of angels.

Seraphim

Isaiah 6:2 says, *"Above him were seraphim, each with six wings: With two wings they covered their faces, with two they covered their feet, and with two they were flying."* These class of angels are in the throne room stationed above the throne of the Lord; where in contrast the cherubim are surrounding God's throne. Their primary function is to lead Heaven into worshipping the Lord continually.

LIVING CREATURES

Living creature angels surround the throne of God. Revelation 4:6 tells us, *"Also in front of the throne there was what looked like a sea of glass, clear as crystal. In the center, around the throne, were four living creatures, and they were covered with eyes, in front and in back."* Revelation 4:8 describes these angels and their realm of worship responsibilities: *"Each of the four living creatures had six wings and was covered with eyes all around, even under its wings. Day and night they never stop saying: 'Holy, holy, holy is the Lord God Almighty, who was, and is, and is to come.'"*

This title presents these angels as manifesting the fullness of divine life, whose chief ministry appears to be worshipping God. And Revelation 5:6 says, *"Then I saw a Lamb, looking as if it had been slain, standing at the center of the throne, encircled by the four living creatures and the elders. The Lamb had seven horns and seven eyes, which are the seven spirits of God sent out into all the earth."*

INDIVIDUAL ANGELS

There are specific angels that the Bible mentions by name, some having special functions and ranking in their class.

Archangel Michael

Michael is a high-ranking warrior angel, a war general in the angel army (host). In other words, he appears to have been given authority and charge by God over the divine angel military of the Kingdom of Heaven and holds a chief position as a prince (Revelation 12:7). He is also the prince of the people of Israel (Daniel 10:13,21; 12:1). Moreover, he is specifically mentioned by name in Daniel 10:13,21; 12:1; Jude 9; and Revelation 12:7 where his role, responsibilities, and assignment in spiritual warfare are mentioned. He is the only angel called an archangel. He has charge over an army of angels. His name in Hebrew means "one who is like God" (Strong's H4317).

Archangel Gabriel

Gabriel is chief angel or prince of angels and his name in Hebrew means "warrior of God or "mighty one" (Strong's H1403). Gabriel is also specifically mentioned by name in Daniel 8:16; 9:21; and in Luke 1:19,26. One of his functions as a high-ranking celestial being is to deliver important prophetic messages from the Lord—including the announcement of the birth of the Messiah and John the Baptist in Luke 19:26—judgment, interpretation of vision, etc.

In Daniel 8:16; 9:21, Gabriel interpreted the vision to the prophet. He played an important role in releasing the mysteries and commands of God. Even though he is responsible for delivering time-sensitive messages from God, keep in mind that he can also fight. All of God's angels are supernaturally equipped and armed, regardless of their role and position to engage in spiritual warfare.

SPECIAL GROUPING OF ANGELS

The Word of God mentions a special grouping of angels in the Book of Revelation of their attributes and themes:

- Revelation 1:4-7 – Seven Spirits around the throne and coming clouds
- Revelation 1:20 – Seven stars representing the angels of the seven churches
- Revelation 4 and 5 – God's Throne, the Scroll, and the Lamb
- Revelation 7:1 – Four angels hold the four winds at the four corners of the earth
- Revelation 8:2 – Seven angels and seven trumpets before the Lord
- Revelation 15:1 – Seven angels who administrate the seven plagues
- Revelation 16:1 – Seven angels to pour out seven bowls of wrath of God

Just as listed in a previous chapter the names of satan and the personality or nature of demonic spirits, here I do the same by high-lighting God's angelic beings—our invisible friends:

- Spirit beings/ministering spirits: Hebrews 1:14
- Holy: Revelation 14:10; Mark 8:38
- Immortal: Matthew 22:28-30
- Powerful/strong/mighty: Psalm 103:20; 2 Peter 2:11
- Unmarried and don't bear children: Luke 20:34-36
- Obedient: Psalm 103:20
- Feelings/emotions: Luke 15:1-10
- Sexless: Luke 20:34-36

- Intelligent: 2 Samuel 14:20
- Speak many languages: Revelation 14:6
- Humble and meek: Jude 9
- Supernatural velocity and speed: Revelation 8:13; 9:1
- Have appetites: Genesis 18:8
- Restless: Revelation 4:8
- Glorified spirit beings: Luke 9:26
- Worshippers of God: Nehemiah 9:6; Philippians 2:9-11; Hebrews 1:6
- Take on invisible and visible forms: Numbers 22:22-35; Genesis 19:1-22; 18:2,4,8
- Innumerable: Luke 2:13; Hebrews 12:22; Psalm 68:17; Mark 1:13; Revelation 5:19

ANGELIC SPHERE OF AUTHORITY AND ACTIVITIES

Angels are given divine and instant access in Heaven. Jesus says it in the parable of the wandering sheep in Matthew 18:10: *"See that you do not despise one of these little ones. For I tell you that their angels in heaven always see the face of my Father in heaven."* Angels are active on earth and also appear in dreams to bring messages of warning— as to Joseph about the baby Jesus (Matthew 2:12). Throughout the Bible there are recordings of people seeing angels.

Angel Assignments in Heaven

- Worshipping: Revelation 4:8; 5:11-12; Isaiah 6:3; Psalm 103:20; 148:1-2
- Excited about the salvation of new believers: Luke 15:10

- Prepared to do the Lord's divine will: Psalm 103:20-21
- Represent children in a special way: Matthew 18:10
- Minister to the dead in Christ: Jude 9; Luke 16:22

Angel Assignments in the Earthly Realm

- Ministering to believers in times of crisis: Matthew 4:11
- Declaring warnings: Matthew 2:13
- Destroying and conquering: Acts 12:20-23
- Declaring judgment on people and nations: Genesis 19:3; 2 Samuel 24:16; Acts 12:23; Revelation 16:1
- Maintaining and sustaining: Matthew 4:11; Luke 22:43
- Defending, guarding, or protecting: Psalm 91:11
- Divine announcement: Matthew 1:20, 2; Luke 1:11-20
- Ruling the nations: Daniel 10
- Teaching/instructing: Daniel 4:13-17; Matthew 28:2-6; Acts 10:3-6
- Strengthening God's people: Luke 22:43
- Interpreting the Lord's will: Zechariah 1:9; Daniel 7:16
- Disclose: Hebrews 2:2; Acts 7:53; Daniel 9:21-27; Galatians 3:19; Revelation 1:1
- Guiding God's people: Acts 8:26
- Answering prayers: Daniel 9:21-22
- Preserving: Exodus 23:20; Genesis 16:7; 24:7; Revelation 7:1

- Uplifting, encouraging, or exhorting: Acts 27:23; Genesis 28:12
- Delivering: Numbers 20:16; Isaiah 63:9; Psalm 34:7; Daniel 3:28; 6:22; Genesis 48:16; Acts 12:1-19; Matthew 26:53
- Intercession: Zechariah 1:12; Revelation 8:3-4

Angels' Future Activities

- Binding the dragon: Revelation 20
- Preaching and warning in the Tribulation: Revelation 14:6-9
- Gather the elect: Matthew 24:31
- Separate the righteous and wicked: Matthew 13:39 and 49
- Involved in Jesus' return: 1 Thessalonians 4:16

Chapter 13

Breaking Demonic Curses and Illegal Soul Ties

No weapon that is fashioned against you shall succeed, and you shall refute every tongue that rises against you in judgment. This is the heritage of the servants of the LORD and their vindication from me, declares the Lord (Isaiah 54:17 ESV).

When we hear the word "curse," some instantly think about witches, warlocks, hexes, voodoo, and even profanity. All of those thoughts are accurately associated, but many are not aware of the unseen dangers and prohibiting forces when a curse is released. In addition, some believers don't understand the invisible threat and the power a word curse has, especial during the pagan holiday of Halloween and its satanic roots. Curses are real and operate very much in the invisible realm. I won't go into full detail of the origin of curses and witchcraft; however, I want to share just briefly what demonic word curses are and how we can avoid and break free from them.

Witchcraft is not a person dressed in black with an ugly appearance, riding a broom with a black cat. Anyone can operate in witchcraft, knowingly and unknowingly. Witchcraft is a term widely and broadly used to describe all sorts of evil employment of mystical superpowers that are released, generally speaking, in a discreet or private manner. Witchcraft, sorcery, evil magic, curses, malediction, the evil eye, imprecation, execration, voodoo, hoodoo, anathema, excommunication, hexes, and other demonic practices are associated in many different cultures, not just in some African societies.

BIBLICAL PERSPECTIVE OF A CURSE

What is a curse? The Oxford Dictionary defines a "curse" as "a solemn utterance intended to invoke a supernatural power to inflict harm or punishment on someone or something, an offensive word or phrase used to express anger or annoyance, and invoke or use a curse against." We also know that swearing, cussing, profanity, blaspheme, execrate, and damnation are all synonyms of the word "curse."

In the Hebrew and Greek languages, the word "curse" has several meanings, but the most common is the Greek word transliteration *kakologeō*, which means "to speak ill of, revile, abuse, to calumniate, traduce or to imprecate evil on, curse" (Strong's G2551). Curses are often manifested and administered in various ways. Some of the most common you may be familiar with includes:

- Barrenness
- Repetitive miscarriages
- Chronic or acute mental torment
- Chronic strife and anger
- Premature deaths

- Continual financial poverty
- Sickly children or infants
- Cycles of delays and denials
- Series of unfortunate events
- Mishaps and mistakes
- Repeated bad news or negative results
- Repetitive suicided cases in the same family
- Poor eating habits
- Poor sleeping habits
- Paranoia
- Fear of failure
- Repetitive business failures
- Multiple accidents and injuries
- Repeated physical illnesses
- Missed opportunities

These are just a few of the manifestation of curses when released. I want to be clear that some of these mentioned that happen are not always attributed to curses. They could be the result of our own decisions. There is power in the spoken word. Words are not simply sounds caused by air passing through people's larynx or vocal cords. Words uttered or verbalized have real power in the natural and unseen realms.

In the spiritual realm our words carry power—like seeds ready to be planted in soils to yield a harvest. We know that the Lord prophetically spoke the world into being by the power of His words (Hebrews 11:3), and we are in His image in part because of the power we have with the words we speak. Jesus goes on to say in John 6:63 (ESV): *"It is the Spirit who gives life; the flesh is no help at all. The words that I have spoken to you are spirit and life."*

THE FRUIT OF OUR LIPS

Words create wombs, spiritually speaking, that have the power to create life from it. One of the favorite Scriptures many quote is Proverbs 18:21 (NLT): *"The tongue can bring death or life; those who love to talk will reap the consequences."* The tongue, according as it is used in context of the Scripture, deals forth life or death; for speech is the picture of the mind (compare Proverbs 12:18 and Proverbs 26:28). The following are a few Scriptures to consider when it comes to the power of our words:

- Matthew 12:37: *"For by your words you will be acquitted, and by your words you will be condemned."*
- Proverbs 10:19: *"Sin is not ended by multiplying words, but the prudent hold their tongues."*
- Proverbs 12:13: "Evildoers are trapped by their sinful talk, and so the innocent escape trouble."
- Proverbs 13:2: *"From the fruit of their lips people enjoy good things, but the unfaithful have an appetite for violence."*
- Proverbs 13:3: *"Those who guard their lips preserve their lives, but those who speak rashly will come to ruin."*
- Proverbs 21:23: *"Those who guard their mouths and their tongues keep themselves from calamity."*

From a biblical perspective, curses and cursing are meant to harm others.

Tyndale's Bible Dictionary cites a curse as an "invocation of evil or injury against one's enemies." Sadly, today in some Christian circles some pronounce curses through prophetic words, preaching sermons that are subliminal messages to invoke harm against someone in attendance they dislike. This is clearly charismatic witchcraft and should not be done as Spirit-filled believers. Historically in Bible days, cursing was the opposite of blessing and should not be confused with cussing or swearing in the modern sense and definition. In the Word of God, curses were often mentioned as the opposite of blessings.

GOD'S OUTLOOK ON CURSES

Deuteronomy chapters 27 and 28 present covenantal blessings and curses, displayed materialistically. Reading these two chapters shines light on how God views both. An obedient person receives the blessings of God through a conditional covenant. A disobedient person was cursed. To break the terms of a covenant was the merit the covenant curse or curses would apply. A curse invoked under other conditions was deemed ineffective or powerless.

However, among the people of God, as His covenant people, cursing was generally prohibited. There were people who would declare a curse upon themselves to prove their truthfulness (read Psalm 137:5-7; Numbers 5:19-22; Job 31:7-10, 16-22). The Mosaic Law forbids cursing parents, (Exodus 21:17; Proverbs 20:20; Matthew 15:4), those in authority as ruler (Exodus 22:28), and even the deaf (Leviticus 19:4). Consequently, those who cursed the Lord were punished by death (Leviticus 24:10-16; cf. Exodus 22:28; Isaiah 8:21-22).

Curses and cursing carried a powerful consequence when done by someone in power or authority. Divine curses were pronounced by God as judgment for an act of disobedience. As God did with the serpent, Adam and Eve in Genesis 3:14-19, Cain the brother of Abel (Genesis 4:11-12), upon individuals who tried to curse Abraham and his offspring (Genesis 12:3), and upon those who put their faith, sole reliance, and trust in human strength (Jeremiah 17:5-6).

The devil sends curses as an invisible dart, or supernatural hindering force to stop a person's momentum. When a curse is operating in people's lives, they are filled with frustration, anger, confusion, and disarray. The person under a curse feels at times unable to reach their full potential and fall short of what they intended to do. This is what the enemy wants for those called to serve and follow God.

But I declare to you that there is good news!

Curses can be broken, removed, and eradicated from your life. Jesus at the finished work of the cross took up every curse and you are not bound by the sins of your ancestors. Jesus' death on the cross at Calvary was the death of the curse: *"Christ redeemed us from the curse of the law by becoming a curse for us—for it is written, 'Cursed is everyone who is hanged on a tree'"* (Galatians 3:13 ESV). It wasn't just the curse of the law but any curse that sin brings upon people; and for this, the "curse" is alienation from the Lord. However, even though Jesus' death on the cross was the death of a curse doesn't mean that we can't give legal rights to the enemy when we sin.

Legal Access for Curses

We give the enemy legal access when there is unrepented sin festering in our lives, unforgiveness, and other ungodliness. The Lord wants every door shut and locked, spiritually speaking, so that the enemy cannot invade our lives with curses. I thought about the following Scriptures when I was studying about curses, iniquities of ancestors, and that we are not held accountable for what they did.

However, there are generational curses that can be passed down from one generation to another. Even when we give our lives over to Jesus doesn't automatically prevent these spirits from oppressing and tormenting us.

- Deuteronomy 24:16: *"Parents are not be put to death for their children, nor children put to death for their parents; each will die for their own sin."*

- Job 21:19: *"It is said, 'God stores up the punishment of the wicked for their children.' Let him [God] repay the wicked, so that they themselves will experience it!"*

- Lamentations 5:7: *"Our ancestors sinned and are no more, and we bear their punishment."*

During my Christian walk I have had to deal with and break free from some of the consequences from sins committed by my natural father. However, through the power of the Holy Spirit and godly wisdom, I overcame and received deliverance, healing, and breakthrough in areas that I was struggling with personally. Generational curses and demonic curses can be broken off our lives. The Lord wants us to enjoy the Kingdom and live a life full of prophetic promises.

The Bible says in Proverbs 13:11-13 (NLT), *"Wealth from get-rich-quick schemes quickly disappears; wealth from hard work grows over time. Hope deferred makes the heart sick, but a dream fulfilled is a tree of life. People who despise advice are asking for trouble; those who respect a command will succeed."* Curses are demonic setbacks, invisible stumbling blocks, barriers, restrictions. It's time to break free from demonic curses sent by the enemy. If God opens your spiritual eyes, you will see what curses look like.

CURSES WITHOUT A CAUSE

Proverbs 26:2 (NLT), says, *"Like a fluttering sparrow or a darting swallow, an undeserved curse will not land on its intended victim."*

Curses have to hit the target. Curses can't just land anywhere. They must have a legal right or probable cause to land on a person.

Curses sent by the enemy is on purpose and for an intended, specific victim.

Proverbs 26:2 shows us how curses operate. Don't be an open target for the enemy to send his barrage of curses against you. Yes, the children of God are on the devil's hit list; however, don't become an easy target.

God wants us to dream and live out those dreams. Jesus is the Hope of glory and will help you win every invisible battle. Again, the main method to counteract the devil and his adverse forces is to remove their legal rights. Satan understands the spiritual realm very well and is governed by it. He needs a legal right to release curses—and he receives that right when someone gives him that right through sin, unforgiveness, bitterness, anger, etc. We must keep our thoughts and actions in line with God's will and plan for us.

So how do you remove curses if you think you may be under one? You must first remove the legal right, cause, or reason that caused it to "land" and function in your life. In other words, if unforgiveness is the cause, or any other open door is the reason, you must repent, forgive, and make it right for the curse to be broken in Jesus' name!

Generational Curses and Word Curses

The enemy has held many as prisoners through ignorance because most people don't realize they are cursed by the devil. This is why I make sure I daily forgive, repent, confess, and love people I also pray to the Father to reveal any open door that I may have given the devil access to. It's about rooting out the cause. For example, if there are mice in a house, to get rid of the rodents, the trash must be removed that is drawing them. When we honestly identify the root cause of a curse working against us and we have become a legal host, we can remove its right by living a godly life after cleaning the slate of any sin.

The Holy Spirit will give you the power and boldness to unshackle yourself from treacherous schemes of the enemy. You are a curse-breaker! Once you remove the cause, the limitations imposed by the devil legally are removed as well.

Many of today's churches are numb from the power of the enemy and left defenseless because of his demonic works. We need Spirit-filled churches that have the power to undo curses of the enemy working against God's people. An unseen curse could have been working against you for weeks, months, even years and you didn't know it. Could it be that you gave the enemy legal access and cause to inflict your life and space with a curse?

Some of what you could be struggling with right now may be due to a generational curse passed down from an ancestor. There may be many factors to consider when facing life's challenges. In this spiritual warfare against the enemy, curses are just one of his secret weapons.

If you are oblivious to what is happening in your life and the lives of those you love, the enemy will take full advantage of the opportunity. Curses can destroy people's destinies and steal their dreams. God wants us to ascend in prayer to the courts of Heaven to dissolve curses in our lives. We can break, shatter, and sever a curse's influence in our lives as we appeal to the courts of Heaven. One warfare method is to soberly, honestly, and spiritually recognize curse are legal issues, not a warfare issue.

We must know the law and our legal rights as citizens of the Kingdom. We make curses a warfare problem, so to speak, blaming problems on the devil when in fact he used the legal access people grant him to wreak havoc in their lives. Know your legal rights and break curses so you can win every battle. This unseen warfare you are facing day to day is intense and real. Is your conflict on the battlefield, or is it in the judicial system of the spirit realm? The answer is that it starts in the judicial system where the battle rages about the legality of it, and then the fight is carried onto the battleground for resolution.

LEGAL WARFARE VERSUS SPIRITUAL WARFARE

Some believe that they are not cursed once they are born again because of Jesus' sacrifice on the cross, being raised from the dead, and later He ascended to the right hand of the Father where He dealt with curses once and for all, legally speaking! However, we must keep in mind that when on the cross when He said, "It is finished!," He was announcing in the earthly realm prophetically and as King, that every legal requirement had been met for the purpose and ministry of reconciliation in the Kingdom while at the same time reclaiming all that was stolen for the Father in Heaven.

Remember, Jesus is the One who hung from a tree. I used to think that I was not cursed anymore because Jesus' death on the cross and death to a curse. But I soon realized that when it comes to spiritual legalities, a judge, once reaching a verdict, doesn't on the same day come off the bench to execute or enforce his or her ruling. There are other law enforcements responsible for carrying out the judge's decision. The sentencing is executed and established until it has the practical and operational ramifications of the judgment.

That being said, when verdicts such as edicts are released from the courts of Heaven, the Holy Spirit equips the body of believers to enforce, execute, and carry out the Judge's orders in the earth realm. In this judicial proceeding and rendering, the Holy Spirit has anointed you to put in place, or establish, the Word of the Lord, the decrees of the King.

We are called to be curse breakers and bloodline generational restorers! It is our spiritual Kingdom duty as citizens and officers of the court of Heaven on earth to dissolve, dismantle, and destroy curses. Jesus provided the legal rights and requirements to enforce His will in our lives. Anything contrary to God's prophetic purpose, will, and plan for your life must be removed. Truth be told, curses will always look for a place to land or dwell. Just make sure you don't give it legal access to do so.

Soul Ties

Last, I want to talk about soul ties. The Word of God doesn't use the term or phrase "soul ties," but it is very present and important issue. What is a soul tie? A soul tie is a spiritual connection or covenant relationship between two individuals, established mutually. Soul ties are established legally through intimacy, contractually, and/or verbally. There are legal or illegal soul ties. There is nothing wrong with building a great partnership, covenant relationship with others.

A godly soul tie is legal and pure. Ungodly relationships are established illegally through multiple sexual partners, or even illicit business relationships that should never have been made. Many times a soul tie begins when two people become physically intimate. Other times, a soul tie forms over time, after an intensely close emotional or spiritual relationship. I would view a soul tie as like a knot in a rope. It's a tying of two soul cords, like shoestrings, that links them together. A person cannot tie their shoestrings with one hand. It takes two hands to tie them together.

Likewise, when it comes to soul ties both people are involved. Sometimes people are unaware of the emotional, spiritual, and mental affect that a soul tie brings with it. The longer the bond of the soul tie exists, the tighter, stronger, and bigger it becomes, making it harder to severe if it becomes unhealthy. People think that once they break off a relationship, the soul tie automatically is broken. This is not true. Common examples of soul ties are marriages, family, business partnerships, ministry involvement, and good friendships, which are considered good soul ties. The ungodly, illegal, or negative soul ties are relationships that ultimately bring a person into bondage or rob or control a person's will that potentially brings harm as a result of the bond. It is a devil's tactic in spiritual warfare for believers to establish unhealthy, toxic, unproductive, ungodly, negative, and life-altering relationships, connections, and commitments with people outside of God's will for them.

Breach the Contract or Agreement

Unhealthy, illegal, unproductive relationships or soul ties to past or present relationships hurts, pains and wounds keeps believers from being able to give their whole selves to God and the person He may have chosen as their true "soul mate." The soul is the seat of the mind, will, and emotions. Unhealthy and toxic relationships of the past and present can negatively play a part in how a person thinks, acts, and feels. A soul tie is the joining of two people of like heart and mind. Again, there is nothing wrong with good, pure, and godly partnerships and connections that produce blessings, favor, fruitfulness, and mutual love, honor, and respect.

But, we are not to get involved in sexual relationships outside of marriage. This, to the Lord, is considered an illegal or illicit soul tie. Having sexual encounters with others who are not your spouse by marriage is spiritually and technically a marriage. In other words, any sexual involvement with someone not our spouse links the two souls together. God showed me an illustration of an illegal soul tie by brings to mind the Disney classic fictional character

Pinocchio by Carlo Collodi. Pinocchio was bound and controlled by his puppet master. The strings controlled his movements.

When a person is involved in an unhealthy, ungodly, and negative soul tie, invisible strings knit the two hearts together and their movements, emotions, and feeling are shared. That's why when a person moves on or ends a relationship, years later they are still thinking about that person and can't break free from that person emotionally. Another prime example is when people are in an abusive (physical or verbal) relationship yet they won't remove themselves from that hurtful environment because of the bond, the soul tie that holds them together.

In the Word of God there are examples of godly covenant soul tie relationships that the Lord established. We can see one such relationship in the story of David and Jonathan: *"As soon as he had finished speaking to Saul, the soul of Jonathan was knit to the soul of David, and Jonathan loved him as his own soul"* (1 Samuel 18:1 NKJV). Some pervert this particular text to make it ungodly, or an immoral relationship. Jonathan loved David as a brother and treated him how he would treat himself. This was not a homosexual or illegal relationship between two men. Jonathan was not in love with David, he loved him as if he was family.

BATTLE BUDDIES

Have you met people and felt connected to them and they became like family? This was the same case and God desires for us to have relationship like this. I do boot camp training, recruits are assigned a "battle buddy." Everywhere you go, your battle partner is with you. This technique can be applied to prayer partners as well. Choose a person who will pray with you and for you. This type of relationship is bonding and will help you to be accountable. Battle buddies in times of war will even die for each other.

When a person has had many partners, a person's soul is knitted together to each individual, whether love is involved or not. We need God-ordained and legal relationships for two to be blessed. What is the point of connecting with a person(s) who is making your life miserable? The Bible says in Amos 3:3 (ESV), *"Do two walk together, unless they have agreed to meet?"* I love what the website Bible Study Tools Commentary shares about Amos 3:3, about believers walking in concert and agreement between humans and God, spiritually speaking:

> Unless they meet together, and appoint time and place, when and where they shall set out, what road they will take, and whither they will go; without such consultation and agreement, it cannot be thought they should walk together; and not amicably, unless united in friendship, and are of the same affection to each other, and of the same sentiments one with another; or it is much if they do not fall out by the way. The design of these words is to show, that without friendship there is no fellowship, and without concord no communion; as this is the case between man and man, so between God and man; and that Israel could not expect that God should walk with them, and show himself friendly to them, and continue his favors with them, when they walked contrary to him; when they were so disagreeable to him in their sentiments of religion, in their worship, and the rites of it, and in the whole of their conduct and behavior. And to a spiritual walk with God, and communion with him, agreement is requisite. God and man were originally chief friends, but sin set them at variance; a reconciliation became necessary to their walking together again.

In this unseen warfare, we must be aware and discerning. We must make wise decisions and seek the Lord about every relationship, whether about a future spouse, business partnership, friendship, etc. He will give us direction and wisdom how to build long-lasting, fruitful relationships.

KNITTING OF HEARTS

Matthew 19:5 says, *"For this reason a man shall leave his father and mother and be joined to his wife, and the two shall become one flesh."* This is how soul ties work. Marital soul ties are acceptable and ordained of God. Soul ties established on fornication, sexual immorality, adultery, and other sexual contact outside of marriage are not of God. Intimate relationships knit two people together as one soul whether a person is married or unmarried (single).

The Lord wants His people to enjoy godly soul ties. A covenant is a legal and binding agreement or contract; a marriage is a legal union or covenant between a man and a woman. Again, the enemy respects no one and would love to establish ungodly and unbiblical unions, even civil unions or marriages between two men and two women. This is not biblical. Just because your nation, country, or state law considers it legal or right doesn't mean it is morally or scripturally right and acceptable. God has ordained marriage to be between the opposite sex—one woman and one man.

The agenda of hell is to make what is ungodly and illegal in the sight of God right and acceptable in the sight of humans. That's why the works of the devil—and what I spoke about in the previous chapter about principalities, power, rulers of darkness and spiritual evils in high places—influences and controls the world system that spiritually blinds people to the truth of God and His Word. I firmly believe that abortion, same sex marriages, and other violations of the Word of God are what need to be abolished and overruled in the systems of the world.

Keep in mind that we can also establish unhealthy toxic relationships with our employers, employees, church leadership and membership, parents, kids, and anyone we invite into our lives. Just because some of these relationships are supposed to be spiritual and godly, they could be relationships that God never directed or intended for us. Again, we need to discern every connection. Ask God if this relationship, job, career, school, church, leader, etc. are ordained of Him. Also, the Spirit within you will also make it clear which relationships are not of the Lord.

SOUL TIE SYMPTOMS

The Word of God says in Second Corinthians 6:14 (ESV), *"Do not be unequally yoked with unbelievers. For what partnership has righteousness with lawlessness? Or what fellowship has light with darkness?"* Clearly, this passage of Scripture is a powerful question and statement to ponder. Darkness and light have no commonality and righteousness and lawlessness are the opposites.

What are soul tie symptoms? Soul tie symptoms are usually what a person feels, thinks, and is emotionally moved by the person after a particularly intense relationship ends. In other words, I call it the aftereffect of a breach in a relationship that causes further codependence manifestations. For example, if a person is used to eating a particular food for some time and when that food is removed, the person will go through some levels of withdrawal.

Soul ties, depending on how long the relationship or connection lasted, can cause withdrawals. These soul tie symptoms can impact a person's mind, will, and emotions long after the relationship has ended, even years later. Soul tie symptoms can cause an irate, erratic, or spontaneous mood swings attributed to that past or present relationship. The following are a few soul tie symptoms:

- Suddenly imagining, visualizing, or hearing the person's face and voice in your head that can trigger a certain attitude, mood swings, memory, or physical manifestation.

- Stalking, overly referring to the person in conversation, obsessing about the individual(s) in your thoughts—particularly at certain times during the day or night.

- Regularly pondering, thinking, fantasizing, or dreaming about this person while single (unmarried) or married.

- Some symptoms are secrets, lusts, or desires from how the soul tie was mutually created.

- Emotionally, mentally, and financially traumatized by the negative results or outcomes of what this person(s) did that hindered, controlled, or manipulated you.

It is possible to move on to another relationship and still be bound by the soul tie with people from your past. People who are married currently can still be emotionally attached and married (spiritually speaking) to their past marriage or intimate relationships. Most are unable to please their current spouse because of their fractured soul that is still knitted with the other person(s). Just because someone moves on or marries doesn't mean the soul tie is broken.

But there is good news, relationships can be severed by the power of God and through the power of our decisions that created them. Just like ungodly soul ties are established by our decisions, they are broken by our decision to be free.

I want you to know that just because a person prophesies or says they are called to be connected to you or walk with you, doesn't mean that they are God-ordained relationships. We must be alert in this hour and especially when it comes to those we allow in our hearts. We must guard our hearts. Proverbs 4:23-26 makes that clear. We are admonished and reminded by the Word of God of all the things that try to come against us. Being wise and discerning through the Holy Spirit, especially in the relationships we build in this hour, is what it means to guard your hearts.

We must overcome temptations every day and the works of the devil. He will use people to get close to us—who will become more like an enemy than a friend. Guarding our hearts is setting the right boundaries and personal preferences for who you allow in. A soul tie symptom has the power to reach levels that can negatively impact your current and future relationships.

Threefold Cord

God wants us to establish strong relationships, friendships, and partnerships whether in business, ministry, family, etc. The Bible talks about the "three-fold" cord that is not easily broken or severed. We need relationships that are God-ordained making it impossible to break them by others or ourselves. It says in Ecclesiastes 4:9-12:

> Two are better than one, because they have a good return for their labor: If either of them falls down, one can help the other up. But pity anyone who falls and has no one to help them up. Also, if two lie down together, they will keep warm. But how can one keep warm alone? Though one may be overpowered, two can defend themselves. A cord of three strands is not quickly broken.

I don't believe we need a whole entourage to feel important, respected, valued, and secure. Personally, I have three amazing, work, spiritual, and God-ordained relationships, and we keep each other accountable. These are godly soul ties of covenant built on trust, transparency, love, respect, and value. We pray for each other, can discern if one is in trouble or in need financially, emotionally, and spiritually. Love has no hidden agenda or motive.

The Lord will send you friends, comrades, battle buddies, prayer partners, associates, people who are filled with the love of God and will tell you the truth no matter what. Not to hurt, harm, or abuse you, but save your life, time, and money.

While writing this book I faced tremendous warfare, especially on the eve of a global pandemic. There were only a handful of people who checked in on me to see if I was OK. There were many I thought were my friends and covenant partners in God, but they weren't when it counted.

You must value and reevaluate those who you allow in your circle. Soul ties are real and there is a silver cord in the Spirit that links us to God and His people. Just like an umbilical cord that connects a mother and her unborn child. All of God's people have an invisible silver cord or ribbon that supernaturally connects us to the Lord.

How to Break Illegal Soul Ties

Ecclesiastes 12:6-7 (GW) says, *"Remember your Creator before the silver cord is snapped, the golden bowl is broken, the pitcher is smashed near the spring, and the water wheel is broken at the cistern. Then the dust of mortals goes back to the ground as it was before, and the breath of life goes back to God who gave it."* This silver cord nourishes our spirits and gives us life; when cut, we return to our Creator. However, spiritual speaking when it comes to illegal, toxic, ungodly, unhealthy, and illicit soul ties of the past and even present, each must be cut, burned, severed, snapped, broken, and shattered for divine breakthrough and liberty.

In other words, severing a soul tie is imperative and a necessary step to take before you can move forward with your life. People are stuck in relationships because they are bound by the contract or terms of agreement established. It's time to rip, tear, and burn the mutual agreement. It doesn't always have to be both parties coming together to break it. One person can actually break free from the soul connection.

So, how do we break soul ties? There are typically four simple steps to break a soul tie:

1. *Acknowledge a soul tie exists* and be honest with yourself that you are ready to move on and be free from it. For example, if a person has an addiction, they must first confess by acknowledging the problem. That is the first step. James 5:16 instructs us to *"Therefore confess your sins to each other so that you may be healed…."* The word "confess" is the Greek word *exomologeō*, which basically means "to declare, to say out loud, to exclaim, to divulge, to blurt, or to profess that one will do something, to promise, agree, engage" (Strong's G1843). In other words, acknowledging is basically confessing. The first step!

2. *Choose to end the relationship.* This could be having a conversation with the person or parties involved in the relationship. Also, praying and/or fasting to sever the cord that was established and calling out their names in prayer to break the cord between you. I do prophetic acts when I pray by spiritually visualizing a cord being severed by calling out the person's name and using my hand as a sword to cut the cord. I see myself cutting the cord and it is broken by faith.

It may seem foolish at first; however, the effect is powerful when done in faith in prayer. I must say, you will know that an illegal, illicit, unhealthy, or ungodly soul tie is really broken when you start receiving emails, text messages, social media messages, unexpected phones calls, or start randomly seeing the person or anyone connected to them. When this happens, you must know that your prayers worked, and now it's up to you not to reconnect. The enemy will test and tempt you to see if you are truly over this person and have moved on.

3. *Choose to forgive*, which is the most powerful form of personal liberty and freedom from an ungodly soul tie. Forgiveness takes action and can be the most difficult step to take. In some cases, this might be because you feel that the other person in the bond should be asking for your forgiveness.

To forgive is the most powerful spiritual warfare weapon to discharge because the enemy doesn't want people to forgive and be set free. Evil wants you to remain the victim or victimized unwilling to forgive the offender. Forgiveness means identifying any outstanding or pending mental "debts" that are keeping the soul tie active, and releasing them. Therefore, you must forgive yourself first in acknowledging that you made a mistake—which can be very difficult to do when you feel that it wasn't your fault in the first place.

4. *Remove any and all physical objects that link you* to the person. For example, if the person was a drug addict, remove all the paraphernalia associated with drugs. Action is required to remove anything closely related to our past and the individual. I will also go so far as to say that you must not connect with people who are associated with that person. However, if you have children with someone from a past relationship or marriage, it doesn't mean you have to cut them totally off. But be wise in your actions so that old

doors will not be reopened. Removing objects such as gifts, photos, clothing, love notes, etc. is vital to moving on. Keep in mind that these objects are symbols of the bond and must be removed from your life.

Also, seek help from spiritual leaders to get spiritual insight. It is possible to seek counseling, a therapist and professional who can help you in your journey to freedom. No longer will you be controlled by the puppet master of your past through a soul tie. Changing your phone number, unfollowing and blocking people on social media, moving to another city, state, or country will not remove the soul tie. Only you hold the scissors to cut the soul tie and keep it cut.

Finally, after all of the physical markers, gifts, substance, mental debts, and spiritual ties that link you to the person have been dissolved in prayer, you should be well on the way to overcoming the power of the soul tie symptoms. If you want to learn more about how to dissolve, disarm, and break illegal soul ties, generational, and demonic words curses, I suggest reading my book entitled *Prophetic Breakthrough: Decrees that Break Curses and Release Blessings* as a powerful resource on the topic.

I pray that the takeaways from reading this spiritual warfare manual will empower you to not only destroy the works of the darkness but to disarm to destroy his works. Jesus came to destroy the very works of the devil not just displace them. He was able drive them out—and remember that you are called to enforce the victory of Calvary that Jesus Christ has already won! The rules of engagement are not the same for every spiritual battle, so you must fight from the position of a winner and conqueror in Christ.

In modern-day warfare, the United States military sends drones into places to spy out the land and later send an air patrol followed by ground troops to fight. Likewise, we must first discern what type of battle you are presently fighting and use the right weaponry to engage and defeat the works of the adversary. This is done through a series of warfare prayers activations that shift and change your spiritual climate for the glory of God.

I salute you, soldier of God, that you are a survivor; and I pray that you are awarded the Purple Heart as a symbol of your dedication to the Lord and your service in the army of God.

SECTION 2

STRATEGIC WARFARE PROPHETIC PRAYER ACTIVATIONS

WARFARE PRAYER FOR BREAKTHROUGH

There are times when the Lord calls us to pray, fast, be still before Him and war in the spirit. Oftentimes it takes prophetic decrees, declarations, and boldly speaking out loud the Scriptures to fight back in prayer. The best method of seeing prayers answered is praying the Scriptures and praying in the Spirit. God only responds to those who are obedient children led by His Spirit as we partner with Heaven. The following prayers are ones I have used to see breakthrough in times of warfare. God wants us to pray faith-filled prayers, believing God will answer them according to His perfect will and timing.

Personal private prayers are reinforced by sometimes including corporate worship, prayer partners, spirit language, reading and declaring the Scripture, and consistency until we see breakthrough. We shouldn't pray amiss as James 4:3 admonishes us, *"When you ask, you do not receive, because you ask with wrong motives, that you may spend what you get on your pleasures."* You may want to use the following prophetic warfare prayer activations as templates to create your own:

Father, I come to you in Jesus' name knowing that You are my Rock, my Fortress, and my Deliverer. In You I take refuge and am safe. Lord, become my Shield and the horn of my salvation, my stronghold so that I am not detected by the evil one (Psalm 18:2).

Father God, I pray in Jesus' name that when my enemies come against me like a flood or sudden tsunami, You will raise up a standard against them (Isaiah 59:19); *for in this hour I need You to contend against those who contend against me; fight against those who fight against me!* (Psalm 35:1).

Father God, I will not be afraid of the evil one who stirs up division, jealousy, strife, and malice against me; all will fall and come to nothing. For the Lord is my Shield and Buckler who will hide me from the evil one, and every tongue that rises up against me in judgment shall be condemned in Jesus' name (Isaiah 54:14; Psalm 18:2).

Father God, I decree and declare according to Your Word that no destructive and diabolical weapon formed, forged, or created against me shall prosper; refute every wicked tongue that accuses me, in Jesus' name (Isaiah 54:17).

Father God, deliver me from my enemies and protect me from those who turn against me. Even though they may be stronger than me, they are not stronger than You. Deliver them into my hands and become the Lord of the Breakthrough in my life, in Jesus' name (Psalm 59:1-2; 2 Samuel 5:18-25).

Father God, supernaturally suit me in this unseen battle with Your armor. For the weapons of my warfare is not carnal but mighty and powerful through You in pulling down strongholds. Give me the supernatural strength to stand and become unwavering, unmovable, and unshakeable in my faith, in Jesus' name (2 Corinthians 10:4; Ephesians 6:10-18).

Father God, according to Your Word, if You are before me then who can be against me? Therefore, I will laugh in the face of evil knowing that when the enemy comes to kill me he will stumble and fall by the power of God. Because I am a child of God and called by Your name, the fear of the Lord shall destroy my enemies now and forever, in Jesus' name (Psalm 27:2-4; Romans 8:31).

Father God, when I am weak You are made strong in me. Give me supernatural strength to win this invisible warfare I face daily. For it's not by might nor by power, but by Your Spirit I shall be victorious, in Jesus' name (Zechariah 4:6; 2 Corinthians 12:9-10).

Father God, in this unseen warfare, teach my fingers to war and hands to fight effectively. For You have given me power to resist the devil. Father, deploy and dispatch Your angel armies to protect, guide, fight, and deliver me from the enemy, in Jesus' name (Psalm 144; 91:11; James 4:7).

Father God, I thank You for the power and authority You have given me as Your child, soldier, and ambassador. I prohibit and bound every demonic spirit fighting against me and cast them into bondage. And I dismantle, severe, cut, and burn by fire any illegal, illicit, and ungodly soul tie or connection that is not of You. I expose every hidden plot of the enemy and bring them into captivity, judgment, and silent the accuser, slanderer, and deceiver, in Jesus' name (2 Corinthians 5:20; Matthew 16:19; Ephesians 5:11).

Father God, I wage prophetic warfare over evil that tries to prevent me from fulfilling every prophetic dream, vision, promise, and purpose of Yours on my life. Give me the supernatural grace and power to wield the weapon of war and mass destruction against the kingdom of darkness, in Jesus' name (1 Timothy 1:18).

Father God, frustrate the plans of the wicked and woe to those who hide their plans from the Lord and hide them in dark places (Isaiah 29:15). *For in time of hardship, crisis, and difficulties, I will stand in my faith and watch and pray with divine supernatural boldness and strength, in Jesus' name* (Nehemiah 4; 1 Corinthians 16:13).

Father God, in this battle I will be strong and courageous like Joshua that I may conquer the places You have given to me. For I shall tread upon serpents and scorpions and what the enemy meant for my destruction will backfire, in Jesus' name (Psalm 91:13; Joshua 1:3).

Father God, let the power of the wicked be broken as You uphold those who are righteous. In times of disaster and in days of famine, let me enjoy plenty. Let Your enemies, Father, be like the flower of the field that are consumed and go up in smoke, but let Your people flourish in times of drought, in Jesus' name (Psalm 37:20).

Father God, I will not rest nor will I be silent until I see my breakthrough and victory in this battle. Since the days of John the Baptist until now, the Kingdom of Heaven suffers violence and the violent take it by force (Matthew 11:12). *Grant the anointing to prevail in the face of adversity* (Esther 6:13; Matthew 16:18).

Father God, let Your Word continue daily to come alive in my life that brings healing, deliverance, joy, peace, and righteousness in the Holy Spirit. I pray as I am willing and obedient, I will be satisfied financially and see tremendous breakthroughs in every area, in Jesus' name (Psalm 119:105; Hebrews 4:11).

Father God, I thank You that according to Your Word, You are doing a new thing in my life and making new ways in the wilderness and rivers in the desert. Prepare a table in the presence of my enemies, in Jesus' name (Isaiah 43:19; Psalm 23:5).

WARFARE PRAYER OF PROTECTION

PSALM 91:1-16

(personalized and paraphrased for you)

Father God, I _____ will dwell in the shelter of the Most High and will rest in the shadow of the Almighty. I will say of the Lord, "You are my Refuge and my Fortress, my God, in whom I will always put my trust."

Surely, You shall save me from the fowler's snare and from the deadly pestilence in this unseen warfare. Supernaturally, cover me with Your feathers and under Your wings as I will find refuge in Your faithfulness.

You are my Shield and Rampart and Strong Tower. I will not fear the terror of night, nor the arrow that flies by day, nor the pestilence that stalks me in the darkness, nor the plague, pandemic, civil unrest, financial uncertainty that destroy at midday. A thousand may fall at my side, ten thousand at my right hand, but it will not come near me. I will only observe with my eyes and see the punishment of the wicked.

I today prophetically declare and decree that, "The Lord is my refuge," and make the Most High my dwelling place, safe haven, and bunker; no harm will overtake me, no disaster, calamity, disease, or unseen and seen dangers will come near my tent. For the Lord the God of the Angel armies will command His angels concerning me to guard me in all my ways; they will supernaturally lift me up in their hands, so that I will not strike my foot against a stone.

I have the power of the Holy Spirit and anointing to tread on the lion and the cobra; and the Lord will trample the great lion and the serpent. "Because God's loves me," is His prophetic decree. And He "will rescue and protect me, as I acknowledge His name each and every day.

For Father God, when I call on You in prayer, I am totally assured in faith that You hear me and will answer me. For You will be with me in times of trouble, crisis, and warfare. Because You will deliver me as I honor You. And Your promise satisfies me with long life and abundance and shows me Your salvation, in Jesus' name, AMEN!

About Dr. Hakeem Collins

Dr. Hakeem Collins is an empowerment specialist, respected emerging prophetic voice, governmental minister, life coach, and sought-after conference speaker. He is known for his keen, accurate prophetic gifting and supernatural ministry. He is the founder of Champions International, The Prophetic Academy, and Revolution Network based in Wilmington, Delaware, where he resides. He is the author of several books including *Heaven Declares, Prophetic Breakthrough,* and *Command Your Healing.* He has been featured on many television and radio programs including Sid Roth's *It's Supernatural!,* The Word Network, and Cornerstone TV. He is a regular contributing article writer for *Charisma* magazine and *The Elijah List.*